# D<sub>e</sub> f a c e ment

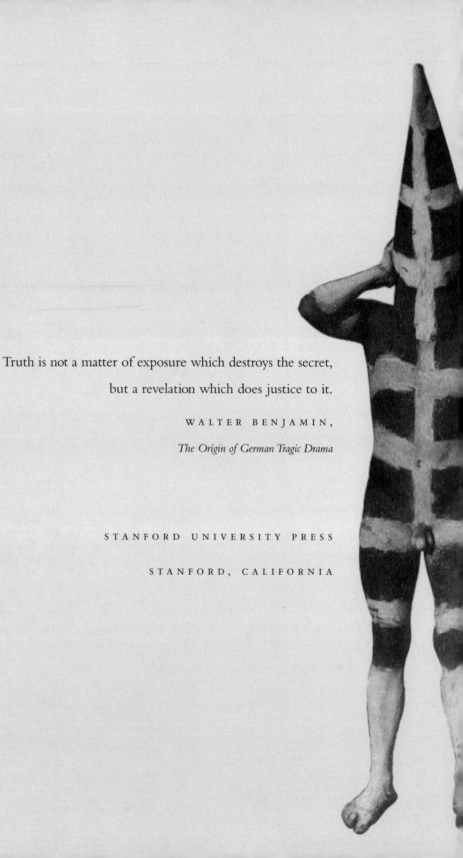

Truth is not a matter of exposure which destroys the secret,
but a revelation which does justice to it.

WALTER BENJAMIN,

*The Origin of German Tragic Drama*

STANFORD UNIVERSITY PRESS

STANFORD, CALIFORNIA

PUBLIC SECRECY AND THE LABOR OF THE NEGATIVE

# De fa
# c
# e ment

MICHAEL TAUSSIG

The Raymond Fred West Memorial Lectures at Stanford University

The Raymond Fred West Memorial Lectures on Immortality,
Human Conduct, and Human Destiny were established in 1910 by
Mr. and Mrs. Fred West of Seattle in memory of their son

Stanford University Press
Stanford, California
© 1999 by the Board of Trustees of the
Leland Stanford Junior University

Printed in the United States of America
CIP data appear at the end of the book

*Frontispiece*: Martin Gusinde, *Die Feuerland-Indianer*, vol. 1,
*Die Selk'nam* (Mödling: Anthropos Verlag, 1931), pl. 32, picture 80.
(Courtesy of Verlag St. Gabriel, Mödling)

*For Laurie, who unmasks only to reenchant*

My first debt is to the ethnographers of Tierra del Fuego, Martin Gusinde, Lucas Bridges, Anne Chapman, the young Charles Darwin, and of course to the extraordinary people about whom they wrote and whose image I carry with me, invested in every line that follows. Many other ethnographers and ethnographized people follow hard on their heels in my subsequent exploration of the peculiar secrecy of secret societies and the mimetic magic therein. To them all I am immensely grateful, as I am to the late Eric Michaels for his essay on photography and secrecy in Australian Aboriginal societies, and for a chance remark by Norman O. Brown, vis-à-vis his work on Bataille, concerning the mysteries of negation. Moreover, readers are assured that any mimetic resonance between my work and Rachel Moore's *Savage Theory* is not accidental but stems from her insight, no less than delight, concerning the traffic between ethnology and the modernist magic of the cinematic image. Finally, casting this book on its way, my thoughts fly to Santiago and Olivia Taussig-Moore, who, bountiful in this respect, led me to understand how the adult's imagination of the child's imagination is indispensable to the gift that secrecy provides the real, as really made up.

CONTENTS

# Defacement

When the human body, a nation's flag, money, or a public statue is *defaced*, a strange surplus of negative energy is likely to be aroused from within the defaced thing itself. It is now in a state of *desecration*, the closest many of us are going to get to the sacred in this modern world. Indeed this negative state can come across as more sacred than "sacred," especially since that most spectacular defacement, the death of God, was announced by Nietzsche's madman: "Do you not feel the breath of empty space?" he demands, lantern held high in the blazing sun.[1]

I take this space to be where the defacing action is, sucking in this book as sheerness of movement within an emptiness so empty anything could happen in a continuous blur—like Margaras, the White Cat, Hunter and Killer, not similar to anything, just similar.[2] "He can hide in snow and sunlight on white walls and clouds and rocks," William Burroughs advises, and "he moves down windy streets with blown newspapers and shreds of music and silver paper in the wind." Margaras is what this book is, an extended commentary on what G. W. F. Hegel called "the labor of the negative."[3]

*Burroughs*

Something so strange emanates from the wound of sacrilege wrought by desecration that rather than pronounce theoretical verdict and encapsulate defacement's mysterious force, I see my task first and foremost to be not its explanation but its *characterization*. Yet this is a cheat for, after all, do I really believe there is such a thing as explanation? And as for having a *task*? Is it not a failure, doomed from the outset, a surrender to the way of the world, want-ing to be one with and even devoured by the subject matter of the negative? The ultimate act of being similar?

For characterization of defacement can never confront its object head-on, if only because defacement catches us unawares and can only be known un-expectedly, complicit with the violence of daily life. The writer must confront the resistances. Why else do we write? The shortest way between two points, between violence and its analysis, is the long way round, tracing the edge sideways like the crab scuttling. This we also call the labor of the negative. And here I follow not only the scuttling crab, eyes protruding on stalks, body armor dripping, but Walter Benjamin's appraisal of Eros in Plato's *Sympo-sium*, for whom truth is not a matter of exposure which destroys the secret, but a revelation which does justice to it.[4]     *truth ≠ destruction of secret?*

Thus, so easily we join *truth* and *secret*; with rapture we skid between them, envelop the one in the other: truth = secret. Yet embedded within this in-grained poetry of daily habit there exists something not so obvious, a finely-tuned theatrical process, thanks to which, as Benjamin sees it, the revelation shall do justice to the secret. In fact, he portrays such a revelation as the burn-ing up of the husk of the beautiful outer appearance of the secret as it enters the realm of ideas; "that is to say," he adds, "a destruction of the work in which the external form achieves its most brilliant degree of illumination."[5]

The just revelation amounts to a funeral pyre, and something else, as well. For beauty has been waiting for this incendiary moment as the fate through which it shall rise to unforeseen heights of perfection, where its inner nature shall be revealed for the first time. At the moment of its self-destruction, its illuminating power is greatest. This decidedly mystical process—which I equate with unmasking—whereby truth, as secret, is finally revealed, is hence a sacrifice, even a self-sacrifice, thanks to an inspired act of defacement, beau-tiful in its own right: violent, negating, and fiery. And this carefully contrived process of the just revelation, be it noted, stands in juxtaposition to exposure, which, Benjamin warns, would only destroy the secret.

Yet what if the truth is not so much a secret as a *public* secret, as is the case with most important social knowledge, *knowing what not to know*? Then what happens to the inspired act of defacement? Does it destroy the secret, or fur-ther empower it? For are not shared secrets the basis of our social institutions, the workplace, the market, the family, and the state? Is not such public secrecy the most interesting, the most powerful, the most mischievous and ubiquitous form of socially active knowledge there is? What we call doctrine, ideology, consciousness, beliefs, values, and even discourse, pale into sociological insignificance and philosophical banality by comparison: for it is the task and life force of the public secret to maintain that verge where the secret is not destroyed through exposure, but subject to a quite different sort of revelation that does justice to it. This is the verge of "a thousand plateaus," resolute in its directionless stasis, my subject, my just subject: the characterization of negation as sacred surplus whose force lies entirely in the mode of revelation we seek and seek to make.

It is the cut of de/facement that releases this surplus, the cut into wholeness as holiness that, in sundering, reveals, as with film montage, not only another view via another frame, but released flows of energy. As Thomas Elsaesser observes in his essay on Dada cinema, "It is the cut as the montage principle that makes the energy in the system visible and active."[6]

If it is the cut that makes the energy in the system both visible and active, then we should also be aware of cuts in language, strange accidents and contingencies, as in the way the *English* language brings together as montage the face and sacrilege under the rubric *defacement*. It is by means of this contingency that I am alerted to the tenderness of face and of faces facing each other, tense with the expectation of secrets as fathomless as they seem worthy of unmasking—one of the heroic tropes, in my experience, of that which we call Enlightenment, no less than of physiognomy, reading insides from outsides, the soul from the face.

I take the face to be the figure of *appearance*, the appearance of appearance, the figure of figuration, the ur-appearance, if you will, of secrecy itself as the primordial act of presencing. For the face itself is a contingency, at the magical crossroads of mask and window to the soul, one of the better-kept public secrets essential to everyday life. How could this be, this contradiction to end contradiction, crisscrossing itself in endless crossings of the face? And could defacement itself escape this endless back-and-forth of revelation and concealment?

Defacement is like Enlightenment. It brings insides outside, unearthing knowledge, and revealing mystery. As it does this, however, as it spoliates and tears at tegument, it may also animate the thing defaced and the mystery revealed may become more mysterious, indicating the curious magic upon

which Enlightenment, in its elimination of magic, depends. In fact, defacement is often the first thing people think of when they think of mimetic
magic, like sticking a needle in the heart of a figurine so as to kill the person
thereby represented, and it is no accident that this was Frazer's first example
in the scores of pages he dedicated to the magic art in *The Golden Bough*.[7]
Defacement is privileged among these arts of magic because it offers the fast
track to the mimetic component of sympathetic magic, in which the representation becomes the represented, only to have the latter die, in the slip-
stream of its presencing.

Defacement evokes a prehistory of the face as sacrifice, as does Georges
Bataille where he rewrites Darwin and Freud with their histories of the almighty consequences of man's ascent to the upright posture from the crouching ape. *This* is the long sought-for source of repression, Freud crowed to his
muse in Berlin, Wilhelm Fliess, because the sense of smell, finely attuned to
the anus and genitals of the Other, thereby lost its ascendancy over the senses
once man strode forth on two legs. Henceforth the eyes were regnant and
shame entered the world, just as sex came to concentrate on the genitals that
had to be covered from sight.[8] Hastening to add that it was mere speculation,
more often than not consigning these thoughts to elaborate footnotes over a
page long, Freud nevertheless clung to this history to the end, over thirty
years, from his 1897 letters to Fliess, through the Rat Man and the essay on
love and the ubiquity of debasement of the loved object, to the ominous *Civilization and Its Discontents* with its prophecies of sexual demise and the total
triumph of bodily repression.

It was not just the nose that was at stake in this millennial struggle for the
rights of the body, but the anus as the sensory button of the world, adrift in
the wake of civilization as a heavy, if occult, presence, heavy enough for the
philosophically trained authors of *Dialectic of Enlightenment* to affirm for smell
an epistemology totally at odds with normal, civilized, perception.[9] For if the
visual settled in with a nice sense of distance between self-enclosed subjects
and other-enclosed objects, this distancing was annulled with nasal perception, such that the senses ran riotously into one another as much as into the
Other, as with the dog, man's best friend, loyal to a fault, never happier than
when its nose is up the Other's rear end. Hence the ambivalence of primal
words, as with "dog," man's esteemed companion through the ages, no less
than the sign of all that is base and degrading. Hence Bataille, canine to a

fault, adding his astonishing fable of the ape's anus to this series of connections between face and nether regions. It all began as a frightening scene at the zoo, the tender faces of children exposed to the blossoming bottom of the ape swinging its scarlet self into focus to dominate the visual field like a gorgeous flower, suggesting to Bataille that the ascent of man to his privileged status in the cosmic design is summed up in the development of a mysterious organ he called the "pineal eye" on account of its ecstatic relation to the sun. Located at the tippy-top of evolutionary development, the crown of the head, with direct access to the heavens above, this eye is in reality a solar anus whose singular achievement is to make the visual olfactory. Like that noble bird of prey and icon of the state, the eagle of mythology, this is an eye that can look straight into the sun and, when it does so, it stimulates immense, offensive ejaculations as the sign of an orgiastic fusion of self with Other, just as the child screams at the sight of the amazing anus on the other side of the bars. All this is the result of the reconfiguration of the ape's anatomy, the migration of its anus headwise, absorbed into the body of man to conceal itself as a mere cleft in the buttocks. "All the potential for blossoming," notes Bataille, "found the way open only toward the superior regions of the buccal orifices, toward the throat, the brain, and the eyes. The human face," he concludes, "is a conflagration that had, until that moment, made of the anal orifice both bud and flame."[10]

Defacement works on objects the way jokes work on language, bringing out their inherent magic nowhere more so than when those objects have become routinized and social, like money or the nation's flag in secular societies where God has long been put in his place. Defacement of such social things, however, brings a very angry god out of hiding, and Nietzsche's madman distraught with implications of the death of God knows of no better return to life than this, although to call this a return would be to muffle Michel Foucault's argument, built on that of Bataille, that with the death of God transgression acquires a different character than before, because now it is transgression itself that is God, most pronounced, most condensed, in what we call sex—that secret we are henceforth doomed to always speak about precisely because it is secret.[11]

This reconfiguration of repression in which depth becomes surface so as to remain depth, I call *the public secret*, which, in another version, can be defined as *that which is generally known, but cannot be articulated*, first drawn to my attention in an extreme form in Colombia in the early 1980's, when there were so many situations in which people dared not state the obvious, thus outlining it, so to speak, with the spectral radiance of the unsaid; as when people were taken off buses and searched at roadblocks set up by the police or military, the secret being that these same police and military were probably a good deal more involved in terrorism and drug running than the guerrilla forces they were pitted against. Likewise, but in a different register, was what people in the towns and hamlets in northern Cauca, Colombia, where I've lived on and off since 1969, call "the law of silence," a phrase I first heard in the early 1980's when, side by side with the suspension of civil liberties and the imposition of military rule via recurrent "states of emergency," mutilated corpses would mysteriously appear on the roads leading to town. Today as I write, in January 1998, the "dirty war" has reached heights nobody would have believed back then, massacres of peasants occurring daily, and it is routine for human-rights people to figure the action in terms of the *smoke screen* uniting paramilitary killers with the regular military forces. We all "knew" this, and they "knew" we "knew," but there was no way it could be easily articulated, certainly not on the ground, face-to-face. Such "smoke screens" are surely long known to mankind, but this "long knownness" is itself an intrinsic component of knowing what not to know, such that many times, even in our acknowledging it, in striving to extricate ourselves from its sticky embrace, we fall into even better-laid traps of our own making. Such is the labor of the negative, as when it is pointed out that something may be obvious, but needs stating in order to be obvious. For example, the public secret. Knowing it is essential to its power, equal to the denial. Not being able to say anything is likewise testimony to its power. So it continues, each negation feeding the other while the headlines bleat "EL ESTADO, IMPOTENTE." And much the same applies, so I am informed, to the U.S. Drug Enforcement Agency, the Internal Revenue Service, and so on. Only the movies tell it like it is, especially those concerning corruption in the New York City police force. But that's fiction.

My examples, as much as the experience within them, seem extreme and tend to weaken the all-consuming banality of the fact that this negativity of knowing what not to know lies at the heart of a vast range of social powers and knowledges intertwined with those powers, such that the clumsy hybrid of power/knowledge comes at last into meaningful focus, it being not that knowledge is power but rather that active not-knowing makes it so. So we fall silent when faced with such a massive sociological phenomenon, aghast at such complicities and ours with it, for without such shared secrets any and all social institutions—workplace, marketplace, state, and family—would founder. "Do you want to know *the secret*?" asked William Burroughs in the journal he kept in the months before his death. "Hell no!" he replies, talking to himself, to us, his cats, and to death. "All is in the not done."[12]

Nietzsche would be smiling in his death sleep at this adroit maneuver with the two-realities model of the world, surface and depth, appearance and a hidden essence, bequeathed the West by Plato and Christianity. "The 'apparent' world is the only one," he wrote just before his final breakdown. "The 'real' world has only been lyingly added."[13] That is another karate-like maneuver with reality's investment in the secret, embracing it in a classic Nervous System play-off. And this mocking language, crisp and timely, reminds us that the point of living, even at the point of death, is not to try to master the secret by evacuating it, as when one says, excited by a sudden insight, that . . . "the secret of the public secret is that there is none." Jackpot! Trembling hands reach out to grasp the negativity.

"Hell no!"

So our writing, as much as our living, becomes extensive, opening out pursuant to filmy trails of the unsayable, not closing down on the secret quivering in fear of imminent exposure. So our writing becomes an exercise in life itself, at one with life and within life as lived in social affairs, not transcendent or even a means to such, but contiguous with action and reaction in the great chain of storytelling telling the one always before the last. Yet how can you be contiguous with the not merely empty, but negative, space?

Elias Canetti pronounced secrecy as the very core of power.[14] And he is most decidedly right. Wherever there is power, there is secrecy, except it is not only secrecy that lies at the core of power, but public secrecy. And there is a distinct possibility of falling into error here. To put it bluntly, there is no such thing as a secret. It is an invention that comes out of the public secret, a limit-case, a supposition, a great "as if," without which the public secret would evaporate. To see the secret as secret is to take it at face value, which is what the tension in defacement requires. According to Canetti, this tension is where the fetishization of the secret as a hidden and momentous thing, made by persons but transcendent over them, verges on explosive self-destruction capable of dragging us all down. This is his foreboding, what he identifies as the vir-tual law of the secret. But against this apocalyptic dread, I regard the public secret as fated to maintain the verge where the secret is not destroyed through exposure, but subject to a revelation that does justice to it.

And the madman in the marketplace agonizing at the death of God? Is he really that worried about God gone, belated guilt at killing the Father, im-petuous deed too easily carried out by the callous, who will live to rue the day? A heavy psychodrama? He certainly is worked up. But about what? Lis-ten to his rant. Is there still any up or down? Do we not feel the breath of empty space?[15]

God is not the problem. Killing him achieved nothing. Maybe less than nothing. The mystery-model of the real continues stronger than before with God-substitutes piling up by the minute. The addiction to the disjunction of appearance and essence goes deep. Before the two thousand years of the Christ-man behind the scene there was the Plato-man with beautiful and true forms hidden behind the sensuous crust of appearance. Secrecy and mystery all the way down. This is why the madman raves and why only the madman raves, because, being mad, he sees that Enlightenment created other gods busy behind the scene of the screen. He smashes his lantern there in the marketplace in broad daylight. "I have come too early," he says. "This tre-mendous event is still on its way."[16]

This then is the breath of empty space. For if we were to abolish depth, what world would be left? The apparent world, perhaps? But no! With the abolition of depth we have also abolished the apparent world!

Canetti's fear of the apocalyptic powers of the secret as exploding fetish: realized.

And Nietzsche leaves us with this picture of a postfictional world bereft of depth. It is movement etched in black and white. Burroughs's cat. "He can hide in snow and sunlight on white walls and clouds and rocks, he moves down windy streets with blown newspapers and shreds of music and silver paper in the wind."

*Mid-day*, says Nietzsche, setting the scene without the screen. *Moment of the shortest shadow; end of the longest error; zenith of mankind.*[17]

Defacement!

# PART ONE

# Sacrilege

> Thus the life of God and divine cognition may well be
> spoken of as a disporting of Love with itself; but this
> idea sinks into mere edification, and even insipidity, if
> it lacks the seriousness, the suffering, the patience, and
> the labour of the negative.
>
> G. W. F. HEGEL, preface to *Phenomenology of Spirit*,
> *trans. A. V. Miller*

## Down by the Lake with Phil and Liz

*A Story of Defacement and Defacement of the Defacement*

"This filthy thing. Why do they allow this filthy thing to be displayed?"

"Clearly, for some people in Australia, the political point of the work embodied in its representation of Queen Elizabeth and Prince Philip as frail and exposed human beings is unacceptable—to them, the 'symbol' of the monarch demands to be preserved untainted and holy, despite the all too obvious reality of recent royal foibles."

"I stood on duty in George Street as a young policeman in 1971 when the Queen went by on her way to open the Opera House. It was a moment I will never forget. I said to myself then: 'I will love you until the day I die.'"

" . . . It has brought disgrace on itself by allowing this filthy thing to be displayed."

"Work of art! Work of art! You're a work of art!" he screamed, right arm raised threateningly.

"'I didn't sleep much last night,' the other one says. 'I knew it was going to happen. I just had a gut feeling that the bastards were going to come around and finish it off.'"

"In the first sledgehammer attack on the figures last week, the Queen's head was removed; then Prince Philip was attacked and on Saturday night the Queen's legs were severed and one of Prince Philip's arms was destroyed."

"'I'm more an abattoir artist,' he said. 'I like to take sacred cows and slaughter them.'"

"The works themselves are quite conservative. They are realistic, life-size. Perhaps if they were more abstract it would be more acceptable. . . . The shock of seeing the queen naked has oedipal overtones."

"Bugger off!"

"Police Sergeant McQuillan shocked hundreds of tourists as he tried to cover the naked forms of the royal couple with a sheet emblazoned with the Australian flag."

"He flashed his police badge and Vietnam medals."

"A scuffle broke out as the organisers, vowing to stop any more desecration of the sculpture, moved in to remove the flag."

"'This sculpture has been ceremoniously vandalized,' said Neil Roberts, co-ordinator of the Canberra National Sculpture Forum 95."

"You're totally bloody disgusting."

"But organisers say it will stay. It is more relevant to be left as it is—as a symbol of intolerance, irrelevance, disintegration."

"The governor general has distanced himself from the debate."

"A decapitated queen and Prince Philip were driven out yesterday, in the back of a rusty ute [pickup]."

"'It's gone beyond a bit of fun now,' Mr. Roberts said."

Two weeks later there were still crowds gathered around the empty bench on which the statues had been sitting.

(Sources: *The Sydney Morning Herald, The Australian,* and Channel 2 News, Sydney)

## Desecration

*"A scuffle broke out as the organisers, vowing to stop any more desecration, moved in to remove the flag."*

Sacrifice has started to preoccupy me. The whole thing seems so mysterious. For a long time I understood the word literally as in Noah Webster's dictionary: *sacer,* sacred + *facere,* make, its very matter-of-factness compounding the mystery. For surely sacredness is something beyond making? And how does one make something from nothing? How does one make such a terrific leap from nonsacredness to sacredness? Very naive questions, no doubt. But persistent. I mulled over attempts to account for or explain sacrifice. Yet, with notable exceptions, they too proved disappointing. But then there is *desecration,* surely the inverse of sacrifice, and about this there seems to be a good deal more certainty and a good deal more passion.

Around me there is no sacrifice. All that was in the past or in faraway places. Avi Bornstein made a short video for my ethnographic surrealism seminar in New York City. He had done fieldwork in the Middle East, on the West Bank of the River Jordan, and knew about sacrifice there. The video showed him sacrificing a lamb in upstate New York in the company of a young cousin about ten years old. Viewers found it shocking in a way that it wouldn't have been if it was a documentary of sacrifice on the West Bank. It seemed sacrilegious, yet exquisitely sacred.

Around me there is no sacrifice, nor much passion about sacred things. The disenchantment of the world still seems to me a largely accomplished fact. What exists now is perhaps best thought of as a new amalgam of enchantment and disenchantment, the sacred existing in muted but powerful forms, especially—and this is my central preoccupation—in its "negative" form as desecration. Then the almighty speaks—indeed, bellows, as we recently witnessed so vividly in the congressional debate over the impeachment of President Clinton, accused of *lying* under *oath*. Has the sacred ever been free of a transgressive impulse? This suggests that desecration is more than the inverse of the sacred or of sacrifice. Something more complicated than inversion is going on.

## Morgue Workers "Robbed Anzacs"

"The Independent Commission Against Corruption was told yesterday how morgue staff at Glebe cherished the annual day of remembrance of the war dead, Anzac Day, for the number of soldiers who died on that day with large amounts of cash on their persons. 'I remember when I first started there,' said Simon McLeod, a morgue assistant accused two weeks ago of washing and drying money he stole from messy and decomposed corpses, 'you know, like, you'd look forward to Anzac Day because the old diggers would be playing two-up and inevitably one would go over.'

"He admitted stealing money on several occasions and had once removed a pair of gym shoes which he subsequently wore, but hotly denied 'he used to love' searching decomposed bodies or exchanging 'really smelly notes' at banks and hated the new polymer notes because they didn't dry properly after being washed."

"As an informer for the Commission on Corruption, Mr. McLeod made secret video recordings of a clerk at the morgue, a Mr. Nichols, who repeatedly denied the evidence therein. 'I never stole off anyone alive so I wouldn't do it while they're dead,' he said. 'They've got no way of protecting themselves.'

"'I'm no fucking angel,' he mused, reminiscing about the old days when he made huge wins.

"'I'm talking about the huge win,' McLeod prompted him, on tape, 'that Frank had with that decomposed woman. She had that money bag around her. . . . '

"'I remember one,' responded Nichols, 'that . . . the sheila had a very small set of tits that she used to walk around like she had a fucking 44-inch bust on her, it was full of dough.'

"On being forced to read the transcripts of the conversations, Nichols said he did not deny the conversations took place but had no recollection of them. The hearing continues."

(Source: *The Sydney Morning Herald*, June 28, 1996)

## Crimes Currency Act of 1981, Commonwealth of Australia

"A person shall not, without the consent, in writing, of an authorized person, willingly deface, disfigure, mutilate or destroy any coin or paper money that is lawfully current in Australia.

Penalty:

(a) in the case of a person, not being a body corporate—$5,000 or imprisonment for 2 years, or both; or

(b) in the case of a person, being a body corporate—$10,000.

And these same penalties apply to those who sell such coins or paper money or have them in their possession."

## Budawangs Fishman

*"Legal opinion was not clear on whether I had committed a crime. One view had it was against the law to deface notes under any circumstance and the other was that is was only against the law if one's intention was to defraud."*

Did John Reid know of the laws about defacing money before he cut up the several thousands of dollars he received from selling his treasured plot of real estate on the south coast, eighth wonder of the world, so as to begin, in 1982, a collage about the plight of political prisoners in Latin America?

In 1984, by which time Reid had cut up twenty-five hundred bills, mainly denominations of one, five, and twenty dollars, a colleague anonymously sent the Fraud Squad of the Australian Federal Police fifty-two of the cut-up bills, with Reid's name attached as evidence. On the wall of Reid's studio the police discovered the unfinished figure of a larger-than-life naked woman, spread-eagled on her back, being beaten by clubs. Below lay the artist's raw materials: cups containing squares, rectangles, and crescent-shaped pieces of money, sorted according to shape and color; Australian paper money comes in gorgeous colors, like Monopoly money, the colors varying in intensity across the bill, perfect for flesh tones, bruises, and wounds. Some bills had the queen's face carefully cut out in sweeping semicircles, leaving mysterious dark spaces between coiffured hair on one side, and the Australian coat of arms, held by a kangaroo and an emu, on the other. Hardened fraud-dicks that they were, the police nevertheless were aghast. They returned with tweezers, gloves, plastic bags, and a forensic photographer to arrest Reid, under a 1959 law, on fifty-five counts of willfully mutilating Australian banknotes in his studio in the Canberra School of Art in the Australian National University.

It turned out, however, that the federal director of public prosecutions was a friend of the arts, and bent over backward to find a solution. The Commonwealth Bank offered officially defaced money to Reid to use instead, but he refused and his case dragged on until 1986 when, taking advantage of a new law, he successfully solicited permission from the prime minister and the treasurer to complete his artwork—which, at least by 1996, when I saw it, remained incomplete, as if official permission by the leader of the country to deface had brought it to an abrupt halt.

Reid is known for his forays into image-politics at the edge of law, as well as his equally spectacular wilderness photography aimed at saving old-growth forest. His favorite site is the Budawangs, a mountain range with eerie escarpments to the southeast of Canberra, where, as he tells it, he has hidden cameras triggered by sound or movement in pursuit of a shy creature, called the fishman, said to be lurking in the watercourses of those remote parts. As yet never seen by humans, this elusive being represents, to Reid at least, the possibility of communication with the wilderness, despite the fact that the fishman is a fraud or, more accurately, a public secret, invented by Australians at large—in Reid's words, "a fine-art discovery, not a scientific one." Working at the edge of the public secret, revealing and concealing at the same time, this photographic pursuit of the fishman in the shadows of the prehistoric Budawangs seems to generate no less a mystery than the contagion released by defacing the nation's currency. Hence the tweezers and surgical gloves?

(Sources: *ANU Reporter*, December 9, 1992, and John Reid's personal file of legal correspondence)

## Texas v. Johnson

" . . . an inarticulate grunt or roar."

"Both Congress and the States have enacted numerous laws regulating misuse of the American flag. Until 1967, Congress left the regulation of misuse of the flag up to the States. Now however, Title 18 U.S.C. # 700 (a), provides that: 'Whoever knowingly casts contempt upon any flag of the United States by publicly mutilating, defacing, defiling, burning, or trampling upon it shall be fined not more than $1,000 or imprisoned for not more than one year, or both.'

"Moreover, Johnson was prosecuted because he knew that his politically charged expression would cause 'serious offence.' If he had burned the flag as a means of disposing of it because it was dirty or torn, he would not have been convicted of flag desecration under this Texas law: federal law designates burning as the preferred means of disposing of a flag 'when it is in such condition that it is no longer a fitting emblem for display,' and Texas has no quarrel with this means of disposal."

Note that Chief Justice Rehnquist, writing for the dissenting opinion, in favor of prosecution, claimed that Johnson's act could *not* be construed as *symbolic* speech and thus was not protected by the First Amendment. "Flag burning," he stated, "is the equivalent of an inarticulate grunt or roar."

(Source: *Texas v. Johnson*, 88 US 155 [1989])

### Farewell to Flags

"Boy Scouts in the Florida Panhandle retired hundreds of soiled American flags yesterday in a ceremony at Barrancas National Cemetery in Pensacola. A Boy Scout aged 12, saluted, after adding a flag to the pyre."

The photograph shows a blond boy in his scout's uniform, body erect, staring down at the burning flags, right arm stiffly at salute. He stands very close to the fire. His white gloves wrinkle as he makes the two-fingered Boy Scout salute. Flames from burning flags leap in the foreground of the photograph. Heat waves cascade over the rest of the image to make a dreamy impressionistic surface, through which the regular white shapes of burial stones stand in columns, stretching to infinity as the soldiers they stand for once did. The boy escapes this filmy fate. His image is crisp as the flames lick toward him.

(Source: Caption to a photograph in *The New York Times*, June 12, 1994)

NOTE: *pyre*, per *OED*: "usually a funeral pile for burning a dead body."

### Nichols Boys Were a Worry, Say Locals

"Decker, Michigan: A town this small does not keep many secrets. . . . Neighbours had wondered why James Douglas Nichols, 41 [charged along with his brother, Terry, and Timothy McVeigh for the horrific bombing of the federal building in Oklahoma City], insisted on driving without a licence, why he put so many anti-government bumper stickers on his station waggon and liked paying for goods with dollar bills he had defaced with an ink stamp."

(Sources: *The Sydney Morning Herald*, May 27, 1995, from *The Los Angeles Times* and *The Washington Post*)

## Survivors Split on Following Trial

"At a meeting of the survivors' group one evening, people repeatedly wondered whether looking at Mr. McVeigh would help survivors make more sense of the incident."

"'I need to see him just one time,' says a survivor. 'I'd like to see his actions, his facial expressions. Right now he's got the nice-kid-down-the-block kind of look. But there must be something about him. Otherwise, how could you even know? If you walk through a shopping center, how can you tell if someone is whacko or not? There must be some way to tell?'

"'No, no!' says a psychologist from the U.S. Department of Veterans' Affairs. 'I guarantee you, looking at him will confuse even more. He does not exude hate.'"

(Source: *The New York Times*, April 19, 1997)

## The Face of the Vietnamese

"In Dispatches, Michael Herr wrote that reading the face of the Vietnamese is like reading the wind. Mr. Bang is different. He does not reflect the subsurface reserve and built-in mystery typical of an older generation of Vietnamese officials. His face softens with childhood memories or at the mention of a favorite poem.

"Mr. Bang throws back his head in delight, often. He is pleased with his new place under the sun [but] the war has yet to be laid to rest. . . . Almost everywhere he goes there are protests. 'Liar' and 'communist' are the cries.

"A congressional source close to Senator Robert C. Smith, Republican of New Hampshire, said: 'Le Bang is a well-trained Communist who thinks that wearing a suit and talking about trade and investment with Washington lobbyists will make us on Capitol Hill forget that Hanoi is still deceiving America on the fate of still-unaccounted for POWs and MIAs. He's wrong.'"

(Source: *International Herald Tribune*, October 6, 1995. The article is centered around a large photo of elegantly suited Mr. Le Van Bang under a portrait of Ho Chi Minh beside the Vietnamese flag.)

**In Miami, Customs Cut Lines and Has More Plainclothes Inspectors**

**(A Shaggy-Dog Story)**

"At the baggage carousel, a young man in jeans and running shoes may give his fellow passengers a passing glance. Then a shaggy dog pads up and sniffs a false-bottomed suitcase and sits down, tail wagging ominously. The man in jeans flashes a badge and escorts the drug courier into a small room for questioning.

"Jay R. McNamara, a rover in jeans and sports shirt, has made 57 drug seizures since he started mingling with travelers.

"'I read people's eyes,' Mr. McNamara said.

"The interdiction effort already used dogs, including beagles and spaniels, to detect illegal drugs. But Mr. Gordon said, 'We found the traffic here so big that the little dogs were being trampled, so we had to change to bigger dogs.' Now recruits from the local dog pound, who are still handled by uniformed inspectors, are as big as Abby, a Chesapeake Bay retriever who recently sniffed out heavily taped 10-pound packets of cocaine sprayed with dog repellent on a couple of couriers."

Recruited to the state-machine of surveillance, physiognomy bears an intimate relationship to the dog's nose, large or small. "Of all the senses," write the authors of *Dialectic of Enlightenment*, "that of smell—which is attracted without objectifying—bears clearest witness to the urge to lose oneself in and become the 'other.'"[1] If true, this would make smell, not vision, the most effective weapon in the physiognomic arsenal. How misguided the physiognomists were! Looking for the look, when all along it was the nose that could do the job, thanks to a truly Dionysian immersion in the body, albeit the body of the Other. Getting to really *know* the Insides. So much so, you lose yourself in them. The only knowledge worth knowing.

So, while vision thrives upon reality as a two-layered entity with a surface and a behind, thereby attaching more importance and mystery to the unseen than to the scene, smell qualifies as "Nietzschean knowing"; depth gone, surface gone too, decks ablaze, mainmast down, and nowhere to put your feet. Smell mocks the scene of the screen.

And what of the attraction? This losing oneself in and becoming Other? Becoming drugs? Whoa! Better to have a human-animal composite tugging at the leash of civilization. Hence physiognomically blessed humans ("I read people's eyes") have channeled smell into vision, as the young cocaine-sniffing Freud made much of in his letters to Berlin nose-specialist Wilhelm Fliess at the birth of psychoanalysis in 1897. Freud speculated that this channeling of smell into vision was *the* basis of repression—the single most important, not to mention negating and mysterious, function of culture. Even more significant (for readers of Bataille, for example), Freud suggested that therefore "libido and disgust would seem associatively linked."[2]

Physiognomy, in this scheme, would be not only a visual substitute for smell, but for animal-like, four-footed sex as well, with the transformation of the latter to a "heightened," more civilized sphere, wherein the scene of the screen promotes depths mysterious and remote. Hence physiognomy itself, the art of reading insides from outsides, is the mark not so much of displaced sex, but of repression and of attempts at supplanting it. No wonder that *Dialectic of Enlightenment* argues that civilization's attempts to suppress base instincts creates a sensuous excess, matter so out of place that it awakens "moments of biological prehistory: danger signs which make the hair stand on end and the heart stop beating."[3] Hence a shaggy dog wagging its tail no less than drugs as prehistoric arousal, ten-pound packets' worth, even if coated with smell repellent.

(Source: Christopher S. Wren, "Traveler's Boon is Smuggler's Bane," *New York Times*, May 27, 1996.)

## The Monument

*I am too tired, I must try to rest and sleep, otherwise I am lost in every respect. What an effort to keep alive! Erecting a monument does not require the expenditure of so much strength.*

FRANZ KAFKA, diary entry, 1914[4]

In *Lenin in Ruins* Mark Lewis quotes Robert Musil to the effect that we never pay much attention to monuments in our city as we pass them by. Quite possibly we don't notice them at all.[5]

Why then, we must ask, all the fuss that suddenly arises concerning monuments during and after the toppling of the regime? "Toppling" of course gives the game away, as if the regime itself is a monument and, what is more, as if there exists a sort of death wish deep within the monument, something in the monumentality of the monument that cries out to be toppled, besmirched, desecrated—in a word, defaced. This is the "law of the base" at the heart of religion and things sacred. Like Flaubert's concept of the act of writing, to erect a statue is to take revenge on reality. And reality in turn exacts its due. Mark Lewis suggests that the lies, or repressed history, of the regime are installed in the statue as a hidden flaw, an invisible fault line awaiting the resurgence of the truth of the past; and it is this, he suggests, that accounts for the fury of defacement and the effervescent magical effect thereof that yields more. But this hopeful suggestion itself suffers, so it seems to me, from the same monumental faith in truth and history, not to mention in memory, that sustains the self-portrayal of the regime. It lacks the defacement quality necessary to any worthwhile theory of defacement. It fails to see the law of the base, the attraction no less than the repulsion of ruins, and the ecstasy therein.

How charming, therefore, the contributions to the defacing art provided to the *New Yorker* by several artists asked in 1993 what to do with the monuments of the recently toppled U.S.S.R.[6] One inverts the statues, burying the tops of the figures in the ground, leaving the base in the air, on which vegetables such as cabbages and carrots are planted. Another artist suggests simply to take the base away, or at least that part of it on which Worker and Peasant are about to place their feet, leaving them both magically suspended in the air, unsure of what the next step shall bring. "One step forward, . . . "

Of course these stirring examples of defacement are somewhat weakened by the fact that they only occur after the regime has, as we say, fallen, emerging from the vantage point of the security provided by another strong state.

## Mucoid Ignominy

Even as he was being apotheosized in the capitals of Europe and the United States, he died in exile with but a handful of companions, coughing his tubercular lungs out on the hot coast at Santa Marta, Colombia. He who had commanded enormous armies and beaten Murillo's Spanish cavalry into the ground. He who had changed the destiny of an empire and brought to a new world new nations. Acclaimed as The Liberator, within a few brief years his fame evaporated under a tropical sun.

But, by some strange detour of the historical imagination, the European

Elsewhere resuscitated him a decade later. And, boy, did they resuscitate him! Statues were ordered from Paris and the States. Ships creaked with the weight of marble. It was prodigious. The return of the repressed, not to mention the insistence on moving the sacred remains of his body from the spanking-new republic to the west, where he had last laid his beleaguered bones to rest. But of rest there would be little. They wanted his remains, they insisted on having his spirit, and in the absoluteness of their claims to the righteousness of possession they defined the very notion of nationhood. "Nobody has the right to go and get 'em but the Nation to which they belong," said General Páez to Congress in 1842, twelve years after the Liberator had died, heaped in vituperation from the very same Congress.

It was, in other words, the foundational act of spirit possession by the new state.

A boat named *The Constitution* was sent along the coast. Simón Camacho, part of the delegation, met with the young French consul and physician Próspero Révérend, who had been in Santa Marta since 1828 and had attended The Liberator in his last days and kept as a relic all those years a small piece of dried-up bronchial mucus retrieved from The Liberator's lung at postmortem. It had "a somewhat oblong shape," commented Camacho, "porous and similar to the tiny bones to be found in the spines of fish."

It was with boundless appreciation that Próspero Révérend hung onto this dried mucus wrapped in the same paper it was put into at autopsy twelve years before. He planned to send it to France in case he died far from his family. Thus from hand to familial hand, and through those hands from nation to nation, the anticipation if not fear of death serves to transfer the mucus of the man coughing to death in exile. Could there be a bond more intimate between nations than that established by this exchange of oddly-shaped mucoid ignominy excavated from the corpse? And by what strange logic of taboo and transgression, by what strange mixture of medical license and ritual lore, could an act of such perfectly base materialism come so naturally to glorify the state of the whole?

(Source: Taussig, *The Magic of the State*, pp. 99–100.)

Cement Fondue was what Greg Taylor used to make his statue of the naked royals, and he coated it with an iron oxide material so it would rust quickly. Active decay, reminiscent of Dada, was thus built into this work, which in the space of three days, beginning with the decapitation of the queen, burst into a riveting "happening" at the center of national attention.

Greg Taylor had gotten into sculpture after a chainsaw accident gashed his leg in the days when he was a farmer and a logger around Bega on the south coast of New South Wales. A doctor advised him to do art so as to relax. "Down by the Lake with Phil and Liz" was his third sculpture. It cost him six thousand dollars. "Washing-machine" money he called it in a generally forgotten Australian idiom, referring to the loose change households of modest means might put aside for a large purchase. An innocent enough tale of an Australian Quixote in over his head. So much for art therapy in country hospitals! So much for art once it gets into the hands of the tough men who cut down the Australian wilderness!

But a quite different and even sinister history was read into his sculpture once it was placed by the still waters of the newly made Lake Burley Griffin, itself a work of art installed to add a certain placid gravity to the new capital city of Australia. On the opposite shore from where his statue was placed stands the National War Memorial, composed of a broad avenue bordered by statues dedicated to many of the wars this little country, in its brief history as a white nation-state, outpost of empire, has been drawn into. There are more wars about to receive their statue, while others are still waiting. It is a slow business. Behind Greg Taylor's statue stood the two houses of Parliament, the old and the new, and while the High Court and the National Gallery lay on one side of the statue, the National Library and National Science and Technology Centre occupied the other.

The setting was too perfect. The precise place for an offensive statue, at least for those who could see the Big Picture. No wonder many people assumed it was endorsed by "the government" itself, the prime minister being vociferously against monarchy and himself seen as the figurehead, if not the instigator, of the extraordinary shift in Australian identity away from its colonial orientation to the British Crown, to its first fumbling steps toward a nation defining itself in terms of a wondrous mix of Australian aboriginality and Asia.

"They are just sitting there rusting away and I love it. They don't even know they are irrelevant," said Taylor early on in the saga, referring to the queen and Prince Philip. It was a prophetic sentiment, in more ways than one. They certainly "rusted away," but much quicker than he anticipated, and as for the attribution of (false) consciousness, or at least the possibility thereof, to the statues—"They don't even know they are irrelevant"—as if they actually were the queen and her consort, we have only to glance at the record to see that this sympathetic magic, in which the copy seems to acquire the properties of what it's a copy of, often accompanies defacement and is what underlies its curious "they don't even know" logic.

But which comes first, chicken or egg, defacement or sympathetic magic? A rhetorical question, no doubt, but let me suggest that defacement comes "first" or at least creates an express lane to the magic of the mimetic, such that defacement of the till-then-inert copy triggers its inherent capacity for life into life. We should recall how the very first example in Sir James George Frazer's famous chapter on sympathetic magic in *The Golden Bough* is a figurine with a needle poked through its head or its heart by an "Ojibway Indian." The hefty number of examples of sympathetic magic, running to one hundred and sixty-two pages, thus gives pride of first place to defacement, and it does this because the author thinks this to be the most common form of magical art. "Perhaps the most familiar application of the principle that like produces like," begins Frazer, "is the attempt which has been made by many people in many ages to injure or destroy an enemy by injuring or destroying an image of him, in the belief that, just as the image suffers, so does the man, and that when it perishes he must die."[7]

What's more, it's not only as if disfiguring the copy acts on what it is a copy of, but that, associated with this, the defaced copy emits a charge which seems—how else can we say this?—to enter the body of the observer and to extend to physically fill, overflow, and therewith create an effusion of proliferating defacements. . . . *As away they rust, so without them even knowing it, I love it.* And the rot spreads in a riot of contagion beginning with (1) the tethering of a live corgi dog to the bench a day or two after Her beheading, not to mention (2) the loving care with which the media highlights its ubiquitous tags of image-befoulment, Her bare breasts and the prince's legs apart, and (3) yet, nevertheless, people of all ages wanted more than anything else to sit with them or between them or behind them, whatever, and to have their photos taken thus. Six-year-old Hope Bush appears between them in a newspaper photograph with a deferential hand on each naked shoulder looking shy, proud, and eminently respectful.

After all, as was pointed out by Ms. Betty Churcher, director of the National Art Gallery, the furor over the sculpture was reminiscent of the row sparked by Prime Minister Paul Keating for touching the queen during the 1992 royal visit. They were inspecting a guard of honor, and in a moment of confusion the PM ever so lightly placed his hand on her "lower back," close to the royal butt.

"It was like he had touched God really," Ms. Churcher said.

He had violated one of the oldest taboos. More than that, one of those taboos that single-handedly created the very concept of the taboo long before Captain Cook put the word into our language after his voyage to the Pacific.

And these taboos regarding the bodies of queens and kings, not to mention God, become magnified by the colonial relationship, more precious and hence more vulnerable. Yet their status is a mystery. And perhaps that's the point. Would your average Australian have known that this touching was a violation if it hadn't been pointed out by the media citing strange authorities, such as the high priests of tradition in Westminster? In any event there must have been considerable power to be galvanized once it became an issue.

We note how Ms. Churcher (four years after the prime minister touched the queen) is quoted as saying it was like touching God, really.

She is in a teaching mode. She is looking for an image to express the inexpressible and get the idea across in clear language, that (a) you simply do not ever touch God or, (b) similarly, royalty.

But as to why you must never touch?

And even more striking and more curious: Why would you want to touch? Because you mustn't? And is touching the statue defaced through nudity as bad as touching the pristine un-defaced object?

But there they are touching the befouled statue, bared breasts, parted legs, and all. "All the perverts of Canberra have gone and stared at her breasts. Some of the sick republican perverts even touched them."

Letters to the editor poured in because, even before it was defaced, it was, for many, a sickening and filthy phenomenon:

"Totally bloody disgusting."

"Obscene."

"Piece of junk displayed in the name of art."

"Vulgar."

"Grotesque."

"Monstrosity."

"Lavatory graffiti."

"Vandalism in the guise of art."

"A revolting display."

"Why was this mess allowed to desecrate the lakeside?"

"I cannot find words. . . . A cowardly attack designed to be as insulting as possible."

"Bad taste."

"Insult and ridicule."

"The Queen has been through difficult times in recent years and has survived with dignity. She cannot, however, defend herself against this sort of attack."

"Profanity."

"A distasteful effigy of my queen."

"These people belong in the trees with the apes, or in cages in the zoo."

"Rot."

"A horrifying scandal."

"Try to do this in any other country, to any other head of state. You would get what you deserve."

"A sick stunt."

"A cheap shot."

"Sexual harassment."

"Human rights violated."

"It is hurtful and uncalled for."

"An overwhelming 94 percent of callers to the *Herald Sun* Vote Line yesterday said they were offended by the nude sculptures of the Queen and Prince Philip. The statues sparked a large response with as many as 1,852 calls."

There was ridicule as well, the attempt to define the work not so much as filthy and sickening but, because of its filthiness, as childish.

A knight of the realm had this to say:

"My own instinctive reaction to that offensive sculpture was to ignore it. After all, isn't that how we are told to treat a spoilt brat of a child who deliberately makes a disgusting mess on the living room carpet, when the natural reaction might be to turn it over and spank its bottom? But I can understand the reaction of those who would prefer to spank the sculptor (*sic*) instead of ignoring him."

The knight of the realm raises difficult questions. For is there not an awkwardness to iconoclasm, paradoxically privileging its target by virtue of ridicule? And does not iconoclasm justify and even insist on violent, childish, debased, filthy, revolting, rotten, disgusting, filthy, insulting, profane, and so on, counterreaction—in this case to turn the artist over and spank his bottom; that is, to deface the defacer or at least his bottom?

Even more than privileging its target, iconoclasm easily turns against itself. Hence the standard option, as expressed by our knight of the realm, to ignore the whole thing, just as you would ignore, so the knight says, a naughty child. (You can see how many naughty children he's been around.) Or the similar claim by one journalist described as a language expert, Jo-Ann Stubbings, that Australians are inherently iconoclastic—they love "taking the mickey out of the sacred and the serious"—such that the final effect, in this instance of Greg Taylor's sculpture, was one of boredom. Indifference is what won, according to her, and taking the mickey out of the sacred and the serious is ultimately boring. Negation falls flat on its defaced face. In fact, she recruits the statuary itself to make her point: "Both the royals seemed tired," she says. "Poor souls. . . . They were, in fact, dead bored. Someone was taking the mickey out of them. And ho hum, disloyal subjects, it had all been be-fore." Of interest here is how in defacing the artist's defacing, in negating his negating, she animates the statues, or at the very least allows their potential for being that which they are copies of to burst forth. Ho hum.

According to this, the artist lost. And perhaps he did even worse than lose, because it may turn out that his defacement was not just ineffectual but added new power to the target of his critique. His work may not only be dead boring but may even raise the stature of the statued, backfiring by virtue of a defacing twist to Hegel's *Aufhebung*, converting a negative into a transcendent positive, the defaced artwork serving as testimony to the truth counter to the countertruth the artist wished to exalt. Curiously, this back-firing twist suggests that to become dead (boring) the artwork must first have become alive in a spurt of mimetic efflorescence, thereby opening up for us a range of interesting possibilities regarding the mimetic faculty: as hav-ing not so much a life but also a death of its own—and even, perhaps, a life in death?

So let us acknowledge this unresolved tension within defacement, first in its cruising along the edge of self-destruction and, second, in the way by which the terms of this self-destruction hover between boredom versus augmenta-tion of the power of the defaced, no less than they hover between boredom and the desire on the part of the bored to be as defacing as the defacement that makes them bored, such boredom created by defacement sliding easily into vexatious irritation where all manner of defacings or bottom-spankings lie parked, awaiting the mad scramble to proliferate.

"It is about time Australia got to grips with what used to be called com-mon decency. . . . Are we now going to have a twelve-metre-high penis called "Prime Minister" or a giant walk-through vagina called Carmen Lawrence?" (Carmen Lawrence was the federal minister of health and a close associate of the prime minister.) "I find either concept revolting," adds the writer of this letter to the editor in one of those offhand negations that en-courage you to think, maybe, the revolting is not so revolting, and could even be funny and enjoyable, as defacement snowballs.

"In my twenty-five years of public relations I have never heard such filthy comments. . . . Some people were crying on the telephone," said a National Capital Planning Authority spokesman.

More than bottom spanking the artist as a child, but along the same axis of punishment and pleasure, were innumerable fantasies concerning the decapitation of the artist, once the statue of the naked queen had been decapitated. The artist's family received death threats too.

"State Returned Soldiers' League chief Bruce Ruxton last night said the sculpture was sick and its creator Mr. Taylor should be tied to concrete and thrown into Lake Burley Griffin."

"Memo Mr. Taylor: Your sculpture can be seen as an act of sedition, and in different times it would have been your head that was removed."

"How lucky we are, I reflect, to live in a country where to be irreverent about authority figures brings letters to the newspaper rather a knock on the door in the middle of the night."

Here the proliferating effect of defacement, with its heavy yield of punning and fast switchback movements between literality and figuration, can draw our attention to the peculiar complexity that art meant to deface acquires in liberal-democratic states in which censorship cannot be physical so much as financial. Legal provision for freedom of expression drastically undercuts the success of the defacing intention. The less censorship there is, the weaker, by and large, becomes the defacing act. This paradox has paradoxical effects, as, when defacement achieves its goal by antagonizing authority and bringing repression down upon itself, the artist then protests in the name of freedom of expression—when the point of the work was to arouse that antagonism, create repression, and strengthen the hostility to defacement that freedom of expression would undermine. The paradox is only deepened by the observation that the artist seems to have no option other than to protest, whereas in truth what one should really be protesting would be the absence of repression. Such is the insoluble illogic of defacement, equally illustrated by the selfless dedication of the censor experiencing all manner of grim pleasures in witnessing obscenity so as to stop it dead in its tracks. Just think of the children.

In any event, be it noted that violence remains a key component; whether it be the indirect violence in the form of financial censorship, as practiced by U.S. Senator Jesse Helms via the National Endowment for the Arts, for instance, and as vociferously expressed by numerous critics of the Canberra statue in the name of defending taxpayers' dollars; or whether it be the physical violence threatened by the off-duty Sydney police officer, attempting to clothe the naked statues, or the physical effort involved in tearing off the heads and limbs of the statues in the days that followed.

There is surely something more to these physical reactions than blind anger (as if anger could ever be "blind"), something almost as calculated, in its own way, as the artwork to be mutilated, even if that calculation uses a language beyond ordinary consciousness, where human bodies and cultural artifacts converse.

"Work of art! Work of art! You're a work of art!!" So echoes the policeman's righteous rage as he readies himself to violate the violation. He looks magnificent by the side of the queen and the prince, their nakedness now concealed by bed sheets bearing the flag and national insignia. "Over my dead body," reads the caption to the news photo as he waves his fist. The sheets have the effect of making the sculptures look like hospital patients, or even corpses. The secret has been reconstrued under wraps. Only the headlessness of the queen pokes through.

For just as the defacing artist violates the norm and does violence to taste and moral standards, so the defacing act seems to demand a mimetic counterreaction, a defacement of the defacement by what can eventually have a disturbing, magical or religious, twist to it. (*"It's as if they really were people,"* I *hear a voice saying. "It's even worse, because they're not!"* I reply.) "It's gone beyond a bit of fun now," Neil Roberts said as the mutilated statues were driven away. "It was almost like the violence level had got too high. We're talking about people attacking them with a lot of violence, not just a casual glancing blow."

The magico-religious moment comes quietly. We sense the mystery that had been there all along in the mimetic magic of the statues, these defacing statues themselves defaced to the point where, no longer mere symbols, they are granted life, becoming soulful extensions of that which they stood for. Just cement fondue, after all. And yet . . .

We feel a corner has been turned and there is little chance of going back, as if, stupidly, violence against a mere representation can be worse than violence against a real person, perhaps because the basis of fiction and of the suspension of disbelief have been violated.

Robert Musil's illuminating comment on monuments takes this further, his point being not only that we rarely (if ever) look at monuments, but that they are (in his phrase) "conspicuously inconspicuous," by which he means, and flatly states, first, that monuments are living beings, albeit endowed with life so as to create their nonbeing, and second, that as part of this extraordinary death-in-life or life-in-death, they incite defacement. "One cannot say we did not notice them," he says of monuments, "one would have to say they 'de-notice' us, they elude our perceptive faculties: this is a downright vandalism-inciting quality of theirs!" And he urges monuments to try a little harder, as we must all do nowadays.[8]

This slide toward bodily realness of defaced statuary ensures that the media itself becomes an extension of the defacement, essential to its proliferation. What catches the eye of the media is the pathos of this challenge to the death of representation. How the words and images now fly!

Note the joy in the wordplay unleashed with headlines such as *Lese-Magesties Unveiled Along the Embankment, Naked Queen Loses Her Head in Australia, Phil Keeps His Head While All Lose Theirs, Heads May Roll over Naked Royals*, and so forth. One wonderfully bad joke after another. "Lucy the corgi was too late to stop the queen being beheaded." Then the lascivious mock-serious serious descriptions of the destruction, in which the prose clamps tight its straight face as it conspires with the suspension of disbelief that allows the statuary to really be what it merely represents. "*The fracas . . . took a new twist yesterday, when the Duke's head was sawn off with a hacksaw [after Mr. Roberts] found the Duke's head detached from the body, standing off on the ¼-inch reinforcing rod that runs through the figure's neck. The left-hand shoulder down to the elbow had been smashed.*" Another journalist wrote: "*The attacks began on Thursday evening when the Queen was beheaded. By early yesterday she had lost her legs. On Friday night, vandals attacked Prince Philip's head, leaving it dangling until organisers took it off with a hacksaw. By yesterday his left arm also had been severed and his chest smashed.*"

*As away they rust, so without them even knowing I love it*, and the rot spreads in a riot of contagion beginning with the hyper-real corgi tied to her bench. The defacements now are legion. And if the written word of the journalist, mediating the image with its public, finds this medium of the defaced image congenial for a newfound wordplay slipping twixt the real and the mirror of the real, no less than between a rollicking good humor and a sad and thought-provoking magic, how much more so with the photography and cartoons! Wave after wave of cartooned defacements roll across the editorial pages to batter down the barriers of censorship and the restraint of taste, secure in their being mere comment on someone else's defacing. One cartoon presents the prince muttering in his good wife's ear, seated, as they are, naked on the park bench, "Imagine if I'd had an erection." And so forth.

As for the media photography, I am thinking of the sort of thing exemplified in the photo of the corgi tied to the park bench on which the statues of royal couple are seated, a photo so perfect it appeared in many newspapers, sometimes in color, sometimes in black and white. The photographer has taken the shot close to ground level just in front of this happy dog, which takes center stage, facing us, sitting on its hind legs in front of the bench, filling the photograph with its brimming, overflowing presence. You can almost see it wagging its tail. The back part of its body is dark, the head and chest white and radiant. Indeed the whole point of this image is the forefronting of the front of the dog, its face bright and alert, elevating the dog to the surface of the photograph, as if, in its eruption from the image, it is drawing along, with its accelerating presence, the otherwise inert statues too. This dog is ready to leap out at you. Only the leash holds it fast. I do not think "animalization" is necessary for the statues to come to life, but it sure helps. Just as does the brutal headlessness of the naked queen, severed neck erect under a cloudy sky.

By using royal body parts, especially the head, other photos achieve this uncanny presencing as well. What creates this almost palpable force is not so much the resorting to the traumatically torn-off body parts themselves, but the way in which the dislocated body disturbs the sense of the whole and, even, the viewer's perceptual apparatus. Take, for instance, the prince's severed head in the *Canberra Times*, April 16, 1995, a photo showing Neil Roberts in the background, hacksaw in hand, trimming the vandalized neck of the queen. The foreground or lower half of the photo, however, due to the distortion of the perspective, is occupied by the disproportionately immense head of the prince, lying on its side on the ground. Something prehistoric stirs in this image. Something cumbersome, yet bespeaking life as the broken object, precisely because it is broken, exhales aura, and returns our gaze.

The same has to be said even when the head has not been torn off the body. After all, the camera guillotines the head in the twinkling of an eye by excluding the body from the frame, so that in the April 16 issue of the *Herald Sun*, for instance, we find most of the photo given over to a close-up of the side of the prince's still intact head, with a slightly blurred figure of a woman spectator in sunglasses in the receding and whitened-out background. His head is pushing at us sideways. Like a crab crawling out of the frame. By contrast, the spectator seems like an object, a mannequin, at best.

But animation and presencing is easiest when the violated bodies are finally moved off their base from the vertical to the horizontal in an unrecuperable transition to base materialism. Life floods the image, as we are reminded by the photo in the *Advertiser*, April 17, in which, from a bird's-eye view, we look down on the headless bodies laid sideways in the back of a pickup. He lies on his back, hands on either side of his thighs. Hers are tightly clasped. Both figures seem to be straining, trying to rise like Lazarus, drawn to the tender glance of the onlookers in the background. Her legs have been cut off as well.

*An empty bench by a quiet lake.* The most convincing image of all, however, relating to the mimetic magic that realizes the statues as living and therefore spiritual presences, is the photograph in the *Canberra Times* displaying the empty bench filled with the gaze of curious bystanders after the statues had been removed. Here, emptiness is as filled with presence as is the adjoining lake gently lapping at the water's edge a few feet away. A complete defacement. A perfectly empty space filled with what was.

*Defacement and the history of the bandit.* Rumor, endorsed by media approval, exhibited this same tendency of defacement for mimetic proliferation of presence swarming with sacral excess. Perhaps least expected was the announcement, a month after the statues were violated, that the queen's head had at last been located! Credit went to the federal police, working with ASIO, the Australian equivalent of the CIA, who discovered the head in the home of a right-wing militia member whose group, so it was now revealed, not only had an arsenal at its disposal, but had infiltrated the computer and communications sections of the Defense Department as well. Senior police officers refused to say more. A "security blanket" was in force. "Both issues are just too sensitive, and no-one will want to talk about it," a police source said. Two days later, however, on May 14, a terse media release from the federal police denied the head had been retrieved. "It's a total fabrication—there's no truth in it whatsoever," a police spokeswoman said.

It was cause for much speculation, this missing head. In his regular column, in the April 18 issue of the *Daily Telegraph Mirror*, Mark Day proposed that the missing head "must rank up there with Ned Kelly's death mask," and if ever found should be displayed in an argon-filled glass case in Parliament House. Was it one of those Australian jokes, Kelly being the icon of resistance to colonial authority and most especially to its head?

For he was a late-nineteenth-century Australian country boy of Irish-convict ancestry who, after many exploits outwitting the law, was captured in macabre circumstances with his brother, both of them wearing quarter-inch steel suits of armor made from ploughshares. A neat reversal on the biblical homily. The suits covered the head and much of the body and the square-can image of Kelly's head, not unlike a TV set, seemingly dislocated from his torso and moving unexpectedly in valiant stops and starts through the Australian bush and townships, features vividly in Sidney Nolan's 1960's series of fantasy-paintings dedicated to him and to the even larger project of creating, ex nihilo, that desperately needed resource, an Australian mythology.

In Nolan's painting *Riverbend*, gloomy dull greens and browns shimmer from the swamp beetled over by dense stands of eucalyptus trees in serried formations like soldiers, nature's sentinels. Ned Kelly is present in only two of the nine panels that constitute this huge painting some thirty-three feet long. Even where he is present he is tiny, about to be swallowed by swamp except for the opalescent detail of his black-bordered square steel head, the "culture," so to speak, that resists the annihilation of the human being by nature, as if, therefore, culture in Australia, at least non-aboriginal male Australia, is to be preeminently defined by an awkward, metallic, masked defiance of the state. Kelly's is a secret, and hence all the more imposing presence, but the fact that he flits in and out of the visual field suggests something more than secrecy, and that is the playing with revelation, a striptease of hidden presence, a public secret, we could say, invigorated by the uncanny head that is his armor, larger than the man himself, just as the forest of a primeval nature also dwarfs the man. And there is nothing, absolutely nothing, where the face should be, in the center of this black-edged box of a head, nothing but a blank, white, empty space. This we call defacement.

And Kelly was the greatest defacer of them all, not only in life, but even more so in afterlife as the figure of the rebel whose love of stealing fast horses and rustling cattle spilled over in ever larger waves of hatred against police and colonial authority. His name is now legend, the legend itself a work of collective art, beginning where the life ended—in that armor made of ploughshares, meant to conserve it. There was a good deal of this armor in Greg Taylor's sculpture of Phil and Liz down by the lake.

There are nine panels in Nolan's *Riverbend*, joined tightly to each other to form something like a movie whose subject, more than Kelly and more than the Australian wilderness, is time itself moving with the waters of the swamp at the base of the looming trees from which the tiny hidden figure of Kelly emerges to kill a man on horseback. Kelly's rifle can be barely discerned. Only the TV box of head stands out boldly as Kelly takes the horse and rides back into the woods, leaving the corpse stiff in the dark water. These waters flow on as our eye scans the remaining five panels. For there is nothing. Nothing but sad forests receding as more and more insipid water fills the canvas.

*Kelly's head featured strangely in accounts of his capture.* Severely wounded, weak from blood loss, and greatly impeded by his homemade armor, Kelly had escaped on horseback from the hotel surrounded by troops, but decided to return in the cold early morning to assist his comrades, which meant he would have to break through the cordon from behind. An eyewitness reporter for the Melbourne *Age* noted that a "tall figure was seen close behind the line of police. At first it was thought he was a blackfellow. He carried a grey coat over his arm, and walked coolly and slowly among the police. . . . It appeared as if he was a fiend with a charmed life."[9] Another source quotes a police sergeant describing Kelly as a tall, aboriginal man, wrapped in a blanket or a possum rug, with an old top hat on his head.[10]

Constable James Arthur, whose gun brought Kelly down, described in writing how at daybreak, in the act of lighting his pipe in the cold morning, he heard Kelly coming up behind him. Kelly's appearance was so extraordinary that the pipe fell from his mouth as he "gazed at the strange object for a minute, not knowing but that it was a madman who had conceived the idea of storming the hotel with a nail-can on his head."

"Go back you d——fool, you will get shot."

"I could shoot you sonny."

Kelly fired but missed, for his arm had been shattered the night before by rifle shots.

They were but twenty to thirty feet apart, and Arthur fired his rifle at the helmet, thinking he would knock it off. It only staggered him slightly.

An opening in the helmet looked like a huge mouth, wrote Arthur. "I fired at that and hit him again." He still came on.

"I fired a third shot and heard it hum off him. I was completely astonished, and could not understand what the object I was firing at was. The men around me appeared astonished too. Someone said, 'He's a madman!' Dowsett, the railway guard, said, 'He is the devil!' Sergeant Kelly exclaimed, 'Look out boys, he is the bunyip.'"[11]

(The *bunyip*, I should explain, is a legendary creature of early white Australian imagination, a figure of the swamp. Sergeant Kelly claimed later that what he'd actually said was "He's bullet-proof."[12] As I guess the bunyip is, too.)

Following the hanging of Ned Kelly, at the age of twenty-five, his head was sawed off, the brain removed, and, stripped of flesh, the head was kept as a curio, its present whereabouts unknown. The headless corpse was covered in quicklime and buried, unmarked, in the jailyard.[13]

With federal police denying the report that they had found the queen's head, its presence grows all the stronger, and I cannot resist imagining how these militiamen arrested by the feds might have, along with their weapons and computer skills, lovingly cared for it in a nice box on a purple cushion as the centerpiece of a strange new cult empowered by defacement. This line of speculation regarding the scene of discovery of a head under a security blanket rests on the notion that such a secret cult in the heart of the Defense Ministry is not only secretive, but the very figure of secrecy, and that it is secrecy to which the proliferation of defacements responds, breaking open, severing parts from wholes, in a tearing of tegument, so as to release a veritably sacred inside, leading to more of the hidden same.

*Hence nakedness was crucial, intermingling the erotic with the secret.* It made a lot of people mad to have the constitutional head of state and her consort presented naked. Moving defenses were made on behalf of the naked human body as central to Western art, and some people—a decided minority—pointed to a strange surge of humanness aroused by what they saw as loneliness and sadness evoked in having an elderly couple gazing over the empty lake, stripped of all pretension and defense along with their clothing—the point here being that, instead of insulting the queen, from this perspective the nudity ennobled her by indicating the emotional burden shouldered by the exalted.

"There was as much dignity as absurdity in those tired, aging, but stoic bodies shivering in the winds of change off Lake Burley Griffin," wrote the senior curator of art at the Tasmanian Museum and Art Gallery (also, be it noted, recruiting the statues—as living, shivering beings—to his ennobling cause).

"To me it was a sensitive study of a couple three-quarters of their way through life," wrote B. N. Mainsbridge of Stanwell Park to a daily newspaper, emphasizing how poignant a picture of human frailty and solitude it conveyed. Stripped naked of all insignia, the majesty of office was reduced "to the frailty of the human condition of which we are all part. What is offensive about that?"

The links between secrecy and nakedness of the human form were given a further twist in the letter by M. Taylor in the *Sydney Morning Herald*, April 19, where she (perhaps inadvertently) drew attention to the important fact that when it comes to secrecy, the head shares a curious division of labor with the genitals and can even be substituted for them. For her, the vandalism of the statues (which began, as you will remember, with the decapitation of the queen) was "reminiscent of those who demanded the genitalia of Michelangelo's David be masked with a fig leaf." The logic exposed here is remarkable. *Defacement becomes equivalent to covering the genitals.* What could be more perfect?

This brings us back to basics, the head being that part of the body generally left naked throughout human history and across cultures, while the genitalia are that part of the body generally covered (as far as I know), even if by a token, a penis sheath or a piece of string. The two zones of the body, the covered and the uncovered, are doubtless selected by a superior wisdom for their stunning contrasts, one zone, the open face, being in fact capable of the most duplicitous covering, on account of its tremendous capacity for self-masking of what I choose to call, too poetically perhaps, "the window to the soul," but which we could now think of as the window to the heart and to the emotions, very much including the sexual emotions and their concentrated erotic repository in the otherwise always covered genitalia. This direct line of connection between the face and one's "private parts" receives its endorsement in that flood of blood which in fair-skinned people creates the blush, a sort of superabundance of connectedness when the face has to hyper-mask or, as a giveaway sign of shame, reveal to the world that one has given away something secret, imposed on secret terrain, or had one's secret revealed.

To the editorial writer of the *Canberra Times* it was the *ordinariness* created by nudity that accounted for the rage many people felt, and such ordinariness of the extraordinary suggested the eternal wisdom of the story of "The Emperor's New Clothes"—"that beneath the artifice of clothing," suggested the editorial writer, "we are all possessed of similar physical assets and liabilities, whether high born or from the common herd."

But is it not also the other way around, that nudity is not only a stripping down to a common humanity but also a dramatic elevation? Surely the long and complicated tradition in Western art of nudity, female or male, is testimony to just such hopes of elevation? How then might we reconcile this opposition and how might it constitute the anger at displaying royalty naked?

The "answer" lies in the derailing of some sort of Hegelian roller coaster in which it is the essence of royalty to "come down" in order "stay up"; hence the hushed yet gleefully reverent remarks as to the splendid humility of the queen, for instance, displaying the marrow of royalness by visiting ordinary working-class people in their ordinary homes and shaking their ordinary hands and drinking tea with them. Not to mention the lust for newspaper photos of topless princesses and the obscene stories and fantasies concerning things royal.

More than a cliché, this is in effect what makes royalty royal and authority authoritative, even when that authority stands remote from the feudal aristocratic culture and structure of royalty—authority of any stripe being automatically aristocratic in its own way. What I mean to say is that "coming down" is prescribed in the heights of power. It is most definitely *not* a sop or a price to pay for being on top, and certainly not a benevolently inspired kindness on the part of society's superiors, although it may well include much kindness and consideration too. No. The "coming down" at stake in power's stake is here nothing more than a requirement of its very being—inadvertently delivered, in this particular instance, by the defacing artist who not only assaults or insults the figures figured, but also (and this is my point) draws out and even exposes that very requirement for those who have eyes to see it.

The Hegelian roller coaster only derails when it is *this* fact of power that is brought out from its hiding in the light of public secrecy, because the real obscenity is not the obscene portrayal as naked beings in statuary, or the proliferation of that as extension and commentary in cartoons playing the double field ("Imagine if I'd had an erection"), but occurs instead in crossing some weird and only half-sensed and less understood line *exposing power's need to "come down."* It is not nakedness per se that is the problem, but the rendering naked of the otherwise concealed authoritative need to be naked that is the problem.

What moves into the spotlight, therefore, and what becomes the appropriate question, is not the attempt at defacement and insult therewith, but rather the exceedingly curious way that *defacement as an inherent property of power's power lies within the phenomenon to be defaced.* Thus we come closer to understanding the mimetic character of the defacement, of the mimetic "fit" between the object and its defacement, and we can proceed to point out that what creates the anger at the actual defacement must therefore have far more to do with this fact of transgressing the taboo, not of nakedness per se, but of daring to indicate that *obscenity is built into the quasi-divine right of authority,* royal or common.

In other words the idea, as expressed in the *Canberra Times* editorial, that the artwork was a clumsy rendition of the story of "The Emperor's New Clothes" has a great deal of merit that is easily overlooked because it seems too obvious. For it points us to the issue of unmasking, in this case uncovering a secret that nobody can give voice to, other than a small boy, the paradox and wonder being that in the case of the story, no less than of the statuary, there were no clothes to be uncovered. To the contrary it was the absence of covering that had to be uncovered.

(Sources: *The Australian, The Canberra Times, The Sydney Morning Herald, The Age, The Advertiser, The Herald Sun, The Daily Telegraph, The Mirror.* Cuttings compiled by Neil Roberts, Canberra National Sculpture Forum Coordinator, in *Media Dossier: "Down by the Lake with Phil and Liz," by Gregory Taylor,* 1995.)

Hegel's parable of bondsman and lord in the story of consciousness becoming self-consciousness is but an instance in the standoff between work and death, processed through vexed equations of Self in Other, as called for by the unfolding of the World Spirit—*work*, because that's what the bondsman does for the lord; *death*, because that's what the lord, but not the bondsman, was prepared to risk. Yet if it was fear of death that determined their respective positions, in this story work triumphs over death to the extent that the bondsman triumphs not only over the lord, but over the original inability to risk death that plunged him into servitude.

If this seems a somewhat romantic story about work, yet incurably intriguing, what of the properties of death and, furthermore, of what we might call death-work; in the *Phenomenology*, for example, where Hegel, in a now famous passage, speaks to the magic thereof:

> Now the life of Spirit is not that which is frightened of death, and spares itself destruction, but that life which assumes death and lives with it. Spirit attains its truth only by finding itself in absolute dismemberment. . . . Spirit is that power only to the degree in which it contemplates the Negative face to face and dwells with it. This prolonged sojourn is the magical force which transposes the negative into given-Being.[14]

Here death-work, if I can use such an expression, would seem to have the potential to go either way—toward the triumph that is properly speaking that of work triumphing over death, transposing the negative into given-Being, or it can instead veer toward that quite other sort of triumph, if triumph indeed it be, which stays with death, stays with the negative face-to-face and dwells with it, finding truth in the magical force of absolute dismemberment. If the first route tricks death by making a theatrical spectacle of it, as with sacrifice in which the sacrificer substitutes an intermediary for destruction, the second sort of triumph is like the auto-mutilation or self-sacrifice of the god, giving without expectation of receiving.

Defacement is that face-off with death and dismemberment that tilts toward this second sort of triumph, if triumph indeed it be, beyond recuperation by death-work or any other kind of work and beyond both lordship and bondage (as Derrida stresses in his commentary on Bataille's Hegelianism "without reserve").[15] Defacement is the confrontation with death and dislocation whose meaning is irrecuperable by a more transcendent system. Why irrecuperable? Because it breaks the magic circle of understanding to spill out as contagious, proliferating, voided force where, no matter how long death is faced-off, contradiction cannot be mastered and only laughter, bottom-spanking, eroticism, violence, and dismemberment exist simultaneously in violent silence. As we have seen.

"A decapitated queen and Prince Philip were driven out yesterday, in the back of a rusty ute [pickup]. 'It's gone beyond a bit of fun now,' Mr. Roberts said."

Two weeks later there were still crowds gathered around the empty bench on which the statues had been sitting.

Behind the empty bench and gently sloping, well-tended lawns stand the houses of Parliament. In front of the bench across the lake stand statues in a line commemorating the sacrifice made by those fallen in the wars entered into by the Australian state. There is a religious service here, once a year, at dawn on Anzac Day. Nowadays, as in the United States, there are Australian veterans from the war in Vietnam who don't exactly fit the bill of the good soldier, neat and patriotic. They are chain-smoking misfits with torn Windcheaters and scraggy hair, a haunted look in their eyes. They make sacrifice more complicated, as if the sacrifice of the war is quite beyond the appropriation sought by the rituals of the nation-state. Instead, the deaths now seem like sacrilege because the war is increasingly seen as such, and this is why these veterans in their very being are effigies of sacrilege. Unlike the statues to the dead, they stand at the back of the group assembled for the service. They seem like living indictments of the very notion of sacrifice which they invert with no possibility of finding resolution, safe haven, rest, or respite.

When the sun rose from behind the low-lying Canberra hills filling the cold April sky, there came three dark army helicopters flying in formation straight up the line of statues until the outer two suddenly veered to the sides. Clack clack clack clack. . . . It was really something, Neil Roberts told me. There was a sort of mass shudder among the vets as their bodies gripped each other. "A thing that remains in mind," Neil writes me recently, was "the lack of space between them—a space so common in straight men's relationships (except in sports) was foregone, breached in trust and need. You don't see men like that *cling* to each other often, brace each other, hold. And the choppers clustered them even tighter than before." For an instant it was Vietnam all over again but only for an instant, for now, neither lords nor bondsmen, do they not, as a mass monument themselves, endlessly stare death in the face?

---

**Tapes Show Johnson Saw Vietnam War as Pointless in 1964**

Austin, Tex., Feb. 14 (AP)—Tapes of two telephone conversations released today by the Presidential Library here showed that almost a year before President Lyndon B. Johnson began the large-scale buildup in Vietnam, he called the war "the biggest damn mess I ever saw, and lamented, "I don't think it's worth fighting for, and I don't think we can get out."

He was on the phone with his national security adviser, McGeorge Bundy.

(Source: *The New York Times*, February 15, 1997)

---

### Critique as Defacement

A critique of criticism? At least an appreciation. Well, what *is* one's notion of criticism anyway? My idea of criticism used to be that of an encounter between two dissimilar entities bound by passion but measured in tone by an implicit appeal for truth and logic, an encounter between a more or less philosophical disposition and its object of scrutiny, whatever that object may be—a history, a text, an attitude, the state of a nation-state. It was like two independent worlds, the critic's task being that of approximating one to the other. And here I have noticed on occasion a curious flip-flop of power and assimilation; by definition the critic assumes the power position, being on top of the object of critique, yet nevertheless in the very act of critique often adds to the power of the thing critiqued. There is a curious complicity at work here that makes me want to ask what happens if we think of criticism as defacement?

Lying somewhere between criticism thus defined and a critique of criticism, this notion of criticism as defacement would seem to get something right about the nature of the complicity between the critic and the object, because defacement succeeds to the degree that it engages internally with the object defaced, enters into its being, we might say, no matter how crude or offensive, subtle or witty, the defacement may be. By virtue or disvirtue of such mimetic and metonymic engagement, the energy emerging from defacement is an energy flowing from an active and activated object of critique and not from a corpse on the dissecting table. Indeed, no matter how crude, defacement and sacrilege thrive on bringing dead and apparently insignificant matter to life—as in the case, for instance, of the desecration of statues or money. The power of the curse and of obscenity speaks to the same awakening of slumbering powers, and this brings us to the unsettling and indeed contemptible consideration that there is a large class of representations that have a strategic, built-in, desire to be violated, without which they are gapingly incomplete. This is Robert Musil's mischievous point regarding statues, for instance, and it implies that the critique supplied by defacement is already inscribed within the object and that what defacement does, like a magic wand, is no more than to tap the object to bring these otherwise obscure or concealed inner powers flooding forth. It is not easy to know how to react to this observation because, in measure equal to the almost magical force of the wand, the sobering conclusion is that negation merely completes the object of critique and was its destiny. So much for critique!

What I have in mind here is critique as repetition of the phenomenon, but repeated in such a way that a defacement and bursting forth of the magic of the negative occurs. This may or may not overlap with caricature and parody, these terms being as highly suggestive as they are complex, but it is certainly mimetic and it is with the power of mimesis that defacement achieves its highest, its most negative, goals. Here again, with the mimetic, we see the intimacy of the bond that connects defacement to its object.

There can be few better examples of this use—or, should we say, spell—of the mimetic than Marcel Proust's miraculous work of remembrance in which, according to Walter Benjamin, physiognomy and mimesis play a creative role. Commenting upon the stimulus the social life of the salons had on the art of mimicry by means of flattery and curiosity, Benjamin suggests that Proust's most accurate and most convincing insights "fasten on their objects as insects fasten on leaves, blossoms, branches, betraying nothing of their existence until a leap, a beating of wings, a vault, shows the startled observer that some incalculable individual life has imperceptibly crept into an alien world."[16]

Of course, Benjamin is doing exactly this with Proust himself, and beyond the subject of Proust we discern this mimetic insect at work in all of Benjamin's writing, the very signature, we could say, of his writing no less than of his philosophy of history and of the famous *correspondences* of which he makes so much in the work of Baudelaire, let alone in his own writings on memory, the doctrine of the similar, and the mimetic faculty.

"The true reader of Proust is constantly jarred by small shocks," says Benjamin, referring to the leap and unfolding of wings by which the insect suddenly reveals its concealed, mimetic, existence. These shocks are the same as those we receive with defacement. For what the latter accomplishes is, first, a mimetic repetition, reproducing the object of critique, gaining power in that very act of copying, only then to immolate the mimicry in a violent gesture of anti-mimicry, the defacement itself, equivalent to the leap and beating of wings.

## Methodology

It started off as *about* but pretty quickly became *mimicry*, close cousin to the *within*. Maybe because what it was about, namely defacement, was too seductive. Yes. Seductive. Which, when you think about it, just has to be the first thing that leaps to mind when confronting the *Thou Shalt Not*. Nothing seemed more right than to jump into the middle and mimic the taboo-defying event, at least as it was reported in the press with all its beauty of rhetoric and direct quotation, the news being the ultimate "social fact," voice of the phantom *them* and *they* whom we invoke to make sense, paranoid yet comforting, of destiny. The world was stories and they formed chains, in every sense of the word. And here was your chance, if only for the moment, to pitch in with yours, or better still (and this is my point, after all), with "theirs," thereby provoking the magical counterpoint that such repetition, depending on the manner executed, may effect. This I call *penultimaticity*, the theory and method of being the one permanently before the last in the great chain of storytelling constitutive of worldly affairs, violence and horror being especially prone to story and repetition. How obvious, therefore, to quote the cherished, if soiled, fragment directly from the media itself, with its countless histories of defacement. Clearly this was realism in high gear (think of Dos Passos's device of the "newsreel," or of Döblin's similar technique in *Berlin Alexanderplatz*), pressed up tight against the object of study, so tight it passes into and becomes one with it, physically, yet therefore also extends it into new fields, so that, thanks to such mimetic immersion and such withinness, the quotation starts to look back at its original self in new ways. Hannah Arendt reports that Walter Benjamin shifted from collecting books to collecting quotations and that nothing was more characteristic of him in the 1930's than the little notebooks with black covers he always carried with him for entering quotations.[17] He understood his first book, *The Origin of German Tragic Drama*, as essentially a book of quotations with his own writing as secondary, and is reported as saying he wanted to write a book with nothing but quotations strung together one after the other. He regarded quotations in his work as highwaymen hidden by the side of the road, ready to rob readers of their convictions. The element of secrecy is striking. No less than the path to truth. To quote Arendt: "To quote is to name, and naming . . . brings truth to light."[18]

# PART TWO

Secrecy Magnifies Reality

At its most literal, *defacement* insists on a certain silliness, shot through with morsels of wisdom in the magic of words and names, as with the face of de/facement pressing close on the heels of sacrilege, bringing faciality and negation into a strange hybridinal wholeness. And because this mix of silliness and wisdom in the magic of words shall dog me throughout this perusal of the face in its relation to sacrilege, let me note that the same magic-of-words treatment is meted out by Sigmund Freud in his influential and extraordinary essay on the uncanny, with the first five pages devoted to faithful repetition of dictionary entries for the word *heimlich*, or "homely" ("uncanny," in German, being *unheimlich*).[1]

But, then, his relating *home* to the female genitalia as the source of the uncanny is not that far off, strange as it may first seem, to what I want to do, which is to render *sacrilege* as a *rend(er)ing of faciality*, especially when taking into account, first, the ties between faciality and the genitalia, the uncovered and the covered, and, second, Freud's main message that the uncanny (to follow Schelling) corresponds to *everything that ought to have remained secret but has come to light*—the *secretly familiar* which has undergone repression and then returned from it. A complicated sequence of oppositions, but easy enough to remember, this "secretly familiar." Whether we choose to place the emphasis on the secretly familiar *item* or, instead, on its *return* from repression, or both, the crucial feature here is the off-kilter, creepy feeling of the uncanny due to an unstable and uncapturable blending, if "blending" be the word, of concealment and revelation of a secret that for all its secretness is not really a secret . . . but what we might call the public secret.

Such a (public) secret may for the moment be defined as that which is generally known but cannot be spoken, and here, at the outset, as the definition sinks in, to the degree it can, let us pay homage to the heterogeneity of the knowledge at stake here with its knowing what not to know, its strategic absences, its resort to riddle and tone . . . a Swiss-cheese reality of unexpected shapes and irregularly shaped holes in the midst of smooth planes, of roller-coaster rides through the carnival grounds of "concealment and revelation," fueled by the intensity of the ambivalence of active not-seeing brought to a standstill by an ineffable fusion of surges so conflicting and contradictory that they overburden language, despite—and hence—five pages of dictionary entries.

In the face of contradiction this intense, precursor of things sacred if not uncanny, there surfaces the problem its demands make on language, as if there is a firm link between the logical possibilities for expression, even with a poetic language, and the exceeding of such possibilities by defacement. Hence not only the resorting to etymologies and lists and antonyms and weird riffs like five pages of dictionary entries in 1917, but the obsession with language—as language—in 1963, as with Michel Foucault ruminating on the meaning of "transgression" in the shadow of Bataille, Foucault running together Nietzsche's death of God with the "limitlessness of the Limit" replacing what had been God's infinitude.[2] Even stranger, perhaps, is Foucault's running together here of sex with language, sex being considered by him not only the repository of taboo in modernity, and hence of the Limit, but the repository of the secret, as well—albeit the *public* secret, as when Foucault in his *History of Sexuality* states repeatedly that "what is peculiar to modern societies is not that they consigned sex to a shadow existence, but that they dedicated themselves to speaking of it *ad infinitum* as *the* secret."[3]

Yet to *dedicate* (as he says) oneself to speech of such a strangely convoluted form of secrecy, or worse still, to be thus dedicated, must be no easy commitment. But do we not carry this off effortlessly most of the time? However, to meet it head-on, this formidable force, to grapple with it philosophically, that is not so easy, at least according to Foucault's essay on transgression. In fact, language itself takes a dive, sabotaged by the demands made on its core by the riddling effect of such secrecy, combined, as it inevitably is, with transgression. For Foucault such talk is perforce *a language transgressed and even actively transgressing itself*, tracing "that line of foam showing us just how far speech may advance upon the sands of silence."[4] In this account, then, such speech is advancing over, yet cut short by, a shifting silence. It is a speech hollowed out by itself, so to speak, working on the secret that works on it. "Perhaps," he says at one point, and we already sense the forlorn note of failure no less than an accelerating enchantment, "Perhaps it is like a flash of lightning in the night which from the very beginning of time, gives a dense and black intensity to the night it denies, which lights up the night from the inside, from top to bottom, and yet owes to the dark the stark clarity of its manifestation, its harrowing and poised singularity." . . . [5] Perhaps.

Was ever a more elaborate and downright mystical figure drawn for the sayable unsayable, painted in the flaring moment of a sky torn dark by lightning to reveal, so as to all the more emphatically conceal? Again and again in his history of sex, written long after the essay on transgression, there is this similar figure of *sex as that secret which has to be spoken so as to preserve it*, the reciprocal, we might say, like pulling a glove inside out, of my definition of the public secret as that which is generally known, but *cannot be spoken*. It is to secrecy, then, most especially to the movement *from* the secret *to* the public secret, tantamount to a "natural history of the secret," and secondly, from that to the peculiar movement implicated in turning the glove inside out, that I feel impelled to turn when contemplating the spiral-like motion and mystical moments implicated by the tongue-tripping transgressive force of negation supplied by de/facement as the site where face and sacrilege abut.

Take one of my opening points of wonder: that rather than offending what is *already* sacred (statues, money, corpse, flag, Liberator's mucus), these acts of desecration seem *to create* sacredness, albeit of a special variety, and now I want to add to this observation my idea that *this is achieved through a "drama of revelation" which, like unmasking, amounts to a transgressive uncovering of a "secretly familiar."*

Think of Robert Musil's statement that the most striking thing about monuments is their lack of strikingness. In fact they are invisible. "Like a drop of water on an oilskin," he wrote, "attention runs down them without stopping for a moment." For him, "the most striking feature of monuments is that you do not notice them. There is nothing in the world as invisible as monuments. Doubtless they have been erected to be seen—even to attract attention; yet at the same time something has impregnated them against attention."[6] Yet, as Marina Warner goes on to note with reference to this observation and its relevance to the statue of *The Law* in the Place du Palais Bourbon in Paris, were it to be removed, "her absence would be acutely felt."[7]

Musil seems to me to be saying more than that statues are invisible; he is saying, first, there is *nothing in the world as invisible as they are*, and second, that to achieve such extraordinary invisibility, statues not only become *animate*, but such animatedness involves *active negation* on their part. "They virtually drive off what they would attract," he says. "We cannot say that we do not notice them, but that they de-notice us." Given this, little effort of imagination is required to understand defacement, as with defacement of statues, as an act whose uncanny capacity to animate dead matter, by magically fusing the representation with what it represents, is already inscribed in the nature of the statue itself. Put otherwise, we could say (following Musil) that the statue barely exists for consciousness and perhaps is nonexistent—until it receives the shock to its being, provided by its defacement issuing forth a hemorrhage of sacred force. With defacement, the statue moves from an excess of invisibility to an excess of visibility.

Sacred things are defined in many Western languages by their astonishing capacity for pollution, danger, and filth, the Latin root *sacer* meaning both accursed and holy. Defacement conspires with this fateful ambiguity, energizing it while accentuating the accursed share now flooding forth in all its loathsomeness of glory—this accursed share that was there all the time, latent, so to speak, hidden, so to speak, all the more effectively granting sacred or quasi-sacred status to the statue, the statue of royalty, royalty itself, the flag, the money, and the corpse. The spy-camera revelation of the morgue workers' desecrations is as much a drawing out of what is already "hidden" in the corpse as tabooed possibility, as it is a revelation of an easily defined obscene act imposed from without. It is a revelation already inscribed in the corpse itself; all that was required was the purer-than-pure straight-backed rituals of the police inquiry into the police to rear its loveliness, reminiscent of the stories—and I stress here the storied nature, as I heard it in Ann Arbor in 1971—about LBJ having sex with JFK's corpse in the back of Air Force One on the way from Dallas to Washington. An article in the *Realist* in 1967 claimed that

LBJ was witnessed by Jackie Kennedy chuckling by the casket, but the manuscript from which the article was drawn is said to have stated that LBJ was "literally fucking my husband by the throat." So the stories extend. The editor of the *Realist* admitted to an inspired wordplay, neckrophilia from necrophilia so as to make his point, à la Jonathan Swift's suggesting the cure for famine was to eat babies, another fine instance of defacement. And Douglas Kahn, from whose marvelous book on mimicry and montage I take these stories, adds the finishing touch, showing us that for all its shockingly bad taste (Foucault's lightning rending the sky dark), this story nevertheless lies on a continuum with everyday life *and humor*, it being one of LBJ's favorite jokes that a group opposed to a Texas sheriff running for reelection suggested spreading the rumor the sheriff fucked pigs. Someone protested. "You know he doesn't do that!" "I know," said the first man. "But let's make the son of a bitch deny it."[8]

These stories are always already there in the corpse that is the beast in the man awaiting ignition. This I call *the law of the base*, playing on the doubleness of the word "base" as both substantial support and as obscene or abject which, in a cavalier gesture, I regard as the base of holiness itself. Such a "law" defines *taboo* not simply as prohibition—and this is the whole and consuming point—but as the prohibition that, illicitly, so to speak, secretly, so to speak, contains hidden yearning, an appeal, even a demand, within itself to transgress that which it prohibits: this, its secret.

Especially intriguing is how, thanks to defacement, images may become real—how the perturbation between revelation and concealment involves an oscillation in deceptively lazy loopings between literalness and metaphor, presence and representation. This ability to blur the distinction, between the representation and that which the representation represents, has in previous pages been amply demonstrated by the proliferation set off by the sacrilegious statues of the queen and her consort, in which the statued objects become what they previously merely symbolized.

With the queen, or should we say with the statue of the queen, this is graspable to some degree in that there is a person within or behind the personage; but what, say, of the flag or the currency? What life, what real reality, lies behind these fetish objects spoliated by the defacing act that all the more effectively establishes their fetish status? Why the cruel penalties carefully provided by the legislature against and in anticipation of such spoliation of tegument? Surely it is the ineffable *presence that behindedness itself generates*—the grandeur of the nation, in the case of the flag, and the extraordinary, indeed super-naturally complicated and taken-for-granted wonder of the socially contrived social agreement to agree on circulation of tokens of wealth that is the state-endorsed thing called money—surely it is the unfathomable mysteries and fragilities of fantasies hardened into workaday facts eluding all rational understanding that are at stake in the fetish quality of flags and money that defacement plunders, against which occurrence President George Herbert Walker Bush the Third valiantly strove, in the case of the flag, to create a constitutional amendment?

So if *behind* the statue of the queen there is at least the comforting presence of the real queen, the two—image and imagized—brought into sudden and unexpected approximation by the magic of the defacer denuding her, then with money and flags it seems like it is the very opposite that emerges with spoliation of tegument, that it is the "great nothing" of the void beckoning, and with it the *mysterium tremendum* of a primal religiosity is reborn. This contrast is paralleled if not explained by the fact that the real queen, like all of royalty, is by definition remote, untouchable, and intangible, while, to the contrary, money (and to some extent flags) is there to be fingered and held close.

Here we do well to figure Nietzsche's famous figure of metaphor as a coin, with the metaphoric magic passing away as active forgetting with the making and continuous remaking of everyday reality as the face on the coin is worn away through circulation from hand to hand.[9] What begins as poetry becomes dulled through usage and we no longer see that the very facts of our existence are not facts but artifacts. *And it is precisely here* in the very nerve center of this active forgetting that, with its burnings, its savage markings, its cruel and often clever cuttings . . . defacement exerts its curious property of magnifying, not destroying, value, drawing out the sacred from the habitual-mundane, illuminating what Nietzsche saw as metaphoric basis of all existence but effaced by usage, passing into the practical illusions of factual truth. *Defacement* puts this habitual operation of *effacement* into reverse, releasing, through its metonymic hands-on downright crassness the magical quality of the metaphor which lies hidden or asleep in the uprightness of the everyday. The true defacement, of course, is precisely this exposure of facticity's hidden dependence on illusion. For who could live in such a world? Midday! Time of the shortest shadow!

On this the art of sacrilege depends.

Thus I keep returning to the physical actuality of tearing and spoliation of tegument, as with the flag and with the currency, the abrupt animation of the statue's somnolent shadow, the feverish attempts to clothe the nakedness of the queen and her prince (with the flag, of course), as if defacement was first and foremost a ripping of surface and thereby an unmasking of hidden capacities waiting behind ready to burst forth with immolation—the immolation defining this invisible border waiting to be crossed, tempting but dangerous, even cruel, guarding some secret awaiting release.

As we ponder Georg Simmel's uplifting statement that *secrecy magnifies reality*, creating a world split between a visible exterior and an invisible depth that determines the exterior,[10] it is possible to be assailed by panic; *first*, and worst of all, that if it wasn't for secrecy, reality would be a pretty drab affair; *second*, that reality itself is like the way the worldview of "primitive peoples" was once crudely pictured by anthropologists as animated by spirits, conspiring in secret as to the makeup of the visible world; and third, that a fair amount of paranoiac sensitivity to invisible determinations of the visible is essential to appearance. I furthermore take this *panic* as complicit with a sense of things as so evanescent and multilayered that attempts to unmask appearances may actually compound the mystery thereof, and it is, therefore, to the mystery-making impact of unmasking that I wish to direct my own dilettantish efforts, unmasking unmasking, so to speak, and the devil take the consequences in my search for a nervous-system poetics of concealment and revelation that can hold a torch to the fabulous magnifications constitutive of human affairs.

Why the devil take the consequences? Because if unmasking is a device for making, rather than dissolving, mystery, then what are to make of its own unmasking? And second, because I feel old Nietzsche tugging at my elbow: "All of life is based on semblance, art, deception, points of view, and the necessity of perspectives and error."[11] Fair enough. Pure Simmel, you could say. But then always this caution, this mocking laugh from Nietzsche, as to the eagerness, indeed the political game we all indulge, striving so much to un-cover semblance as to miss if not make the greater truth hiding in the light. Curious, though, the metaphor he insisted on using here. *Truth as a woman? Not to be unveiled?*[12] Doubly curious given what we shall learn about Isla Grande and sacred flutes.

But the hypnotizing hold of the two layers, surface and depth, is unbreakable, and Nietzsche's mockery is as naught. Take Elias Canetti's fearsome dictum in his book *Crowds and Power* that "secrecy lies at the very core of power," no less than Michel Foucault's statement in his *History of Sexuality* that secrecy is not in the nature of an abuse of power, but is indispensable to its operation. "Not only because power imposes secrecy on those whom it dominates, but because it is perhaps just as indispensable to the latter." Thus the intense and awesome absoluteness of Canetti—"Secrecy lies at the very core of power"—is no less arresting than the sequence of images and concepts to which it stands as prelude, designed to plunge us into baneful zoomorphic fantasy of hunter and prey, where infinite patience and camouflage is abruptly trans-posed into speed of attack, the flash of exposure, "like lightning," says Canetti, "illuminating its own brief passage," followed by the slow and deliberate ab-sorption of the Other via the mouth, sliding down the sliding mucoid surfaces of the intestinal tract on its way to oblivion.[13]

Face is left far behind as it opens up to an unknowable interior, and it is with this daunting picture that Canetti is able to then vent secrecy as a thing in itself, even Godlike, transcendent over mere mortals as "the secret" with laws of its own. "Everything is subordinated," writes Canetti of the secret, "to its apotheosis." And as Godlike fetish force made by persons, yet coming to stand over them, so there is in Canetti's eyes a mystical inevitability to the destruction that will be unleashed by the secret's equally inevitable exposure. "Every secret is explosive," he grimly warns, "expanding with its own inner heat." You feel the fear in his writing.

The outstanding thing about exposure is its speediness ("like lightning," says Canetti), the stark alternation between absolute stillness and speed as prelude to the transmutation of meaning into force, the alternation marking the transformation in which the secret is exposed—unmasked, we might say—*so as to lead from invisibility into explosive force, apotheosis as prelude to apoc-alypse*. Could there be a more dramatic statement regarding the mysterious consequence of revelation? For it is at this precise moment of exposure that forms flow into one another, as when the prey is absorbed into the body, and when the secret explodes into itself "with its own inner heat."

Besides its terrible truth and equally terrible romanticism, there is this to consider; that in becoming fetish as prelude to eventual self-ignition and self-and-Other destruction, secrecy achieves its Godlike status by passing from what we might call "true secrecy" to become something else, a void with a halo encircling it, an entity now perceived from the outside by all as a secret, yet with its contents inviolate. The point is that while "true secrecy" is a virtual impossibility outside of the considerable powers of fantasy, this impossibility is unimportant to what we might call the ideology or secret of secrecy. The fact is that when the fetish status of the secret is achieved, it is the skin of the secret that vibrates with sacred light, intimation of the *public* secret within.

Canetti's morbid picture only gets worse. For there are others who tell us that
secrecy is not only inevitable but *essential* to social process and the health of
social institutions, an ambiguity skillfully rendered by Julian Pitt-Rivers in
his study of a remote mountain village just west of Ronda, in the south of
Spain, during the Franco dictatorship, some unstated time in the late 1940's
or early 1950's. In the 1971 preface to the second edition to Pitt-Rivers's book,
first published seventeen years before, he describes how he has come to realize that his was essentially a study of secrecy. It was, in retrospect, intended to
be a theoretical book, and the village was, perforce, more than a village, being an interface of secrecy, let us say, between its visible self and the Spanish
state. "In short," he says, "the whole book can be read as no more than an example of Simmel's great essay on secrecy and the lie."[14]

No doubt there is some exaggeration here, in that secrecy per se does not
in fact feature all that much in the book, which in my reading is primarily
about the way friendship mediates law, meaning the state, meaning Franco.
Yet insofar as secrecy accompanies this mediation of friendship and law, Pitt-
Rivers's retroactive insight as to what he was really writing about makes
sense. Such a reframing of the intention of a work by its author would also
imply, so it seems to me, a meditation about what it means to conduct ethnographic inquiry into people's lives in a dictatorship and, more important still,
the vexing problem of what can, and what cannot be revealed in writing

about other people's secrecy. Small wonder that this second preface should conclude with a pungent formulation of the meaning of anthropology, its yield in human understanding and self-understanding.

Following Simmel, Pitt-Rivers emphasizes the great cultural achievement that lying represents and, loyal to a fault to his informants, also emphasizes how "Andalusians are the most accomplished liars I have ever encountered." Insofar as a great deal of training in the arts of dissimulation is required, there is nothing natural in this, especially with regard to the "rapid ability to know when the truth is owed and when it is to be concealed," no less than the ability "to acquire conscious control over facial expression, an ability which takes practice from childhood."[15] Lest one assume this is a purely psychological trait, it should be reiterated that the author sees secrecy as the grease which allows the wheels of society to function. Deeply embedded in the personality and in all interpersonal relations, secrecy comes across in this brilliant book as a principle without which both the reality and the very notion of "structure" would founder, it being secrecy that provides the ambiguity and hence the flexibility without which structure would shatter.

The beauty of this view of the structurality of structure (and here I anticipate the author's ideas concerning method) is that it inevitably makes the reader reflect on his or her own situation with regard to secrecy as social grease, and hence see the world anew. Not least interesting here is the play underlying the presence, no less than the absence, of Being, vividly expressed in this ethnography of southern Spain, in the figure of the *heart*, because it is the "state of the heart" that provides the palpitating certainty as to Being in this reality riddled by deception and flux.

Now, of course this is the state of the heart of the Other—your intimate friend, your neighbor, your patron, or your client (in what Pitt-Rivers calls a "lop-sided friendship") . . . even your informant, in whom you put your trust as an *amigo de confianza*. And of course this heart stands out precisely because it cannot itself be seen, plunging the certainty it represents into an ever more obscure realm where secrets nest and strange plots are concocted. With typical adroitness, Pitt-Rivers gathers the many paradoxes within this where he writes that "the state of the heart is important not because society demands constancy but precisely because it does not. Where so many relationships are, in response to the fluidity of the structure, unstable, the heart provides a guarantee of fidelity in time."[16] It is the state of the heart, then, this

anchor embedded in the shifting sands of truth, that allows for the margin of
fiction separating the laws of the state from their actual observance, in which
not only the law but also the system of community values is largely honored
in the breach.[17] "As long as the law is 'upheld' to all appearances," he writes,
"the power of the state is inviolate and the authorities are satisfied."[18]

What we have here, therefore, is not only the makings of a theory of corruption, but one which emphasizes the power of fiction in the makeup of social reality. Indeed, why not see these as one and the same, reality itself being
always honored "in the breach," a corruption of itself?

## The Secret of the Gift (of Friendship)

In retrospect, writes Pitt-Rivers, this is an ethnography of the secret. Yet what
stands out for me is not so much the secret, but *friendship*, and the way that
friendship folds into secrecy. For friendship is the shock absorber that allows
Pitt-Rivers's binaries to coexist—like law with its corruption, hierarchy with
equality, patron with client, state with *pueblo*, and even maleness with femaleness. Here, friendship is synonymous with ambiguity, paradox, and instability,
and this is because friendship, like sacrifice, is built on the contradiction of
ends and means. For on the one hand, friendship is an end in itself and disinterested, while on the other it serves as an instrument of self-advantage, or is
at least vulnerable this way. In politics and bureaucracies the world over, this
is second nature, the name of the game being how to blend the energies of
these opposed principles. In Pitt-Rivers's village it is the "female" element of
shame that a man forfeits if he pushes the contradiction too hard toward the
means-pole at the expense of the ends-pole of *simpatía*—and this is where
one of the several senses of the (public) secret fortifies friendship, as when
Pitt-Rivers observes that in the village, a friend, without actually forfeiting
his honor, "may through skilful evasion manage to maintain his friendships
with both sides [i.e., factions]. These people are famed for their skill with
which they dissimulate their feelings. . . . Hence the importance of gossip."[19]
In other words, everyone knows that the ideal of friendship is being betrayed,
but depending on the skill of the manipulator and the interests of other parties, the fiction of friendship is upheld. Even better examples exist in university departments than in Spanish villages, but this is hardly a secret.

Friendship, in this view, behaves like Marcel Mauss's famous notion of the gift, which likewise "cements" much of social process and lies at the heart of what we often call "corruption." Mauss drew attention to just this duplicity in the gift which is, as he stated on the first page of his book, in theory voluntary, disinterested, and spontaneous, but is in fact obligatory and interested. The form usually taken, he went on to note, "is that of a gift generously offered; but the accompanying behaviour is *formal pretence and social deception*" (emphasis added).[20]

Not only is the logic of the gift implicated in friendship, but friendship in most situations is, I believe, likely to presume the gift or be itself a gift. For if we reflect upon it, friendship seems to possess a delightful mix of everyday taken-for-grantedness *and* something wonderfully serendipitous emerging from short circuits of social life so as to build and build on an ineffable bond of confidence between two or more persons. In this sense, friendship is a gift that an otherwise indifferent society now and then bestows on those of us fortunate enough to be so blessed. Moreover, friendship becomes the locus for secrecy and sharing secrets, just as it is the locus of gifts and sharing gifts. Conversely, gifts can be like secrets and come nicely wrapped as part of the element of *surprise*. For surprise is the precise Maussian point where the contradiction in the gift discharges itself. But over and above this, friendship is in itself a gift.

All the more fascinating and all the more poignant, therefore, the secret within the gift, and therefore within friendship, concerning the impossible but necessary coexistence of generosity and calculation. This is of course no secret other than the classic public secret—that which we all know but cannot easily talk about . . . and the logic of the contradiction is giddying. Still, most of the time we get along. . . .

### Will and Wave

It is at this point that I need to ask why so many things in the analysis of this village in Franco's Spain are accorded the status of what I would call "buffers" as between center and periphery, law and lore, state and community. Friendship is a buffer. So is secrecy. So is the *caciquismo* or patron-client relationship vital to these villages and most else beside. It seems like first we are to be seduced by the elegance and drama of oppositional pairs, but when this analytic device proves to be too analytic and too much of a device and falls victim to its own revelatory power, then the byzantine twists in the dependencies holding each side of the opposition apart and together are evoked by reference to the opacity of a blurring mechanism. In the pages preceding his conclusion, the author writes:

> The formally constituted institutions controlled by the ruling group or the state and the activities wherein the pueblo avoids them stand in opposition to one another. The latter spring from the network of interpersonal relations within the community and depend upon the memories and cultural traditions of the pueblo rather than on the written word. The former owe their existence to authority delegated to a central power. Pairing them together one can see, in place of the sanctions of law, the sanctions of the pueblo's mockery; in place of food control, the clandestine mills and the black market; in place of the matriculated shops, the *revendonas* and the illicit traders; in place of Civil Guard, the bandit and the smuggler. In place of the schools, the *maestros rurales*; in place of the doctor, vet and chemist, the *curanderos*; in place of the *practicanta* (trained nurse), the *parteras* (country midwives). And for the purpose of invoking the powers of religion in such matters, in place of the priest, the *sabia* [or wise woman].[21]

And so it goes on. Oppositional pair following oppositional pair. The whole scheme is then designated as a "structure," with the pueblo or community "side" being designated as the "infrastructure" of the structure's structure.

But what has to be immediately added is the nature of the space between, what the author repeatedly refers to as the *ambivalence* joining the two halves of each pair, "for it must be realised that neither could subsist without the other," and that "the two systems are, at the same time, interdependent and in opposition. They are both parts of the same structure," and what requires explaining, he concludes, "is not only the source of this tension but the ways through which it is resolved."[22]

In other words, the whole is sundered into dialectical halves that are then put back together again, thanks to the buffer of the "space between," yet what is buried from view, in this vigorous effort to sustain the oppositional pairs, is that it is actually the buffer, inaccessible to analysis by means of binary distinctions or contradictions, which is the savior of the binary. The secret, we could say, the secret of the system, is that it is held together by some sort of deus ex machina, some sort of mischievous genie called "secrecy" or "ambivalence" or "instability" or "friendship," and this applies no less to the state and its practice of law than to the ethnography of those very forms. When the ethnographer tells us that the secret is what allows "complex" society to function because secrecy "permits conflicting social forces to co-exist and gives to this structure the resilience which enables it to persist," I accept this functionalist explanation with surprise and gratitude as a powerful insight.[23] But what the invocation of this secret conceals is another order of secrecy within the analysis itself, the existence of an oppositional pair without which all the others would self-destruct, namely, the structured opposition between *binarism* and *buffering*, in which, it turns out, buffering becomes the Joker in the pack. For the buffer is immune to and cannot be reduced to the same move of the intellect. It cannot be subject to the same splitting process. It resists. It is too fast and too slippery, and the paradoxical upshot of it all is that the instability attributed to the society and to truth is actually denied by the analysis itself, the very elegance of which rarely allows us to contemplate the mischief on which it precariously rests.

## The Secret of Anarchism

So much for secrecy! But then how does one write about it without being trapped in it? I ask this maladroit question both because I feel the logic of secrecy impels me, and because it emerges from Pitt-Rivers's text, for now, in retrospect, in the preface to the 1971 second edition (two years after Franco declared an amnesty and four years before Franco died), he reveals his own secrecy as an anthropologist back in 1954 publishing his book, withholding not only the name of the village and of his informants, but also, out of the same "need for discretion," he "judged it premature," he says, "to publish my materials on religion and Anarchism at that time and decided to reserve them for a later book, which I still intend to write."[24]

It is a pity that this volume, as far as I know, was never written, because on the author's own admission it seems like he is caught in a cleft stick, having to omit, together with anarchism, much of what would seem to make an ethnographic study worth doing in the first place. This is the result of what he himself states to be the significant entailment of anarchism in religion.

Hence, not only is religion out of bounds, but also, I would presume, many subtle aspects of life into which religion percolates—a diffuse array of everyday attitudes and premises woven into notions of fair play and justice, spiritual aspects of honor, shame, and so forth—it being his clearly stated opinion that in this part of Spain, at least, anarchism and religion densely interpenetrate one another. In his own words, "It is not possible to discuss the plebeian religion of Andalusia, other than as folklore, without treating the agrarian Anarchists who, in their iconoclasticism, their temperance, and their respect for education and the sanctity of words, recall the Puritan revolutionaries of the English seventeenth century." And he concludes on this definitive, even strident, note: "The distinction between politics and religion, as we conceive of it in our own society, has no anthropological validity."[25]

What then, we are forced to ask, is "the anthropological validity" of this anthropological monograph that has to omit anarchism and, therefore, religion? Is it intended that "the plebeian religion of Andalusia" can be transfigured as "folklore" and therefore be discussed in this transmuted form? And if so, why all the fuss?

The omission of anarchism (and therefore of religion) is not only a pity, but also rather curious given that anarchism appears to be the main reason this anthropologist chose the village in the first place, on account of the area being, as he put it, "the cradle of agrarian Anarchism."[26] The locus that is "the village" thus operates in a strangely fictitious world eclipsed by anonymity, pseudonymity, and the evisceration of an anarchism left as a ghostly presence.

Yet given the police-state character of the Franco regime at the time of his fieldwork, and of publication in 1954, was there any alternative?

This question becomes all the more poignant because the secret as to the name of the village and its illustrious anarchist identity was, according to testimony that will be quoted further on, in fact no secret but a public secret, and what I am led to conclude is that, far from Pitt-Rivers's book being an ethnographic explication of secrecy, as in retrospect he says it is, it is actually using a discussion of secrecy to make a secret out of something that is (apparently) not a secret. If this sounds confusing, then surely it no more confusing than the unsettling game secrecy plays with reality and with those who dare to enter into such. The preface to the second edition thus inadvertently stands as a case study of what the revelation of public secrecy entails, stirring the mix of the known with the half known, moving rumor and ambiguity along the chain of storytelling, such that the instrument of revelation may even backfire and become instead another form of concealment.

### Footnotes: Primitive Rebels

This is brought out in a reference Pitt-Rivers makes by way of footnote to Eric Hobsbawm's *Primitive Rebels*, published in 1959 with a chapter on anarchism in southern Spain. This note is so out of character with the otherwise lofty tone Pitt-Rivers strives to achieve throughout his book that it would seem to indicate a fascinating problem concerning rival styles for the appropriation of the play of the secret. In *Primitive Rebels*, the secret was duly brought to light of day *by footnote* four years after the initial publication of Pitt-Rivers's account.

> It may also be worth mentioning Pitt-Rivers's *People of the Sierras* (1954), an anthropological monograph of the *pueblo* Grazalema. Its observations on local anarchism are useful, but show too little appreciation of the fact that this little town was not just anarchist, but one of the classical centres of anarchism and known as such throughout Spain. No attempt is made to explain why Grazalema should have been so much more powerful a centre of the movement than other *pueblos*, or to explain the rise and rhythm of the movement, and this detracts from the value of the book, at least for the historian.[27]

Even the precious name of the pueblo is calmly outed, as if Hobsbawm's strategy is to be crushingly open in a world that is anything but that, calling for a moratorium on all this silly hiding behind false names, dark glasses, and beards. And as for the invisible presence of anarchism, we are here informed that the pueblo was not just anarchist, and not just a "classical centre" of anarchism, *but was known as such throughout Spain!* In keeping this public secret secret, presumably so as to protect the village and his informants, Pitt-Rivers has run the risk, it would appear, of falsifying a profound reality or, as the author of *Primitive Rebels* judiciously understates, of detracting value from the book, "at least for the historian."

Just a footnote.

Now, Freud taught that the return of the repressed—another way of positing revelation—stimulated all manner of fabulous displacements and condensation by way of resistance, and even if the revelation is by means of a mere footnote we should nevertheless expect some skillful recuperation on the part of the exposed. And of course, given the rules of the game, of professional courtesy as much as of the psychoanalytic mechanisms of resistance, a mere footnote is probably going to be a more effective challenge than open confrontation, and hence it will push those fabulous displacements and condensations to considerable heights. Even so, I must admit to some surprise, even awe, at the adroitness with which Pitt-Rivers chose and positioned his 1971 footnote intended to flatten Hobsbawm's, my point being that in this curious interchange of footnotes we are being given an extraordinary demonstration of the poetry of secrecy that Freud brought to our attention. As for footnotes, let it be remarked as an aside that it is, after all, into this skirmishing in the underbrush of footnoting that one is inevitably drawn, as to the twilight zone, where scholarly norms are sharpened to the point of self-destruction, one of the better known secrets of scholarly *écriture*.

Pointing out in the body of his preface (to the second edition) that it is when "knowledge is something to give or to deny you become concerned with its exact worth," and that "it takes a money-changer to detect false coinage," Pitt-Rivers informs us, with considerable zest, how Andalusians feel a particular mixture of indulgence and admiration for the British (read Pitt-Rivers, read Hobsbawm . . . ?) because they are poor liars, hence poor truth-tellers, and are regarded therefore like children, yet admired for still cherishing the bold ambition to be frank. "Let us face it," advises our ethnographer as he relaxedly stretches the long legs of his sentence, which shall terminate in his gouty footnote, "we are all fumblers by Andalusian standards, but they envy our innocence even while they also take advantage of it."[28] And it is not lost on us readers, this "we," that the writer, having thus included himself and thereby shown this degree of self-consciousness, has earned the right to detach himself from such fumbling.

Then comes the footnote:

> It appears therefore rather inept to label the Andalusian rebels "primitive," as Eric Hobsbawm has done (*Primitive Rebels*), unless one is to adopt a point of view similar to that of Victorian anthropologists who called all people primitive who did not share their ideas and assumed that they "advanced" if they came to do so. Hobsbawm was referring to their political conceptions which he believed would inevitably evolve to become similar to his own. In fact they showed no signs of doing so and

the recent resurgence of anarchist ideas among student rebels elsewhere does nothing to validate such an evolutionary scheme.[29]

It is not so much the content of this footnote, as its relation in time and space to the main text, that is breathtaking. This is one of those occasions whose artistic perfection make it seem like some sublime agency is afoot, testimony, I would say, to the high degree of theater spontaneously involved in the play of revelation and concealment in human affairs. By locating Hobsbawm through the agency of the footnote at this exact spot, the latter is *as it were* disposed of as a child and as a fumbler, admirable in some ways with his naive attitude to truth, but fundamentally naive as to the complexity of secrecy and its revelation.

Yet none of this is stated directly. Pitt-Rivers does not need to call his antagonist childish and clumsy. To do so would be counterproductive. And like the public secret, this is the beauty of the footnote because, as with Freudian parapraxis (with slips of the tongue and with jokes), its relation to the corpus of the text is intimate, yet distanced, both within and without, providing therewith the raw energy, as well as the mechanisms for making implicit and powerful connections, while at the same time denying them. In this respect the footnote resembles the foot so beloved of the fetishist, beholden to the wondrous logic Freud suggested in 1927 of dis/avowal, namely, the art of recognizing a charged absence *and* denying it at the same time.[30]

And let me emphasize how, on this analysis, the fetish owes its power to something a good deal more than its function in both revealing and concealing. For what it both reveals and conceals is *a nothingness*, a glaring absence, which in Freud's bloody story is symbolized by the wound that is the nothingness of castration, the ghostly presence of the mother's phallus, but for us is the absent-presence of the silent ghost of anarchism in a Spanish village in the late 1940's and early 1950's, when people all over Spain, it would appear, most of the time kept their head down and their mouth shut or else acted stupid or crazy, and disguise and spying was a way to stay alive.

*In Hiding*

Two sorts of problems, two sorts of tension, emerge from this with regard to writing. There is what I would call the political problem, determining the overall character of the text when it comes to the issue of revealing the absent-presence of anarchism in the ethnography of a village in a country seized by civil war in 1936, resulting in the violent death of some three hundred thousand persons and thirty-six years of right-wing dictatorship.[31] And there are the "empirical" or "technical" questions concerning (1) the reliability of anything the anthropologist is told or in turn chooses to tell the reader in such a circumstance, (2) why one would presume to carry out an ethnography of a village in such a situation anyway, especially one famous for its anarchism, and (3) why, finally, one would dwell upon the legendary stereotype of an almost supernatural capacity for dissimulation on the part of Andalusians, rather than on the cruel political situation in which they practice the alleged dissimulation?

After all, it seems not so secret a public secret that, at the pinnacle of control of the society, by Franco himself, corruption seems to have been regarded, as Stanley Payne puts it, "as a necessary lubrication for the system that had the advantage of compromising many with the regime and binding them to it." As Franco remarked, "I must tell you that I really don't trust anyone."[32] What is salutary about this distrust, in other words, is not that it led to an anticorruption policy, but, on the contrary, allowed public secrecy to be a principal arm of statecraft and wise government. Much of the brilliance of Pitt-Rivers's ethnography of secrecy would seem, therefore, to owe its genesis to a script written far removed from any specific genius of Andalusian cultural style and character formation, no matter how much that style may give expression to such a script. Dissimulation as the lifeblood of social structure turns out to be not so much the "infrastructure" of the "structure," but the quintessence of the state itself, occupying the moral high ground of the public secret.

Manuel Cortes spent thirty years, from the end of the civil war in 1939, secreted initially in a closetlike space and then in an upstairs room in a house in the village of Mijas, twenty miles as the crow flies, from the village studied by Pitt-Rivers. The account of this astonishing but by no means unique event, compiled from interviews a few months after he came out of hiding following the amnesty granted by Franco in 1969, gives one plenty to think about as regards secrecy and the political situation Andalusians found themselves in after the civil war ended. A barber, he had been a socialist and mayor of his village prior to the war in which he had fought as a soldier on the side of the Republic. "I lived in fear all the time," reflected his wife, Juliana. "The people in the village went round saying that the *Guardia Civil* had some sort of machine with which they could find anything that was hidden. I got it into my head that it was true. . . . It terrified me. . . . Of course it wasn't true, they hadn't a machine or anything like that, it was just the people talking to create fear."[33]

Of course, it wasn't true . . . and at the end of the narrative, looking back over the experience in 1969, and worrying about what he sees as a monstrously deformed view of the past held by young people, Manuel Cortes tells us that there "was terrible fear. I know that as well as the next person. Some of the comrades whom I considered firm turned out to be the weakest, the most cowardly, in the end. Not because they were threatened but because of the fear. But the others, those who retained their convictions, did nothing to teach their children about their beliefs. 'And when you die,' I say to them, 'what's going to remain? . . . What hope is there with a youth that knows nothing and cares even less.'"[34]

Nothing could seem further from Pitt-Rivers's portrayal. His village seems more like a village of jolly pranksters where, with a nod and a wink, the illegal millers mill away and the black market flourishes under all too conspicuous shop counters and behind all too firmly closed doors, while at night women scurry between farmsteads carrying black-market eggs in covered baskets across the moonlit sierra to Málaga.

And in asking ourselves what's the price of omission of the side of life conveyed by Juliana and Manuel Cortes, what they talk about as much as the way they talk about it, let us dwell for a moment on the continuous fear that they describe, as when Juliana Cortes says offhandedly, about the fantastic machine the *Guardia Civil* were at one point supposed to possess so as to detect anything hidden. "Of course it wasn't true," she says in retrospect, "they hadn't a machine or anything like that, it was just people talking to create fear." Yet all the same it terrified her. So here's the issue. Why would the people she is referring to talk like this? Why would they talk to create (further) fear, especially when "of course it wasn't true"?

There are many possible explanations emphasizing the propensity to outlandish fantasies in situations of fear and stress. But I would like to single out something else that is perhaps not so obvious, that comes to me after thinking more about Stanley Payne's remark about Franco and his attitude toward corruption, namely, that Franco saw it in a positive light as "a necessary lubrication for the system that had the advantage of compromising many with the regime and binding them to it."[35] In other words I think that, in becoming a link in a chain of storytellers passing on fearsome tales, and in acting as a purveyor of public secrecy working at several levels, a person is compromised in a complicated emotional and epistemological manner into the system exactly the same way that Payne describes as intended by Franco's regime of (un)truth.

I am reminded here of two stories related to me by Angela Giral. The first concerns a progressive coeducational school in Madrid, set up under U.S. tutelage prior to the Franco dictatorship and continued as such after the civil war, despite Franco's prohibition of coeducation. In the Franco years, when the inspector arrived for his routine visit the principal would invite him for coffee and press a concealed button. As they sipped their coffee they pretended not to hear the scraping of furniture and pounding of feet on the floor above, and when, after a decent interval, the inspector arrived at the classrooms, to find boys and girls in separate rooms, the entire charade was passed as satisfying the law. A victory for the school. A victory for the antifascist forces. And, given Stanley Payne's observation, a victory for Franco's lubricating use of corruption binding people into the system.

As the years went by and the system of corruption itself became corrupt, there would be no scraping or rapid pattering of feet. The inspector would be shown a classroom with boys on one side, girls on the other, a teacher in the center at the front of the room, and a curtain running down the middle. Voilà!

It is a remarkable image, and one we could well use as the arche-scheme for thinking through the power of charade and of public secrecy sustaining the regime. One point worth adding is that it is precisely because it is built on charade that the regime lends itself with such perfection to stagelike, theatrical images like this one. All of Brecht's work springs from this, and Marxists have yet to catch up with him.

Angela Giral's second story takes us back to fear of fantastic machines that are supposed to detect hidden things. It is told that having executed many men as "Reds" in the opening weeks of Franco's campaign in the south, at the beginning of the civil war in 1936, Franco's commander in Seville assembled their widows and, by threatening to harm their children, forced them to tell their children that their fathers had been killed not by Franco's troops but by the "Reds." And this they did.

We could see this as part of the propaganda by which one side to a conflict tries to make its version of reality dominate the other side's, but it seems to me to be something else as well, namely that in telling the lie, and in telling it so it stuck and stuck good over decades, the mothers were compromised in the same lubricating function of the public secret we have now come to see as state practice. In other words, it is not one reality being pasted on top of another so as to conceal it. It is not a war of opposed ideologies, worldviews, and so forth. Instead it is far cleverer and more insidious than such wars of content. It is a war about confusing reality and living one's flesh and blood in that compromise.

What the omission of anarchism would really seem to amount to, therefore, in Pitt-Rivers's ethnography, is the omission not of anarchism, but of dictatorship. Behind the secret that is the absence of anarchism lies another secret, encysted in the first as "revealed" by the second preface. For in fact there are plenty of big-time secrets revealed in this ethnography. We are told for instance that all of the fourteen water-powered flour mills in the vicinity of the village are not only illegal but are functioning entities. We are told in some detail how millers obtain black-market grain secretly at night on loaded donkeys and what measures the millers adopt to hide their milling from the state inspector—who of course, given the public secret that greases and glues the society together—also "knows" about these illegal mills and is rewarded with money through chains of friendship for pretending not to know. We are told how farmers cheat the state of 50 percent of its wheat quota, how poor women carry the sizable contraband trade in their covered baskets, how a stupendously intense *vito* (public manifestation of ridicule concerning adultery), proscribed by Franco, was carried out in 1951, how bandits course through the adjoining sierra, and so forth. So, who cares about revealing anarchism, dreadful as it may be, when the underbelly of the village is laid bare like this?

*Marx and Bakunin*

It is here that I would like to consider the rancorous footnote that springs from "Let us face it , we are all fumblers . . . ," the footnote that takes Hobsbawm to task for his "rather inept" terminology of *primitive* rebels because such an appellation verges on Victorian disdain toward other cultures and encourages a view of Andalusian anarchism as not only an inferior political philosophy, but one destined to succumb, as if by natural evolution, to Hobsbawm's "own." Not only is this morally inappropriate, concludes Pitt-Rivers, but history (as of 1971) has disproved it, as demonstrated by the resurgence of anarchist ideas among contemporary student rebels.

As for the lessons of history, however, it is surely the case that anarchism did die in southern Spain, as elsewhere, and that, secondly, the anarchism of the student rebels in Paris, Berlin, London, and the United States in the late sixties was hardly the same as that of southern Spain from 1870 to 1936 and was every inch motivated by despair and hatred of the anticommunism of the United States's raining bombs and napalm down on Vietnam. The context of this jab at Hobsbawm was the context of the Cold War in which, from the 1950's, Marxist professors had been hounded from the United States and insidiously attacked and blocked in England, too, albeit to a lesser extent. By the late 1960's and early 1970's, when Pitt-Rivers was writing his second preface, however, Marxism was ascendant in the British university student body, and Marxist professors were considered a political problem by university chancellors and others in a position to wield power. Hence what seems left violently silent here, *as if it were a secret*, and therefore all the more sinister, is what is referred to as Hobsbawm's "own" politics. What was meant here, of course, was his Marxism and rumors in academia as to Hobsbawm's ties to the British Communist Party at that time.

And if history is seen to repeat itself here, in this quarrel over naming and secrecy, revelation and concealment, it is the history of the First International brought to a stormy end in 1872 by the quarrel between Bakunin and Marx, anarchists and Marxists. For what is at stake here, I believe, in this dispute relegated to the obscure position of a footnote, is something of frightening importance, namely the treacherous place of the intellectual in revolutionary movements, and the role of the historian in times of fascism and war. What this boils down to, in other words, is the place for secrecy in revolutionary ethics, the famous means versus ends debates that gripped revolutionary councils for well over a century, remembering that, while communists after Lenin in the twentieth century became feared as cloak-and-dagger operators, there could have hardly been, nevertheless, at the outset of modern revolutionary history, a more secretive personage than the anarchist Mikail Bakunin, who is universally accorded the awesome power of having introduced, virtually single-handedly, through his deputy Fanelli, anarchism to Spain, like some sort of food fad or virus. Bakunin was the leader whose sine qua non was the secret brotherhood, disguises, and invisible ink. "One of the many issues not discussed at the famous interview between Bakunin and Marx," writes the eminent biographer of Bakunin, E. H. Carr, "was the issue between secrecy and publicity in revolutionary organization. Marx, like Herzen, was a lifelong believer in publicity. Bakunin had clung, ever since 1849, to a rooted conviction of the necessity of secrecy for serious revolutionary work."[36]

As regards Spain, not only did Bakunin score one of the great successes of his stormy career there, taking advantage of Marx's International to introduce anarchism to Spain through the Secret Alliance and maintain it there in a chain of secret societies, but this very secrecy made his endeavors there susceptible to damaging exposure later on by Marx's son-in-law, Paul Lafargue.[37] In her study of the history of anarchism in Andalusia, Temma Kaplan tells us that "Bakunin was obsessed with conspiracy. Were the issues of secrecy and conspiracy not so fundamental to early anarchism, they might seem comical."[38]

*Human Science*

And let us not underestimate how high the intellectual stakes are here, concerning method in the human sciences. At the end of the second preface, Pitt-Rivers once again raises the specter of anarchism, advising us that, in his delineation of beliefs in the village, he has studiously avoided judgment of them. What I might feel about their political and religious ideas, he writes, "does not appear to me to be capable of adding anything to my analysis."[39]

Thus the issue of secrecy and its revelation passes at its climax, toward the end of the preface, into ethics and methodology as a vehement plea for revealing the concealment of one's political views. What is more, it is argued that such concealment of ideology is fundamental to the human sciences. Pitt-Rivers refers us to the "attitude of detachment" whose "methodological roots" allowed him to "forego the joys of partisanship," and, what is more, separate description from theory.[40]

We note the spiritual call to self-discipline with its promise of future re-ward, the self-denial required by law, not the law of the state, as in Franco's Spain, but the laws of "methodology" stipulated by social analysis in the search of truth. But surely there is a secret, even a "lubricating corruption," in all of this, right where there shouldn't be, "methodology" being designed, so to speak, to be the site of luminescent openness and purity thereof? For is it really possible not to judge the judgments of others, either when in the company of the persons who express them, or in describing them later on in writing?

I try to imagine what the face looks like in this situation, the face of he who does not judge the Other, especially when the Other, Andalusian fash-ion, is bent double (not) judging also. Its terrible blankness would surely give it away or frighten us all. Or is it perhaps a dissimulating face which, in avoiding poker-facedness as too obvious, adopts all manner of deceptive gri-maces and twitches? So much for the scene of fieldwork.

And as for the scene of writing! For finding a prose form that is value-neutral with respect to the belief of the Other! How on earth can one create a language that can do justice to the passions and nuances of the Other, while at the same time refraining from revealing something absolutely crucial about one's own life-world, prejudices, fears, values, and enthusiasms? After all, it is all there in your *style*, and it is style and stylishness that leaps from the pages of this witty and elegant ethnography. There is a "voice" here, clear and loud, opinionated without having to directly state its opinion. As is so frequently the case, power lies in the unsaid.

And as for the style of detachment, surely the posture of neutrality is just that, a posture recognized as such, a charade acknowledged as a public secret by one and all? This would make most social scientists and their funding agencies even better material for study than Andalusians.

Hence the methodology of human science unites with the ancient method-ology of public secrecy as both blur into the charade of scientific detachment, and this cuts to the heart of anthropological or "cross-cultural" knowledge, as when Pitt-Rivers goes on to eloquently work through the dialectic in-volved in "penetrating behind the natives' eyes," so as to "reinterpret what [the natives] saw through them" and then be able to "transcend the values by which he [the anthropologist] lives at home."[41] His point is that the ethnographer has to set aside "his own culture" so as to "project himself into their lives," the lives of the Other, "leaving his own behind or he would never grasp their viewpoint." But, and here's the rub, "if he fails to regain his detachment he will never know what it is he has learned." In other words, detachment from one's own values is followed by projection of oneself into the Other's, which in turn is followed by detachment from that projection so that one can then detach oneself from one's own.

Yet from here stretch endless questions and uncertainty. What passion does one have to muster to become passionless and detached, for instance? How does one switch it on and off, and off and on again? Surely this whole approach, which to greater or lesser degree involves us all, requires the most meticulous practice of deception and self-deception, secrecy and public secrecy? It goes without saying, therefore, how wonderfully spirited a thing it is to hear that the ethnographer, at the end of this trek, would not be displeased if the reader detected in him a resemblance to those ardent liars he has spent so much time studying.[42]

### North and South

Let me return to the arresting assertion that what Pitt-Rivers calls "complex" (as opposed to "primitive") society requires secrecy for its very existence, that therefore "the most important knowledge is not common," and that such knowledge generates elusiveness to language, to time, and to memory, not to mention social relations. Such is the ubiquity of secrecy as diffuse necessity. I lie, therefore I am. Not so much Machiavelli as Zeno. My question, then, bearing all this in mind, is what of the English and what relation do they bear to the reader?

The English are the necessary underside of the secret, as we witness with the observation that the Andalusians pity the English for the ineptitude they display with lying, which thus surely makes the English less appreciative of truth. This observation would seem to call out for even more self-reflection on the part of its English author, providing an incentive to rethink the secret that we can now see as located between an English ineptness with the art of lying, a virtual guarantee of a robust ethnographic authority, and the dissimulating skills of Andalusian peasants and bureaucrats. For surely what is ref-

erenced here in this epiphanous encounter between north and south, between the cultivated man of letters from the north and the sun-drenched
tillers of the southern soil of untruth, is an uneasy acknowledgment as to a
certain secret of the secret in which the south has long had the function of
mirroring, in its dishonesty, the dissimulation of dissimulation in the north?

> Thus the villainies of the Venetian thieving system formed one of the secret bases of the capital wealth of Holland to whom Venice in her decadence lent large sums of money.
>
> MARX, *Capital*, "The So-Called Primitive Accumulation"[43]

Modern Western history revolves around a deep split in the secret in which truth's dependence on untruth is ethnically and geographically divided between north and south. Both Nietzsche's and Freud's theories of truth, let alone their travels to Italy, fantasies, and modes of figuration, provide abundant testimony to this assertion culled from my preceding meditation on an English ethnography of secrecy and lying in southern Spain. What struck me as of chief importance emerging from that ethnography was, *first*, the mischief of the distinction, north as honest and industrious and repressed, the south as anything but, and *second*, how deeply insinuated and ultimately inseparable is truth in deception. We have already borne witness to Pitt-Rivers's salutary observation that by virtue of their lying, Andalusians put a higher value on truth than the naive and honest English, and my feeling about this paradox is that it serves as a blind for evasion and deception on the part of those, who for the sake of this equation, are called the English. If all of this points to a profound impossibility of ever separating the intertwining of truth and deception, and even worse, of never even being able to be aware of the intertwinement, due to the way it conceals itself, we can at least speculate about the profit entailed for the different parties, beginning with Marx's observation regarding the early modern formation of capitalism in the epigraph to this chapter, in which the villainy and decadence of the south serves as a secret source of capital for the north.

This early modern history of capital's dependence on the secret of the south is, moreover, a relation between trading ports, the Venetian empire in decline, and the burgeoning port city of Amsterdam, the former representing the history of the Mediterranean, the second the history of the Atlantic and the Far East. Not only are these maritime cities, but both are built on canals along whose turbid waters came the spices and silks from the east, and much else beside. Indeed the canals not only *are* the city, but remind us that these cities, from their remote beginnings to the present day, have been in reality continuously operating salvage operations squatting on swamps and mud precariously rescued from the ravages of the sea. These places where the coast breaks into neither one thing nor the other, these anastomoses of islets, lagoons, and estuaries—natural canals, we could say—seem to have been selected out by an omniscient nature as the generically fertile zones for generating money and trade, just as the prehistoric zone that is neither water nor land, is where life began, and to which it will return.

It must be a deep thing, this secret of the secret, in which the south in its dishonesty mirrors the dissimulation of dissimulation in the north. Marx's language in the epigraph above is florid, like opéra bouffe. Purely "southern," we might say. Villainy, thievery, and of course, *decadence*. "Grotesque Renaissance," is how John Ruskin refers to this period, in which Venice, he says, exhausted itself "in deformed and monstrous sculpture . . . jesting in its utmost degradation."[44] Yet the surprise must be that in its decadence, and one would assume precisely because of such decadence, there was generated a flow of capital to the north, which, if I understand the history being told here, formed the basis for modern capitalist takeoff with sober Dutch merchants and then with their Protestant British counterparts, first with their arduous voyages of discovery across the globe to places even more "decadent" than Venice, then the trade in slaves, and later the English factory system and child labor as described by the young Friedrich Engels for that most northern of cities he knew so well, Manchester. Since World War Two—with southerners migrating north, Turks to Germany, Algerians to France, West Indians and Africans to England, not to mention slightly earlier waves of Spaniards, Italians, and Greeks—the tension generated by the north-south axis of truth and dissimulation has reached dangerous levels of racism.

This curious contract between truth and falsity, uniting the land mass of Europe along a north-south axis, is present in other histories of Europe as well.

Take the history of the plague in relation to closeted homosexual attraction, as depicted in Thomas Mann's 1912 novella, *Death in Venice*.[45]

Grappling with his attraction to a young Polish aristocrat, a beautiful boy of around fourteen years of age with a complexion as white as ivory against the dark gold of his surrounding curls, fifty-year-old and very uptight professor Gustav (now "von") Aschenbach from Munich, scholar and aesthete, becomes aware, albeit in a confused and fitful way, of the hidden presence of death while holidaying in Venice. Now and again—in the barbershop in his hotel by the beach, for instance, or from a waiter—he gathers that something terrible is happening behind the scenes. But no sooner does he gather an intimation, than it is dispelled by one or more of the gamut of dissimulating devices with which humanity is not only blessed but seems to delight in using. Indeed, one has to wonder why these Venetians of the serving class keep on revealing the secret, only to pull the curtain tight after the merest glimpse. It's as if the secret of the plague—a public secret, be it noted—demands to be revealed; and yet this very same exciting tension has to be turned back, as it were, into itself, through ever-greater expenditures of dissimulating energy.

Finally it is a tweed-clad Englishman who tells Aschenbach the truth. He is a clerk in a British travel agency, "still young," writes Mann, "with his hair parted in the middle, his eyes close-set, and having that sober, honest demeanour which makes so unusual and striking an impression amid the glib knaveries of the south."[46] Yet in fact this Englishman does not so much reveal as confirm the truth, for Aschenbach has already read about it in the German newspapers in the hotel. It is this English face which, in its struggle to conceal, then reveal, provides the stamp of confirmation. Yet there is no face without an Other, and it is that other northern face, belonging to von Aschenbach, that forces the truth out of him: "But raising his blue eyes, he met those of the stranger, which were looking wearily and rather sadly at his lips, with an expression of slight contempt. At this the Englishman coloured."[47] We take note of the blush, displacement of secrecy via the autonomic nervous system, a veritable defacement preceded by this act of ethical access, the gaze locking onto the lips of the Other, the face as witness for the southern secret that under pressure cannot be contained by the northern visage.

For the secret is overdeterminedly southern. But at the risk of enormous and enormously-forgotten banality, note there can be no south without a north.

The secret then is "Asiatic Cholera," and its lair is the innermost recess of the Third World—originating in the "sultry morasses of the Ganges delta, rising with the mephitic exhalations of that wilderness of rank useless luxuriance, that primitive island jungle shunned by man, where tigers crouch in the bamboo thickets."[48]

The secret, then, is not only southern but of the sun—the fiery sun that Bataille wrote of, in the opening pages of the first volume of *The Accursed Share*, as emblematic of the principle of exuberant expenditure, because, unlike other gifts with their demand to be paid back, *the sun gives without receiving*.[49] The secret is Zarathustra's sun overflowing, Nietzsche's sun to which the sea adds its aqueous depths in mockery of all that is deep—where the heavens collapse into the base materiality of beach and swamp. This is Mann's "sultry morass of the Ganges delta," made even more explicit in the figure of the secret's rising with the exhalations of *that wilderness of rank useless luxuriance*. Indeed, this dizzying interaction of sun and plant-life is central to Bataille's picture too, as in the prelude to his exposition of *general economy* (the art of profitless spending, as opposed to the *restricted economy* of capitalist profit-maximization):

> I will begin with a basic fact: The living organism, in a situation determined by the play of energy on the surface of the globe, ordinarily receives more energy than is necessary for maintaining life; the excess energy (wealth) can be used for the growth of a system (e.g., an organism); if the system can no longer grow, or if the excess cannot be completely absorbed in its growth, it must necessarily be lost without profit; it must be spent, willingly or not, gloriously or catastrophically.[50]

Compare this with Aschenbach at the beginning of Mann's story when, caught off-balance by the sight of a strange person in the portico of a mortuary chapel in Munich, he is spun into a hallucinatory seizure.

> His imagination, still not at rest from the morning's hours of work, shaped for itself . . . a tropical swampland under a cloud-swollen sky, moist and lush and monstrous, a kind of primeval wilderness of islands, morasses and muddy alluvial channels; far and wide around him he saw hairy palm-trunks thrusting upwards from rank jungles of fern, from among thick fleshy plants in exuberant flower; saw strangely misshapen trees with roots that arched through the air before sinking into the ground or into stagnant shadowy-green glassy waters where milk-white

blossoms floated as big as plates, and among them exotic birds with grotesque beaks stood hunched in the shallows, their heads tilted motionlessly sideways; saw between the knotted stems of the bamboo thicket the glinting eyes of a crouching tiger; and his heart throbbed with terror and mysterious longing.[51]

In other words, Bataille's "principle of expenditure," of the necessity to spend without profit, gloriously or catastrophically, holds for the "origin" of this secret connecting the wilderness of rank luxuriance to the animated, compressed, figure of concealment of the tiger, wild and magnificent and, of course, glinty-eyed, crouching in the bamboo thickets. We can almost see one of the Henri Rousseau's tigers, vintage 1910 (cf. *Death in Venice*, 1912), winking at us, its sad, wandering eye the most human thing in this jungle of waves and stripes like a prisoner's, blending with the bamboo stalks pressed tight under a silver moon. This is also Canetti's zoomorphic figure of the secret (1960) as a wild animal, epitome of a violence made all the more fearsome on account of its infinite patience, stalking its prey.

Yet for Mann, as for Freud, the sun most resolutely *cannot* give without receiving. No Such Thing As a Free Lunch. There must be payback time, the restrictive economy of death in Venice, civilization and its discontents. And there is this further difference to contemplate as well: From a Bataillian and Nietzschean perspective, spending the secret would be built into the secret itself, essential to its spreading power and joy, with none of the checks and balances built into a sense of duty, as with "the calling" of a writer such as Aschenbach, who invests in the suffering of self-discipline in the hope of a good idea or even a neat book. In the former case, the secret cannot be anything else but the public secret—for it is there to be spent, not invested— while in the latter, it is like a capital investment to be carefully harvested as narrative tension, of which, in *Death in Venice*, there is plenty, beginning with the title.

Originating in the entrails of the "south," the secret inevitably spreads—east to China, west to Afghanistan and Persia, and then by Syrian traders to Toulon, Málaga, Palermo, and Naples. Until recently, northern Italy had been spared, but when an Austrian tourist in Venice died of cholera, the city authorities took the first steps to ensure the public secret; stating that the public health situation had never been better. At the same time, they sprayed the canals with carbolic, leaving a sick and sterile smell floating over the city, and it was this disturbing odor, mixed with his delirium for the beautiful Polish boy whom he pursues through the narrow streets and turbid canals, that first suggested to Aschenbach the presence of a secret hitherto intimated by obscure signs and unexpected confessions, aborted no sooner than begun.

Duplicity breeds further duplicity. The city plunges into crisis, provoking "an activation of the dark and antisocial forces, which manifested itself in intemperance, shameless licence and growing criminality." People even murder their own kin, claiming the deaths are due to the plague, and "commercial vice now took on obtrusive and extravagant forms which had hitherto been unknown in this area and indigenous only to southern Italy or oriental countries."[52]

The tension within the secret, the need to reveal it, no less than the need to conceal it, reaches its climax when Aschenbach struggles between his desire to tell the boy and his family about the plague, and thus provoke their flight, or instead maintain the secret and thus the boy's physical proximity, at least for a little longer, a few days, till the boy's vacation ends.

Aschenbach chooses not to tell. And what is noteworthy about this tremendous choice—if choice is the word—is that it is first and foremost not a pragmatic calculation, but a seduction by secrecy and an act of voluntary enlistment to the growing morass of the public secret. Dissimulating energy wins out, harvesting the vitality of the secret in the form of splendiferous fantasies, Simmel's magnification of reality magnified further by the uncanny coalescence here of the public secret with the personal secret growing between Aschenbach and the boy, who never speak to one another and barely exchange glances. "They want it kept quiet!" whispers Aschenbach to himself. "I shall say nothing!"[53]

Aschenbach's dream that night after deciding not to reveal the public secret of the plague, so as to all the better cherish his personal secret, is Mann's attempt to express the peculiar reality of this compounded secrecy, an impossible task, overloaded with melodrama and predictable images of extremity, testimony to something more than the dream of a haunted individual's subjectivity. It is another world opening out, rendering the fetish powers of the secret, magnifying reality even further.

The dream begins with fear and sound, a "compendium of noise, a clangor and blare and dull thundering, yells of exultation and a particular howl with a long drawn-out *u* at the end—all of it permeated and dominated by a terrible sweet sound of flute music: by deep-warbling, infamously persistent, shamelessly clinging tones that bewitched the innermost heart." (We shall encounter these flutes in other secrets as well.) Odors begin to predominate: the pungent reek of goats, the scent of panting bodies, the flat, acrid, smell of stale water, the smell of wounds and disease—and in fragmented light tumbling from the wooded heights comes a raging human swarm becoming intense, becoming animal, mouths foaming, bodies melting into one another laughing and moaning in an ecstatic, orgiastic, bleeding mass . . . on the trampled, mossy, ground.[54]

Canetti's figuration of the secret as tied to animality *and* godlike powers of the fetish seems here amply confirmed, even though we are now in the midst of the public, not the private, secret. Indeed, what makes *Death in Venice* singularly important for my purposes is the character of the merging between these two qualities of secrecy and the implications such merging offers for rethinking transgression and theories of repression, in which *faciality*—no less than the *dream*—exposing the soul, is crucial.

*This merging of the secret with the public secret* achieves fantastic form in the architecture and waterscapes of Venice. On reading of the plague in foreign newspapers, even before his interview with the tweed-jacketed Englishman, Aschenbach feels "an obscure sense of satisfaction at what was going on in the dirty alleyways of Venice, cloaked in official secrecy—this guilty secret of the city, which merged with his own innermost secret and which it was also so much in his own interests to protect."[55] Indeed, it is precisely at this point, where he learns of the plague, that he begins his optical pursuit of the boy through the narrow streets and canals of the sickening city that, by means of its fluctuating light and shade, figures the judicious obscurity of its secret. Steered by a gondolier with an uncanny ability to take shortcuts and make neat interceptions, gently gliding and swaying on soft black cushions, Aschenbach experiences the stagnant and malodorous air, the sun burning oppressively through the haze that turns the sky the color of slate. "The gondolier's call, half warning and half greeting, was answered from a distance out of the silent labyrinth, in accordance with some strange convention." Blossoms spill over crumbling masonry. Moorish windows are mirrored in the murky water. The marble steps of the church dip below the surface. And Aschenbach can think of nothing but the pursuit, a pursuit in which heightened sensory details of sight and smell are pronounced.[56]

It is eye standing in for touch, this eye of the hunter secreting itself so as to drink-in the object of visual pleasure. We note this with Aschenbach's first encounter with the boy, which, like all encounters in this novella, is marked by pointedly physiognomic practice: "With astonishment Aschenbach noticed that the boy was entirely beautiful. His countenance, pale and gracefully reserved, was surrounded by ringlets of honey-colored hair, and with its straight nose, its enchanting mouth, its expression of sweet and divine gravity, it recalled Greek sculpture of the noblest period" (as contrasted with his sisters whose "expressionless" faces had "a nun-like emptiness").[57]

Trapped in what he sees as his ugly old body, and scared by his feelings toward the boy, Aschenbach can do no more than look—at dinner, in the hallways of the hotel, and especially on the beach. Yet the moment at which Aschenbach becomes conscious of the depth of his passion and finds a situation in which he can—inadvertently, as it were—lay his hand on the boy's head or shoulder while passing by on the boardwalk by the beach, the drama of repression of physical contact, and consequent return to the semisecrecy of just looking, is created. It is a zero-sum game, a plumber's system of valves and feedback whereby pressure in one part creates a reactive pressure in another. The boy comes close. Aschenbach's heart hammers wildly inside him and he feels so breathless that he can only speak in a strangled and trembling voice. He hesitates, struggles to control himself, makes another failed attempt, and hurries past with his head bowed.[58] Sensations dam up so as to explode silently within the fastness of the isolated and ever-so-miserable body.

The "south" would not be what it is in this scheme of things concerning secrecies and transgression were it not for its glorious sun and, better still, its beach: where children play at building sand castles and adults play at becoming children, bodies stripped of clothing (but nothing like today); where bright awnings flap in the sultry breeze and colors leap in the reflections of the sun playing on the water's moving surface. It is also the place for looking, a looking that is relaxed yet attentive. Here, then, on the margin between land and sea, is where the repression sustaining civilization takes a transgressive dive and where, moreover, it can be seen doing so. And, beyond the beach, the sea, and beyond that to what in this tale is the empty eternal, the great nothingness into which Aschenbach's gaze dissolves.

On the beach, then, we are suspended between two forms of letting go, two forms of distraction. There is the sparkling chaos in colorful play, the eye active. And there is something quite different, the utter sameness of the sea stretching forever. Venice combines these contraries, for it stands at the intersection of sea and city, like some vast sea anemone, with its innumerable canals from which the greatness of Western architecture emerges heavenward. In Western high culture, then, Venice *is the beach* with the playful elements subdued and re-wrought, succumbing to Marx's "decadence" and Ruskin's Grotesque, with its "unscrupulous pursuit of pleasure."[59]

Aschenbach's own body, if only he knew it, is to serve as Mann's beachhead for passion let loose, like line from an angler's reel, only to be jerked back into place. We travel south to the beach to stoke the fire of the flesh, and we return north to Munich and other cities to advance the spirit. An eternal return. Geography of the human soul. But what if one day we got stuck and didn't come back?

As we contemplate this question, our thoughts dreamily lost on the limitless horizon, a figure abruptly emerges from the sea, like Venice itself,

> standing upright with his hands clasped behind his neck, slowly rocking to and fro on the balls of his feet and dreamily gazing into the blue distance, while little waves ran up and bathed his toes. His honey-colored hair nestled in ringlets at his temples and at the back of his neck, the sun gleamed in the down on his upper spine, the subtle outline of his ribs and the symmetry of his breast stood out through the scanty covering of his torso, his armpits were still smooth as those of a statue, the hollows of his knees glistened and their bluish veins made his body seem composed of some more transparent material. What discipline, what precision of thought was expressed in that outstretched, youthfully perfect physique! . . . Was it not well known and familiar to Aschenbach as an artist? Was it not also active in him, in the sober passion that filled him as he set free from the marble mass of language that slender form which he had beheld in the spirit, and which he was presenting to mankind as a model and mirror of intellectual beauty?[60]

The beach can even allow miracles, *physiognomic miracles*, in which spirit and flesh will match and reading from one to the other is reflex. For, according to Plato's *Phaedrus*, here invoked by Mann, erotic love should be but the stepping-stone to higher realms of truth and beauty. What is left unclear, however, is where the pleasures of the flesh end up in this scheme. Are they destined for self-annihilation, having served their loftier purpose? Yet what dangers lie in store, surfing along a steamy carnality in the hope of catching that iridescent wave of philosophy otherwise known as "Platonic love"? For might you not get stuck, unable to elevate yourself to the higher realm, blocking the intricate sequence flowing from flesh to spirit? Plato leaves us to grapple with these doubts, confident in the power of logic and dialectic to uncover the secret that is the Form of the Good hidden deep within. For Aschenbach, however, things are not so academic. Not there on the beach, they aren't. Getting stuck or derailed on the way to revelation is a real possibility.

But there is always this utopian hope that a surface of such compelling beauty shall of itself supply the magic required of a physiognomic reading that not only accesses the soul, but in so doing shall reveal the ultimate forms of the universe and bond with them as well. This we call love, cunningly contrived by Eros as servant of philosophy. But in Plato's view, ideally, the love between a man and a boy had to be reciprocal. What, then, are the implications for physiognomics and the fusion of mask and window if, as in this case, the love is one-sided, the status of the boy's feelings is unknown, and the stated social norms, unlike Plato's Athens, are hostile to homosexual love? Logic suggests that the physiognomic eye would turn with extra intensity from the beloved into one's self.

Eros has its face. And so does the devil—the devil, of course, that is created by repression if not by Eros—and this face appears throughout *Death in Venice*, from the very beginning of the story that spring day in Munich when Aschenbach, worn down from years of service dedicated to art, comes across a strange man by a mortuary chapel, the sight of whom inexplicably makes him want to travel—to exotic lands, to the eye of the tiger, no less, to Venice, to death in Venice. All this comes about, let us note, by nothing more than what Aschenbach reads into the figure, and especially into the face, of this silent stranger, with his milky complexioned, snub-nosed, redheaded face held on high, a face from nowhere, bereft of national or ethnic signature, his Adam's apple stark and bare, two pronounced vertical furrows by the nose, colorless red-lashed eyes peering sharply into the distance with an air of imperial survey, posture bold and wild, and last but not least from this somewhat incomplete list, a sort of facial deformity with the lips too short, leaving the teeth exposed, bared to the gumline.[61]

This is a face which *reappears* with the gathering tension of the public secret *as it fuses with* the personal secret of homosexual fantasy. It will reappear on the boat to Venice, with the eerie gondolier who takes Aschenbach from the ship to the hotel, and it will reappear once again in the face of the gypsylike entertainer who similarly comes out of nowhere to mysteriously disappear.

Mann gives more attention to this entertainer's face than anybody else's. It is an overworked and overworking face whose elements, in particular its mouth and grimace, display not only great plasticity, but draw attention to the human face, in general, as a medium of expression that, thanks to this power of expression, conceals or confuses attempts to discern from it the inner state or truth of the person. It is above all a detachable, recurring face, a more-than-stereotypical face, the very mold we might say not of a specific type, but of faciality itself.

Moreover, this face is always referred to negatively with regard to regional or national identity. He "was quite evidently not of Bavarian origin" we are told at this face's first appearance at the mortuary chapel in Munich.[62] Why should nationality be an issue here, let alone its absence? As for this curious face's reappearance as the gondolier, when Aschenbach first arrives at Venice, we are told how by "the cast of his face and the blond curling moustache under his short snub nose, he was quite evidently not of Italian origin."[63] The singer at the hotel "with a mimic gift" is a further metamorphosis and also subject to a process of ethnic and nationalistic determination that is expressly negative or, at least, strategically indecisive: "He was quite evidently not of Venetian origin."[64]

I take this recurrent face-without-a-country as the sign of detachability, plasticity, and great radius of action. It is more than a mask. It is the face of the permanently Other, always a not-from-here, not-from-there. More important still is its mediation of north with south, of Munich with Venice, of the British with the Andalusians, of those who cannot tell a lie with those who lie all the time . . . with plague itself, stirring in the Ganges.

This recurring, detachable face is also one of disguise and makeup. On the ship to Venice, for instance, we meet one after another of the passengers and crew members, each one marked by a face and gestural score that sug-

gests a clumsy disguise, notably the raucous young passenger who, Aschenbach realizes on closer inspection, "with a kind of horror," is falsely young:

> There were wrinkles round his eyes and mouth. His cheeks' faint
> carmine was rouge, the brown hair under his straw hat with its coloured
> ribbon was a wig, his neck was flaccid and scrawny, his small stuck-on
> moustache and the little imperial on his chin were dyed, his yellowish
> full complement of teeth, displayed when he laughed, were a cheap,
> artificial, set, and his hands with signet rings on both index fingers,
> were those of an old man.

Ashenbach recoils and feels reality slipping away as the ship casts off.[65]

It is the hallucinatory impact of these faces that leaps out at us. As faciality itself they transform Aschenbach or at least fill him with the desire to be radically different, and each time he sees the face of faciality, he becomes sick
and frightened, overcome by a dreamlike state. With the dancing man in
Munich, his first encounter with the face, he becomes conscious "to his complete surprise" of "an extraordinary expansion of his inner self, a kind of roving restlessness, a youthful craving for far-off places, a feeling so new or at
least so long unaccustomed and forgotten that he stood as if rooted."[66] The
expansion of self is here couched in the motif of travel to far-off Third World
places, but the travel is also a seizure that stands for instantaneous transformation of Aschenbach's very identity, as he imagines tropical forests and lush
landscapes centered on the figure of the tiger—the figure, we could say, of
the "south," it being this particularly exotic animal, camouflaged by jungle,
that provides the formula for beauty, danger, secrecy, *and* wild release.

When he sees the face of the falsely young man on the ship to Venice
something similar transpires.

> Aschenbach put his hand over his forehead and closed his eyes, which
> were hot from too little sleep. He had a feeling that something not quite
> usual was beginning to happen, that the world was undergoing a dream-
> like alienation, becoming increasingly deranged and bizarre, and that
> perhaps this process might be arrested if he were to cover his face a little
> and then take a fresh look at things.[67]

Again the context is travel, as at that very moment "he had the sensation of
being afloat," and "noticed that the dark heavy hulk of the steamer was slowly
parting company with the stone quayside."[68] But it is not travel of the body

or of ships that is here at issue, so much as self-transformation consequent to facing the face of faciality, and the transformation seems all the more laden with portent for its being constrained and massive, like the heaving of glaciers. The steamer is a dark and heavy bulk. The parting from the stone quay is slow. Inch by inch the engine pounds. And first the steamer has to reverse. The water between the ship and the quay is both dirty and glinting, and it is only after clumsy maneuverings that the ship turns its bow to the open sea.[69]

When he gazes into the face of the gondolier upon arrival at Venice, the same sort of dream state heralding a transformation of identity occurs, and again events seem to arise from without, leaving Aschenbach a witless victim of facial circumstance. "It was wisest to let things take their course, and above all it was very agreeable to let them do so. A magic spell of indolence seemed to emanate from his seat . . . so softly rocked by the oarstrokes. . . . The thought that he had perhaps fallen into the hands of a criminal floated dreamily across Aschenbach's mind."[70]

As for the face of the gypsylike entertainer outside the hotel, the penultimate in this series of faces, its furious grimacing and changes of expression culminate when "he suddenly discarded the mask of the underdog, uncoiled like a spring to his full height, insolently stuck out his tongue at the hotel guests on the terrace, and slipped away into the darkness." At this point Aschenbach finds his thoughts returning to the house of his childhood and he imagines he has, right there before him on the table, an hourglass from that time of so long ago. "Silently, subtly, the rust-red sand trickled through the narrow glass aperture, dwindling away out of the upper vessel, in which a little whirring vortex had formed."[71] This vortex is the mobility of the face set free at last into that other realm, the realm of defacement, disappearing into itself. Only its movement and its whirring exist now, sheer defacing presence we might say, the elementary form where mask and soul are left to fight it out as Aschenbach sits alone on the terrace in the darkness by the sea.

What is fascinating in this series of faces—all the same strange-appearing out of the blue and disappearing right back into it, hallucinatory omen of an expanding night—is that right after the momentous dream that followed his decision not to reveal the plague to the boy's family, Aschenbach finally "outs" himself and does so emphatically by entering this same defacing realm by changing his own face, wearing jewelry and scent, and making frequent

visits to the barber who volunteers to rejuvenate him. Now his journey has
reached an end. He is becoming one with the tiger, this tiger that is the secret crouched in the bamboo thickets of the south. Now he too is that
"wilderness of rank useless luxuriance" that is the secret from which comes
all manner of plague. The barber dyes and curls his hair and then sets about
to freshen his complexion. "And like a craftsman unable to finish," writes
Mann, "unable to satisfy himself, he passed busily and indefatigably from one
procedure to another." Incapable of resistance, Aschenbach

> gazed at the glass and saw his eyebrows arched more clearly and evenly,
> the shape of his eyes lengthened, their brightness enhanced by a slight
> underlining of the lids; saw below them a delicate carmine come to life
> as it was softly applied to skin that had been brown and leathery; saw
> his lips that had just been so pallid now burgeoning cherry-red; saw the
> furrows on his cheek, round his mouth, the wrinkles by his eyes, all
> vanishing under face cream and an aura of youth. . . . [72]

"An insignificant adjustment, signore," says the barber.

Aschenbach's real face is rather different and it is important that we recognize why this is so—and not only because Mann spends a lot of time describing it. His head seems too large for his body, and his hair, graying on the
temples,

> framed a high, deeply lined, scarred-looking forehead. The bow of a pair
> of gold spectacles with rimless lenses cut into the base of his strong,
> nobly curved nose. His mouth was large, often relaxed, often suddenly
> narrow and tense; the cheeks were lean and furrowed, the well-formed
> chin slightly cleft. Grave visitations of fate seemed to have passed over
> his head, which usually inclined to one side with an air of suffering. [73]

"And yet," Mann concludes the elaborate facialization of this big-headed
man, "And yet it was art that had here performed that fashioning of the physiognomy which is usually the work of a life full of action and stress."

"You see," said a friend in Munich, "Aschenbach has always lived his life
like *this*," and he closed his fist tightly. "Never like *this*." And he let his hand
open once more. [74]

Aschenbach's fist-face betrays no passion, other than its determination to
hide passion. Such a face is so manifestly a mask that it is no mask at all, and
when it is unmasked, thanks to the barber by the sea, it shall fulfill its preor-

dained potential as the plastic face of the devil that from the very beginning runs through this novella, each time different but the same.

It is of course crucial we not fix the face of the devil, that arch-mimic whose great mischief is to play with the face of things so as to cheat on the cheat that is physiognomy. For this is the recurrent face, the detachable face, the face of movable elements that can be arranged this way or that, *the face therefore of defacement*, and it is this that comes finally to open out like a flower on Aschenbach's fist of a face, revealing how masklike all faces are—sets of meaningful features, like pictures or texts, trading in apparent permanence or realness for a mobile facade, not unlike writing itself.

That this applies to writing as a form of masking also, Mann leaves us in no doubt, it being Aschenbach's self-discipline that brings home the accusation that writing, no less than the face, is the container of repression—that "the magisterial poise of our style is a lie and a farce [masking] an incorrigible and natural tendency towards the abyss"—a struggle within one's being no less than in the text, a struggle between what Mann refers to as the "warrior of repression" and "the woman that is passion," reminding us once more, if reminding we need, of how gendered is the south—let alone the death in Venice—that allows for the masking of masking in the north.

Writing here is portrayed as like lying; a continuous, living, conflictful process of negotiation between repression and transgression, each stamped with a sex, the warrior of repression and the woman that is passion. Hidden in every line of prose lies a tormented bisexuality, as it does in every furrow of the face of Aschenbach the writer, whose genetic endowment, it turns out, has ensured this fate. Aschenbach's dad was an important legal official descended from a long line of military officers, judges and state administrators noted for discipline and austerity. His mom, on the other hand, introduced a "strain of livelier, more sensuous blood," including musicality and "exotic racial characteristics" that "betrayed themselves in his appearance." And it is clear that Mann's text is invested in the notion that it is the union of these oppositions that underlies repression as the motor of artistic production.[75]

With his privileged means of access as creator of this tale, Mann thus leaks the inside story, stripping away the veil to reveal the mechanics of artistic production and the bitter costs thereof. Yet all along this secret was there for the reader on the surface as a public secret, the sort of thing that so vexed

Michel Foucault in his labored chapter on "the repressive hypothesis," chasing in circles nineteenth-century Western European sexuality as the secret bound to exposure so as to remain concealed.[76] And has it not always been thus? Especially with the secret of Realism? That it is a property of such art to "inadvertently" display its hidden mechanisms whereby and wherein the face of things connects to dense interiors, hidden histories, and illicit desires? Indeed the outstanding thing about *Death in Venice* is not merely the minute needle-worked intricacy of its symbolism, every element connected to every other element, but the labored quality thereof, calling incessant attention to itself as "great art" whose symbolic force merges organically with the real.

Ultimately this notion of art is the notion of the secret and its defacement. It rests on the notion that the world of appearance is a surface, a tensed surface, concealing a hidden and deeper world providing a treasure trove, so to speak, for a certain kind of storyteller who skillfully exploits the play of facades and the repression holding facades in place. Everything becomes in this sense a "symbol" dripping with mystery. Yet ultimately this cheapens both truth and repression because it assumes and reinforces the sense that if only we can get through the facade, the truth is there for the asking—as if truth was some thing, some entity or presence, that could exist outside of our presentation of it in yet other facades. As for sex (à la Foucault), so for representation in general. The secret is unmasked so as to conserve it. North and south cartwheel in each other's embrace all the way down the beach into the surf and the setting rays of the sun. Which also rises.

As he sinks into the transgressive realm, thanks to his rejuvenated face, Aschenbach can see in the mirror his masking turn in on itself. This is where his life will now for the first time meet and transcend his art, where life and art will change places; and it must needs be that this fatal encounter will occur on the artwork that is the surface of his awakening body, notably on his fake-face, window and mask to the soul. Now he is on the beach, where life forms began, but from which people now flee. He is watching the boy playing his last game in the sand before leaving Venice. A playmate wrestles the boy to the ground, buries his face in the sand, suffocating him with the cruel force of his knee. "His attempts to shake off the weight of his tormentor were convulsive; they stopped altogether for moments on end and became a mere repeated twitching." When finally released the boy walks away, ignoring the calls—laughing at first, then anxious—of his playmate who was brushed aside. The boy is locked in Aschenbach's gaze. He is walking now into the water, wading to the sandbar. He is slowly pacing back and forth on this narrow strip of unsubmerged land divided from the shore by a width of water, an apparition walking as if on water with his floating hair "out there in the sea, in the wind, in front of a nebulous vastness." On impulse he turns toward Aschenbach his eyes seeming to call and beckon to the horizon. He is still. Everything is frozen. And as Aschenbach struggles to clamber out of his deck chair to project his body into the flight path of his eyes, Mann kills him. This sun does *not* give without receiving.

In a charming footnote to his ethnography of those great southern liars and cultivators of secrecy, the Andalusians, Julian Pitt-Rivers evokes the philosopher Schopenhauer explaining that men have beards because, unlike women, they do not possess a natural talent for dissimulation. "The rarity of beards in Andalusia," comments the anthropologist dryly, "might be explained by the same theory."[77]

To invoke Schopenhauer and his beard is first and foremost to raise the maleness and femaleness of secrecy as a worldly trope of excessive proportion, and at the same time to be made aware of the absurdity of an all too familiar commitment to what we anthropologists, swallowing hard, call "functionalism," which is really nothing more than assuming that it is a good thing (1) to explain things, and (2) that explanation consists in demonstrating "causes," as in mechanics and a purported logic of profit and efficiency—familiar terms, after all.

Take the list Schopenhauer gives us of things to be explained as prelude to understanding the world as will and representation, this list that terminates in *beard* on its way to displaying what he calls the necessary and indeed marvelous conspiracy connecting "efficient" to "final" cause. Before getting to beard he runs through:

why lice on Negroes are black
why the plumage of tropical birds is colorful

same for butterflies

why the health of pregnant women with tuberculosis improves until they give birth, and then their health does a dive to the extent that they often die

why men with tuberculosis often beget a child in the last days of their life

why a fly poisoned with arsenic still mates (from an unexamined impulse), and dies in copulation[78]

Moreover, this concatenation leads directly if not obviously to the human genitals, starting with the mons veneris of the female, which the World as Will designed so that the pressure of the *ossa pubis* grinding against that of the male during sexual intercourse should be cushioned and thus not excite aversion. Schopenhauer calls this the "final" cause.

The "efficient" cause, however, is to be sought in the fact that wherever mucous membrane passes over to skin, hair grows in the vicinity, and also in the fact, so the philosopher informs us, that the head and genitals are, to a certain extent, opposite poles of each other. They therefore have many different relations and analogies to each other, one of which is their being covered with hair.

With this identity between face and genitalia hinting much in the way of an underlying design, we finally arrive at beard—whose efficient cause is the same as the pubic hair (where mucous membrane meets outer skin) and whose final cause lies in the fact, so Schopenhauer writes, that "rapid changes in the features of the face which betrays every hidden movement of the mind, becomes mainly visible in the mouth and its vicinity. . . . Woman, on the other hand, could dispense with this; for with her dissimulation and command of countenance are inborn."[79]

Hence a peculiar and irresistible attraction, especially for men, to practice an art of defacement, not to mention all those jokes about women's facial hair; Marcel Duchamp's 1919 *Readymade* of the Mona Lisa with a faint moustache and few chin whiskers, or René Magritte's 1934 oil painting *Rape*, of a woman's "face" with breasts for eyes, umbilicus for a nose, and pubic hair for the mouth—the odd and disturbing thing being how face-like and -unalike the whole thing is.

Now surely the point to mull over is the self-assured way the philosopher assumes the inborn nature of what he calls woman's capacity for dissimulation and self-control. Yet no less basic is the marvelously surreal and quirky way he relates both face and beard, in all seriousness, to the genitals, in a series of oppositions, relations, and analogies focused on the beard.

It's as if the great design that is the World as Will and Representation lies in a magical connection (in his words, "their wonderful working together," or "a marvellous conspiracy") between that part of the body that everywhere in the world and world history (as far as I know) must be covered, and that Other part, which—with some notable exceptions—is always naked: the face. As for analogies, surely the leading candidate would be the oft-cited and oft-abused notion of the sudden and secretive glance that the little boy bestowed on the mother's genitals, seeing only hair, and swiftly looked away so as to absorb the shock—so the tale goes—of the absence, the absence of the phallus. In a famous essay the good doctor Freud wrote, "To put it more plainly: the fetish is a substitute for the woman's (the mother's) penis that the little boy once believed in and—for reasons familiar to us—does not want to give up."[80] Here then is beard sprouting from what was the setting for the Great Deception, whose name hereafter must be Woman, hair without penis—or, as with the phallic mother emergent in dream, the woman with both hair and penis—proving, if proof be needed, that all other women are hiding it. Either way, deception; so that the hair he later grows on his face is not only virile assertion when it's his turn to be suitor and father, but is also—so the tale might grow—the sign of having weathered Oedipal storms, ready to take on all comers in the wars of castration, now to be understood as the original deceit read into that (female) anatomy upon which much else depends. As a mask for men, then, Schopenhauer's beard is not only nature's beneficent way of allowing men to compete with women's natural mastery of the arts of dissimulation, but is also the mask of castrated pussy that mimics deception itself. Small wonder that Nietzsche's figure for truth as a play of surface and depth, revelation and concealment, should be woman too.

# PART THREE

# In That Other Time: Isla Grande

The "apparent" world is the only one: the "real" world has only been *lyingly added*.

NIETZSCHE, *Twilight of the Idols*

There in 1832, on the beach of what had come to be called Tierra del Fuego, Land of Fire, young Charles Darwin was taken aback by what he saw as the mimetic prowess of primitives taking off on his language and mode of walk, all lit up by fierce body paint and importunate soliciting of buttons and knives and good red cloth. Pausing for a brief moment in his diary, he asked how one might account for such mimetic skill, suggesting that maybe it was a result of living close to and keenly observing nature.

We who come a century and a half later to this diary have the power, bequeathed by colonialism, to encapsulate his equation of primitivism and mimicry within a perspective more self-conscious as to the place of mimicry both in colonization and in thought itself. To do justice to this perspective requires a curious sort of excavating of colonial history in the present, of the tropes it leaves as unexamined residue in world historical reckoning, whereby the mimetic faculty can be approached as the nature culture uses to create second nature, an achievement of sympathetic magic using likeness to become like. Justice here also requires acknowledgment of the sheer excitement and even love of such becomings and transformations, just as it requires acknowledgment of the need for acknowledgment—namely, by the women and kids who sit over there, and in their being set apart from the secret, allow its power to expand so as to keep the world turning.

The question shall turn, therefore, not so much toward whether the women and kids know the secret—whatever we might mean here by "knowing"—but what we might ourselves come to tentatively think, first, about audience and witnessing, and second, about the disturbing possibility that it is the art arising from this elusive force of concealment and revelation of public secrecy that lies at the core of power and of sacred representation, as well—foregrounding the need for contrived illusionism as cultural truth, for the real to be really made up.

For post-Darwinian investigation into the closeness to nature and the vivacity of the mimetic faculty in Tierra del Fuego reveals an enormous distance between men and women, a distance articulated around the ceremonial theater that, for want of abbreviation, I shall call the Big Hut, following Lucas Bridges's memoir and the detailed 1918–1924 ethnography of the Selk'nam and the Yamana, published by the German-Austrian priest and anthropologist Martin Gusinde. The point is that on the largest island, *Isla Grande*, every few years for months or more, initiated men adorned great masks and painted their naked bodies with red, white, and black, so as to *represent* (or should I say *become*) certain spirits, while the women and children in an on-and-off fashion served as witnesses of such spiritual performance when it emerged from the Hut, the women threatened with death if they intimated by whatsoever means that these were not spirits but performing men—their kinsmen, at that.

In contrast to this was the orchestrated *un*masking of spirit in dramatic confrontation with an initiate in the all-male confines of the Big Hut. Indeed, such unmasking could be said to provide the central and consuming point initiating initiation.

In a world saturated with spirits such as Temaukel, the Howenh, the Yosi, and the spirits of the dead, these particular spirits of the Big Hut formed a class apart, "a strange and weird position indeed," wrote Gusinde, given that once the secret ceremonies were over "they appeared, so to speak, as if erased from the women's consciousness to be never spoken of again. And the men would never once mention, not even the tiniest detail, that might reveal the true nature of these spirits."[1]

We are confronted, then, by an ensemble of escalating mysteries such that this ritual theater, ostensibly concerned with male initiation, could also be thought of as both a deadly serious game with the secret, and as a philosophical toy for the investigation of the place of men and of the place of women in magnifying reality by means of public secrecy and its revelation.

It is important to grasp the magnitude of this. Gusinde says that among the Selk'nam the ceremony lasted four months, at other times ten, and even longer. "It was not unusual for the ceremonies to last more than a whole year." "Two summers and one winter we spent," says his informant shaman, the famous Tenenesk, referring to times in his youth before the Europeans had inflicted so much death on the natives through the disease and calculated murder associated with gold mining, and then sheep farming, in the late nineteenth century.[2] The 1886 population of roughly 2,000 had dropped to 279 *indios puros* and 15 *mestizos* by 1919 at the time of Gusinde's ethnographic researches, and the number plummeted thereafter.[3]

### The Big Picture

It should also be emphasized how far-reaching this theater of truth and secrecy extends, geographically and mythologically. As regards the Selk'nam, it is said that once upon a time, long ago—in that Other time, shall we say—women were supposed to have run the show on Isla Grande and had the magic and powers of shamanism and sorcery. In that Other time, the men had no theater. Instead it was the men who had to bear witness to the women's great performances yet, one day, were able to rise up against the women and massacre them, except for the tiny girls, and take over the Big Hut out of fear the women would reassert their earlier privilege—women being blessed (as Schopenhauer informed us) with innate if not supernatural powers of dissimulation.

Moreover, this history of the public secret rooted in the original matriarchy, together with its postmassacre theater of secrecy and revelation, is recorded in many other parts of the world, as we shall see in succeeding chapters, such as Amazonia, New Guinea, Melanesia, Australia (with modification), and Central and West Africa, to name only the best known, a fact that would not only grant Schopenhauer's beard an awesome place in the world-reckoning of universals—including the place of woman in the workings of truth and knowledge, mimicry and deceit—but that also turns inside out the family romance assiduously mined by Sigmund Freud, with the murder of magically-empowered women displacing the murder of the father so as to obtain, not sex, but the spirit-theater of the secret.

## *On Not Knowing*

Before I examine this theater of truth and secrecy in detail, let me point to the insolubility of the problem of whether those supposed not to know, really don't—bearing in mind the need for witness by these strangely unknowing women and children of the men's elaborate deceits. On the basis of much experience, having been born in Isla Grande in 1874 and having befriended many Selk'nam, Lucas Bridges put the matter succinctly.

> When once I ventured to suggest to the men that the women only did
> it to please them, their reaction left me under no misapprehension as to
> their firm conviction of the women's blind credulity. To me it seemed
> impossible that the women were utterly deceived. . . . One thing is
> certain: that if any woman had been indiscreet enough to mention her
> doubts, even to another woman, and word of it had reached the ears
> of the men, the renegade would have been killed—and most likely
> others with her. Maybe the women suspected; if they did, they kept
> such suspicions to themselves.[4]

Let me further point out how this uncertainty resists analysis, demonstrating vividly, if indeed demonstration be necessary, that this "object of study" curls back on one, enmeshing in its coils the analysis supposed to master it. What I am saying is that the uncertainty of the object of study "contaminates" its study yet does so in instructive ways. It is no longer a question of what the women and kids think, but of the possibilities of determining truth in a social field in which knowledge is power and the reality of illusion serves the social contract—a situation fraught with allusion for all social worlds, built as they are on the noncontractual elements of contract. And even more to the point than identifying the *question* here, is *method*, staring us in the face. All we have to do is sit still and think about our thinking, so to speak, as it takes the form of attempting to disentangle truth from fiction in this specific situation. The very analysis itself, as it drags us along in its inner life and being, serves as a most marvelous illustration, exercise, and sort of laboratory experiment, for observing, feeling, and participating in the play of power with knowledge—of how what I call the public secret parodies and subverts our most cherished tools and categories of thought recruited for the pursuit of truth and the unmasking of appearance. Observer melts into the observed in confusing ways, subject and object keep changing places in unpredictable

rhythms, language becomes manifestly treacherous, both sharpening and dis-
arming the critical faculty through hazy ambiguities—and all of this serves
as salutary reminder of Canetti's opening statement that secrecy lies at the
core of power.

Surely such mischief puts in jeopardy the very notion of unmasking the
secret, reinforcing the move Canetti makes when he gives to the secret fetish
powers, as if the secret is itself a spirit standing over those who created it, con-
trolling them in its animate intensity, vibrating with explosive force.

And it is precisely this explosive force which, on my analysis, separates the
secret from the public secret. For with the latter, *the explosion never comes*, and
remains instead as tensed possibility. Indeed it is the task of unmasking, in
such circumstance of public secrecy to both reveal and conceal, and so *augment the mystery that lies not behind the mask but in the act of unmasking itself.*

Witness Gusinde himself, tossed hither and thither in his response to the question as to whether the Yamana women believe the figures they see emerging
from the Big Hut are not men dressed up in masks and body paint, but spirits. "The terse answer," he says, "is that the women without doubt are more or
less definitely informed about the deceptive performance of the men, but at
the same time they cling to their firm faith in the existence and activity of the
spirits that are mentioned or appear."[5]

The ambivalence is unsettling, not merely on the part of the women in
question, but also on the part of the ethnographer. The very language starts
to curdle, the women *without doubt* being *more or less* informed as to the deception *but at the same time clinging* to their *firm faith* . . . not just in the existence of spirits (in some abstract, general sense), but in the notion that those
"spirits" emerging from the Big Hut are not mortal men painted and
masked, but spirits proper, and that the men are not practicing an elaborate
deception.

As if this is not disorienting enough, he continues on still another tack,
saying that "in particular it cannot be determined which of the two opinions
predominates in this or that person and whether there is any kind of common
evaluation of the many different details, for the women never exchange detailed opinions among themselves."[6]

But then he would seem to immediately contradict himself, relating a story
told among the women as to how, in years past, one of them, fearing an attack

by the spirits, painted her own body like one of them and crept into the Big Hut so as to secretly paint a stripe on the back of each man by means of which the women could later see it was only their husbands sitting in the hut and not spirits. "Sure enough," continues Gusinde, "when the men stepped out each bore the line drawn on his back and since then all the women have known the true state of affairs."[7]

Just a story. And please note how in getting to its demystifying point so quickly, the story has something wonderfully implausible about it, something magical and miraculous, as if matter-of-factness and demystification in this situation can do naught else but self-destruct because of their dependence on magic. Hence, "knowing," as in "since then all the women have known the true state of affairs," becomes more than knowledge. For it is remarkable how the men inside the Hut do not notice this newcomer and even more strange that they do not feel her passing behind, painting a stripe on their backs. It must be true, then, that women are innately blessed with magic? And perhaps it is significant that she was able to accomplish this because the men were "sitting crowded by the fire, their heads bent low in serious med-itation," for we have to ask ourselves, first, why such sham-artists would in-dulge in meditation, and second, what sort of "meditation" is this?—given that the ethnography later on informs us that meditation, depending on how we define this elusive word, is what brings certain spirits if not into being, then at least into the consciousness of shamans. In any case, meditation raises a slew of issues cutting across "belief" and "disbelief" and concealment thereof, for now we are faced not just with the marvels knocking at the doors of perception, but with altogether different questions about certainty and subterfuge in relation to what William Blake would have called "the in-ner eye."

Yet the uncertainty seems endless, pushing us this way and that, a dialec-tic of truth suspended in frenetic stasis. "It must be admitted," continues Gusinde, "that probably all the women actually recognize their own husbands in their roles as individual spirits, but nevertheless their faith in these spirits is unshakable. A European observer can hardly explain how their knowledge and their faith can be reconciled."[8] And this from a Catholic priest, minister of the Eucharist—his problem being not that of the *efficacy of symbols* in which, by definition, faith and knowledge are adequately reconciled and mu-tually confirming, but rather the problem of *deliberate and fantastic deception.*

*Love Disporting with Itself*

The challenge, as I see it, is not to indulge an empirically-based skepticism grinding away in its infinitude on yet another disputable or disputing fact, trying to maintain one's balance in so much heady contrariety by clutching at yet another destabilizing observation, but instead to allow oneself to be brought face-to-face and remain within the ambiguity, grasping it whole, so to speak. I am at a loss to put a name to this stance but it must imply location no less than mobility, location within struggle, the struggle with ambiguity itself, with the fact of ambiguity as opposed to the facts that constitute it. I am reminded here of Hegel, especially the Hegel suspended from his moorings by Bataille in the struggle over the fate of resolution of contradiction where, in the famous preface to the *Phenomenology*, Hegel warms to the need for the labor of the negative when confronted by contradiction as a necessary component of Understanding.[9] Let me then call this struggle with ambiguity "the labor of the negative," and while underlining the suffering no less than the patience here required, let me also recall the gloss Hegel gives to Understanding as not only "the most astonishing and greatest of all powers," but as "love disporting with itself." To me this suggests that far from Understanding being an attainable and stable goal, its very greatness implies a profound instability, as when Hegel speaks not only of love disporting with itself, but of mind as the power that can look the negative in the face and dwell with it as with death in a sundered wholeness, providing the magical power that converts the negative into being.[10] But what sort of "being"? Everything revolves around this question.

Let me therefore assert the following constellation of principles by which we can navigate our way into the maze of deceptions and counterdeceptions formative of social realness, principles that in no way, shape, or form, can be restricted to so-called "primitive societies" but very much include my social world too, and most pointedly the world of the writer and analyst: *first*, that men mime the spirits, women mime belief in such, and the men mime belief in the women's belief, thus perfecting a decidedly curious circle of dissimulation, faith, and skepticism; *second*, the obsession with secrecy occasioned by the public secret is associated with a marked degree of fear and violence, beginning with the threat of death against revelation, yet also entailing licentious, carnivalesque behavior on the part of the performing men; *third*, within all this, *unmasking* acquires enormous dramatic, no less than philosophical and religious, importance, bringing us back once again to the magic of revelation, the exhilarating labor of the negative. Allow me to expand on these points, beginning with that Other time in Isla Grande, the time of women, of their deceit, the time of their secret. But *finally*, please note that there is an obsession with the secret that cannot be underestimated, especially on the part of the initiated men, to the degree that it seems not only to hang over and drive most everything, but to make a mockery of neat distinctions between reality and unreality and, indeed, at the end of the day, to make it difficult to be sure of anything, beginning with the ethnography no less than my meta-ethnography.

No magic here. No guarantee of getting through to that Other side of the secret and the secret's secret. Indeed to even assume that possibility is profoundly naive, profoundly spiritual, we might say, as when we see truth itself as a religious passion and frenzy, unable to admit to its inseparable dependence on untruth. "I needed a shared blindness," wrote Nietzsche, as if he too was willingly locked into this world of dissimulation binding Europe to Tierra del Fuego, no more no less, as if indeed "truth was a woman," and he was a woman, too, knowing what not to know. "I needed a shared blindness," he said, "with no suspicion or question marks, a pleasure in foreground, surfaces, what is near, what is nearest, in everything that has color, skin, appearance." And he continued: "Perhaps one could accuse me in this regard of some sort of 'art,' various sorts of finer counterfeiting." Perhaps. But how could you trust an admitted deceiver, let alone such a desperado? "What do you know," he shrieks, "what could you know . . . how much falseness I still *require* so that I may keep permitting myself the luxury of *my* truthfulness?"[11] Welcome to the men's Big House. Welcome to the Massacre. Of Women.

In that Other time, the one before now on Isla Grande, when sun and moon, stars and wind, mountains and rivers, were people, in that Other time when women ran the show and the men were at their beck and call, the men did not know. The world was strangely complete in this unknowing, as if waiting to be made. They suspected nothing. Not only did they have to hunt big game as well as rodents and birds, absorbed in ingenious tasks like making bird traps from whales' whiskers, but they had to do the domestic work as well. Can you imagine what it was like for the bird hunters to go into the drizzling night to be lowered naked down the cliffs covered with bird droppings, grabbing the cormorants sleeping with their heads tucked under their wings and biting their heads to kill them before they could cry out, and then to go home and prepare the meals and look after the children? Sowing the furry guanaco hides together to make cloaks was the least of their chores. You know how it is in the fall and early winter, when there are plenty of goslings on the Isla Grande, when the guanaco are plentiful and leave clear tracks and the time is good to begin the Big Hut.

And the women were hardly ever at home. Rarely would they sleep with their husbands, and before dawn they'd be off back to that Big Hut of theirs a quarter of a mile distant from our camp across the open ground. Have to go! Have to go now! they'd say. Got to attend to Xalpen, she with her voracious appetites—and I don't just mean for the fresh meat that we had to supply dragging in guanaco carcasses all the time, either, downright lascivious old bitch. And now all she wants is young men, especially novices, dragging them down. Fresh meat indeed! And she the wife of Shoort!—living underground most of the time she was under the Big Hut away from the camp where the men would huddle with the children, scared the spirits would come darting out like Shoort smashing the houses, screaming abuse, making everyone cover their heads with skins so they'd see nothing.

But now it's all changed. The men run the show. The men have the secret. And it is the men who impersonate the spirits—exactly the same spirits the women impersonated in those far-off times. History is important here; but history as eternal return, history as repeated revelation of its concealed self. In his story of the killing of the father as prelude to the development of human civilization, Freud writes in *Totem and Taboo* of what he calls the totem meal as "a repetition and commemoration of this memorable and criminal deed which was the beginning of so many things—of social organization, of moral restrictions and of religion."[12] In the Tierra del Fuego story, which is also the story of many other people, the "memorable and criminal deed" is utterly different. Nevertheless the obsession with the deed is the same and the need for repetition is urgent, except that while Freud would have us assume it as hypothetical, for the Selk'nam men it seems all too true. Repetition and eternal return by means of astonishingly imaginative ritual life are here the hallmarks of magical force unleashed by the initiated men as they repeat to the male novices how, for so long in that Other time, men labored in ignorance, deceived by the women and how (inexplicably) these same dupes were one fine day able to rise up and violently kill them. A real bloodbath. It's the first thing told the novice in the Big Hut immediately after the "spirits" have been unmasked to reveal mere men, thereby creating, in effect, a twofold unmasking with one revelation folding into the other: first, the taking off of the masks, revealing men, then, the unmasking of the secret history of that secret, as the making of the world through matricide.

*The Cosmogenic Consequence of the First Unmasking (of Women by Men)*
*and the Transformation of the Secret into the Public Secret*

> In ancient times there were already many ancestors here in our
> country. In those days sun and moon, stars and winds, mountains
> and rivers walked the earth as human beings, exactly as we do today.
> But at that time the women held sway everywhere.[13]

It seems to me that the very nature of the secret changed and the world
changed with it, precisely because the men can never forget. Before, in that
Other time, the men really did not know. The secret, if I can put it this way,
was sealed and pure. The men were truly ignorant, as only men can be. There
were no hints or innuendos. There was no calling attention to itself. "Hey!
Look, but don't look! There's a secret over here!" There was, in other words,
no "skin" or "outer edge" of the secret, no membrane pulsing with an inner,
hidden, and presumably magnificent, life. But *now*, after the massacre and the
appropriation of the secret, *not-knowing* is a whole lot more complicated because it is haunted by a secret history and by what seems to me like a revolution in the very basis of identity and of relationship, a revolution in mimetic
facility and hence the ability of humans to transform themselves, into animals and other elements of nature, and vice versa.

In that Other time, before the massacre, it seems like the basis of identity
and of being was utterly different from what they became afterward. For
there was then an enormous capacity for flux in the universe, with all sorts of
identity-switching going on, back and forth, but after the massacre such flux
ossified, although it is far from easy to conceptualize this, given that identity
before the massacre was so fluid and would therefore seem to be a burlesque
of its very self, something no less defining, than disappearing, temporal, and
evanescent.

Sometimes in the accounts recorded by Martin Gusinde, this form of
identity becomes expressed by his Selk'nam shaman informants as a hybrid,
like Moon-Woman, or Sun-Man. Other times, identities are switched with
no warning or explanation from one dimension or one manifestation to another, as when the Sun-Man discovers the women's deception and the men
send spies into the women's Big Hut to confirm that indeed, there are not
spirits there but simply women masking and painting themselves to look like

spirit-beings. We are told that first the men sent the little Kaxken, and are informed in a separate commentary that *Kaxken* is the name of a small bird that lives in long grass and has feathers the color of the earth and a long beak.[14] "He bent down, pressing against the grassy ground, and thus he stole close, unseen," returning to the camp to tell the men "I only saw our wives and girls. . . . Apart from that there was nobody there in the Big Hut."[15]

Is this bird or man?

And this spying is repeated by sending two more men-as-birds/birds-as-men, each bird being of a different species. There is no sign that such transformation is surprising, or that there is any need to clarify the confusions entailed.

*It's as if two quite different forms of transformation are being signaled here, one natural, the other artificial and theatrical.* The first form is dependent upon the flux in being that defines that Other time of matriarchy, the time of the women's secret. Here it seems like a natural thing evolving from the being of being. A man becomes a bird and returns to his human status at will, as natural as breathing. *But then there is this other form involving secrecy*, as first developed by woman, with body painting, masking, and the creation of fake spirit performance through sound, fire, and choreography. (Perhaps this helps explain how the men were for so long so totally ignorant of the women's secret, because where such transformative ease of being exists, where identity is so fluid, the very notion of secret identities makes little sense?)

The two forms of transformation, the natural and the artificial, converge—and this is of the utmost importance for what we might call "the history of the secret"—when we are told that the man-as-bird scurrying unseen through the women's Big Hut accidentally knocks over two of the women's great masks standing against the wall. Gusinde tells us that the masks are venerated and, when not in use, are placed against the inside wall behind the owner's seat. "Its falling over means bad luck for the owner and a great disturbance in the spirit world."[16] In this tiny detail, almost an aside, it seems to me we are being told of the world-shaking decisive confrontation between the theatrical and the natural forms of mimesis, in the ominous collision between the auratic masks, on one side, and this naturally transforming, little bird-man, full of flux, secreted in the heart of the women's secret, on the other.

The "history of the secret" thus lies in two overlapping movements, the passing of the secret from women to men, and the transformation of the mimetic faculty from nature to artifice as the very basis of identity is changed and a new type of supernatural presence is created by means of theatrical illusion, both movements mediated by the massacre and preserved by an overwhelming concern—itself partly fake and whipped up, as far as I can see—with maintaining all of this secret so that the history of the secret is itself tightly wrapped in a cocoon of secrecy from the women.[17]

What is so fascinating is that each of these two movements is dependent on a sort of ontological freeze in which, as a result of the massacre of the women, the inherent capacity of beings to transform ceases. What amounts to a revolution in the very nature of being occurs, the notion of such a "revolution" being clear in the relevant native exegeses.[18]

The upshot is that *the men did not simply exchange roles with women*. It was not a neat reversal. And what deserves emphasis, in my opinion, for it is crucial to all these marvelous and intricate changes across the line of violence and death of women from that Other time to Now time, from natural to artificial mimesis, from matriarchy to patriarchy, is that the *secret* was transformed into the *public secret*.

In other words, when the secret was discovered by the men, and they had killed all the women, the world's capacity for flux ossified, and at the same time the line dividing appearance from reality was enforced. Having thus *detheatricalized nature*, so to speak, by sharply limiting transformative flux, the men's action *theatricalized society*, not merely through mask and spectacle, but through the brilliant exploration of the possibilities offered once the line separating appearance from reality was scored across the face of being. Thus the license to indulge the mimetic faculty as theater passed from nature to man, via the massacre of woman. Yet this involved ever so much more than "theater" as the enchanted space of fiction, designated by Coleridge as the suspension of disbelief, carefully sealed off from reality—by double negatives, no less. It involved more because the terms of the contract the public secret establishes with reality are distinctly different, as if deliberately and painstakingly designed to be conscientiously confusing, and because the "theater" or "ritual" thereof is deliberately designed to this end. If the term "theater" is appropriate, it's a "Brechtian" theater in which the "fourth wall" is very deliberately played with and indeed could be thought of as the main focus of the theater, tracing the power-implications of such a play with the curtain that separates reality from illusion. There is no hermetic sealing off. The very notion of a seal or of a line dividing illusion from reality is itself really illusory.

The massacre of the women jolted the cosmos into another state of being, spreading victims in spirit-metamorphoses out into the stars and bodies of animals where they cling today, in casually experienced and familiar after-images composed of color and line interpolated in fur and feather, the sun in fiery pursuit of the moon across the heavens as night gives way to day, her profile filling out with the passing of the month. "Now there was a revolutionary change," records Gusinde after conversations with the Selk'nam men Tenenesk and Halemink. "Most of the women turned into animals, and one can still tell from their colors what designs they had been wearing at the time when the men were so completely deceived by all the women."[19] Indeed "the totality of the animal kingdom, with few exceptions, was thus created in this time of the integral revolution."[20] In this respect, Lucas Bridges lists stars, mountains, lakes, trees, rocks, animals, birds, fish, insects, and yellow, red, and white clay (presumably used for body painting).[21] Almost fifty years later than Gusinde, with a catastrophically reduced population, Anne Chapman recorded some 650 Selk'nam toponyms, and one of her informants, an elderly woman, "insisted that nearly all natural features had a mythical history."[22]

History thus passes into nature, creating a poignant tension in the world of things, most manifest in the situation of the moon. In the account told Gusinde by Tenenesk and Halemink, Moon-Woman was the first to be attacked when the men massacred the women. They pushed her into the fire and she sank to the ground, her face burning, and as she fell the sky thundered and so the men desisted.[23] When she's full you can see the scars on her face where her husband, Sun-Man, beat her with a burning log. And when she's thin, she wants to eat people, especially when there's an eclipse. Her face is flushed with the blood of men condemned to die. Everyone gets scared, especially the men shamans for they're the ones most responsible for her wounds and flight. She has great power. Two elderly women told Anne Chapman that it was the moon who predicted whom the whites would kill when they set foot on Isla Grande; and when, as they recalled, there was an eclipse, the men shamans would gather everyone, all the household fires would be extinguished, and the women would paint themselves red and draw a stripe across their faces from ear to ear under the nose. The shaman painted a red circle on each cheek to represent the moon and put on a headdress of the feathers of the kex eagle, while the women tried to sweep away the moon and chant to make her less angry toward the men. "Beautiful heart," they sang, "Ample face . . . " as the shaman started to imitate the call of the eagle when it flies high, preparing his spirit to soar to the heavens where she lives. "Let us go to the daughter of the sky," he would chant. If he was invited by her to a seat corresponding to his sky, he would be happy, because he knew he would not be killed. But if he saw the feathers of his headdress in her shadow, he knew he would die within two, maybe three, months.[24]

It is precisely because of the freeze on the mimetic facility that existed prior to the massacre that there now exists, so it seems to me, a most wondrous animation of nature. Humans no longer swim across lines of identity as they did before, and hybrid types have ceased by and large to exist, but natural forms have as a consequence become the "masks" for humanlike agency within. "First the ancestors were like us, now they're what we see: animals, mountains, stars, or winds," an informant tells Gusinde, who thus entitles an entire section of his ethnography "The Integral Animation of the Visible World," referring to the fact that with the passing of prehistory into nature, so nature has become endowed with a mysterious spiritlike being into which people can now fearfully enter by design or accident.[25]

That Other time has passed, so to speak, into present, patriarchal, time, as a stratum accessible to dreams and altered states of consciousness, "access" perhaps being too benign a word here for the way that fate or special procedures generate supernatural power and phenomena. Both men and women shamans, for example, can enter into and arouse this hidden stratum through their chanting and meditation, which brings on dream, and it is dream that the shaman Tenenesk calls upon to invoke that Other time:

> Whoever sleeps in the Máustas mountains sees in his dreams how the Big Hut of men was enacted in those days for the first time, and how those men planned and arranged everything. That mountain range brings good luck! Whoever thinks of it and calls: "Máustas, Máustas!" will find many sea lions or a whale on the beach. For these mountains used to be a big Big Hut. All the men, who played here at that time, turned into mountains, rocks, and hills, and have remained there since. Whoever falls asleep there sees in his dreams everything that happens in those mountains, including the men who played there at that time.[26]

The natural world is to some degree a repository in allegorical form of that Other time, which, when unmasked by dream, grants miraculous power. "Almost from the beginning of our acquaintance," wrote Lucas Bridges, "I had noticed that the Selk'nam would sometimes speak to a bird as though in response to something the bird had said."[27] But it is in dreamlike states that such communication is more likely to flourish. People daydreaming, walking in the woods or along the shore, may suddenly encounter a spirit, a figure, a sound. Gusinde tells us how a Yamana man (although it could just as well be a woman) may be roaming the shore alone,

> as though sunk in a world of dreams, without definite thoughts. Sud-
> denly he finds himself in a visionary state, known as *asikaku*; before him
> swarms a vast number of herring, whales, swordfish, vultures, cormorants,
> petrels, and other animals. They all speak flatteringly to him. . . . They
> act like the most friendly of human beings. The man is completely out
> of his mind. His whole body is numb, and he sinks down and lies there
> motionless.[28]

Gusinde was told that the spirits of these creatures are now communing with the soul of the man, who feels a great happiness descend. When they depart, he wakes from his "dream" but is disoriented and goes home to bed, only to have them arrive once more, enticing his soul onto the high seas. One of them may become his spirit-guardian, prelude to the man becoming a shaman. Other times a huge whale arrives, in which case the call to shaman-hood cannot be delayed, as the creature gives the person a song to chant. With the chant, body rocking back and forth or slumped over, face painted, comes a dream again, and with this dream one acquires the power to see and hence use the powers hidden within the natural forms that the cataclysm of prehistory has deposited.[29]

Thus seeing is power, and a quite incredible power at that. It seems to me no accident that in his remarks on sorcery and shamanism, Lucas Bridges was drawn to the eyes of the great Selk'nam shaman, Houshken, eyes exceedingly dark, almost blue-black. "I had never seen eyes of such color," mused Bridges, and he wondered whether Houshken was nearsighted. Far from it. For not only was the man a mighty hunter, but it was said that he could see through mountains. What is more, these are the eyes that can look deep into the hu-man body, as was brought out when Bridges allowed another famous shaman, Tenenesk (who twenty years later became one of Father Martin Gusinde's most important informants), to induct him into the ways of the shaman. Reclining on guanaco skins by the fire sheltered by a windbreak, Bridges's chest was gone over by Tenenesk's hands and mouth as intently, said Bridges, as any doctor with a stethoscope, "moving in the prescribed manner from place to place, pausing to listen here and there. He also gazed intently at my body, as though he saw through it like an X-ray manipulator."[30]

The vision involved here is tactile. Yet it is also a seeing-into and a seeing-through, with those penetrating eyes joined in some perceptual endeavor with the shaman's hands and lips journeying across the surface of the body. Even more tactile is the succeeding penetration and fusion of bodies as when, from his own body, the shaman then produced a lifelike feathery form to implant in Bridges's chest and then asked him if he felt something moving in his heart, or whether he saw something strange in his mind, something like a dream.[31]

This strikes me as physiognomy, the whole nine yards, the eye of the shaman being the eye of physiognomy par excellence. What needs pointing out, however, and this is not so obvious, although equally marvelous, is how such visual power of penetration is equivalent to unmasking and unmasking is equivalent to "beaming in" to the perturbations of that Other time, as that time is incorporated, especially through the massacre of women, into the constitutive Being *and* un-Being of the world. So dazzling is this unmasking that I would prefer to call it defacement, so as to emphasize the radical nature of the changes that can occur in the very heart of Being.

Let me emphasize that it would be a mistake to attribute this to the power of an all-seeing eye. To the contrary I would say that the key to such power of vision lies in a physiognomic potential within the world at large, with its twofold Beingness of identity closure and identity flux, corresponding to Our time and Other time. Hence the extraordinary material power attributed to such vision lies in working back and forth across the line of tension lying in Being itself, revealing and concealing the materialization of matricide in the life-forms of today, no less than the transformation in the very basis of mimesis. Such dreamlike unmasking of Other time also occurs at times of danger, as we saw with the eclipse of the moon, with illness, and, in other places in the New World, in ritual involving psychoactive drugs, like *yagé*.[32] This suggests an equivalence between the secret, drugs, danger, and dream, linked together by the wonder of defacing things in which prehistory reposes.

It is a marvelous thing, this secret, the way it theatricalizes everything as if with a magic wand. Writing about the days and nights after the major events of the Big Hut, when there was a soulful peace lying like a mantle over the camp, Martin Gusinde wrote that every night a different man would stay in the Big Hut and suddenly you would hear this terrible cry, *Waaa*, shattering the silence. The women then knew that Xalpen was hard at work, and when some poor fellow came limping back into camp, worn out and quietlike, his women kinfolk never beleaguered him with questions. They would care for him so he'd more easily forget his ordeal. When a man was missing for several days, the men would casually inform the women that Xalpen was still fucking him.[33]

In addition to being an ethnographer, Gusinde was a priest of the Catholic Order of the Divine Word outside of Vienna, with his own Big Hut to go back to, presided over by Father Schmidt. Once, he heard the terrible cry and it was his very own voice! Waaa. Waaa. The women were upset and some were deeply ashamed.

"Leave him alone," they shouted. "How much longer are you going to violate this poor man! You really go for white men, don't you! That's why you won't let him go!"

Occasionally, five men formed a semicircle outside the Big Hut and the one in the middle had a bladder tied to his penis stretching down as far as his knees so he could barely walk and then only with his legs astride. Round and round the Big Hut they went so the women would believe the man's scrotum had become grotesquely swollen due to the demands made on him by Xalpen.

Sometimes the men panicked and fled from the Big Hut to escape her, each whirling a blazing brand in the night air. The cries would be terrible. Waaa, Waaa. Some would go back into the hut, others would be ejected. This could go on for over half an hour. The men would pair up and race round the Big Hut, the one behind holding his fire-stick up against the one in front to make him go faster. Other times the man behind would be carried upside down against the back of the man in front, so that his head dangled down near the ground, looking backward as they raced along chased by a third who threatened them with a burning log, the air filling with these awful cries, Waaa, Waaa, the women wailing for the fate of their men and mad as hell, screaming at Xalpen.

"So that the women can see these different scenes," explained Gusinde,

> a huge bonfire is lit close to the Big Hut. The wavering flames throw a filmy pink light over the naked bodies of these strange groups of men. Gigantic shadows leap across the snow, their moving forms changing in an uncanny mix of magic, color, and nerves on edge. When the night is dark they allow the women as close as eighty paces to the Big Hut.[34]

It was spectacular. But, then, what else would you expect? You see, it's a full-time twenty-four-hours-a-day performance, day in, day out, death threats flying, the women being watched and spied upon all the time. But even Gusinde, after all he'd heard, was taken aback when told that *if* a woman got close to the Big Hut she would be dragged in by a Shoort spirit and strangled.[35] Did he really believe this? This is the sort of problem an ethnographer of dissimulation has to squarely confront.

Yet he himself was almost killed when Nana, who disliked him, told the other men that he had told Nana's wife about the secret. (According to Gusinde, the men would have killed Nana's wife too. So what does that tell you about Nana?) What startled Gusinde was how even his best friend, Tenenesk, was so paranoid that he was more than ready to believe Nana's story and, in panic at the prospect of the revelation of the secret, couldn't see how implausible Nana's story was. Gusinde was in no doubt that his own life was in danger through the long night of waiting to see what the men decided. "This shows better than so many words," he later wrote, "to what degree the mentality of these men is dominated by the omnipotent preoccupation with the security of their secret."[36]

But the ethnographer proved to be no less preoccupied. Take the night he brought his camera and tripod to the Big Hut when the men were painting their bodies. The agreement was that he should have their permission for each photograph, but he couldn't resist the urge to unobtrusively set up his camera to take a picture when the men were almost finished painting.

"I had set up the tripod thirty minutes ago," he related,

> the body painting was almost done, the magnesium powder was ready for ignition, and so I pulled the flap [la solapa] off the film mounted in the chassis. [The word la solapa for the flap covering the film, can also mean "secret" and "on the sly."] Now the Indians knew from previous occasions how my camera worked and that pulling off the flap was followed by taking the picture, and in that very instant my throat was clutched to the point of strangling in the heavy hands of Tenenesk who had, without my knowing, been watching from the corner of his eye.
>
> "What the hell are you doing!" I heard him say. "You want to take a photograph? And what if it falls into the hands of the women who will see there's no spirits in here, only men, and they'll say, 'Oh! It's just men in there painting themselves, just our husbands, all these figures in there are just our husbands!' How dare you do this! Can't you see the men are painted but are not wearing their masks! With your photo we would be betrayed to the women! Stop at once!"
>
> The faces of the other men showed profound disgust and emotions rose to a dangerous point. . . . My salvation lay in a dramatic display of submission. With a sweep of my arm I knocked the camera to the ground where it lay covered in snow. Tranquillity returned. It was the decisiveness, the unexpected blow, that deflated their passions.[37]

So what bravado possessed him to try and take a photograph without permission, using a magnesium flare for lighting? Is this mad disregard a tribute to the seductive magic of the secret, combined with the need to unmask it? Only the "decisiveness" of the redeeming gesture, as he explained, could cut through this—the camera and its tripod sailing through the air to lie abject on a snowy bed in a drama of nonexposure, no less magnificent than revelation.

Improvised and spontaneous as it was, this was a great piece of theater as far as the secret and its demands for revelation are concerned, illustrating that ease whereby whatever approaches the secret becomes theatricalized—at least in the retelling. After all, storytelling is the art of revelation through concealment. But above all, what I want to suggest is that this theatricality emerges in the "leap" from the secret as made by persons, to the secret, in its turn, making persons. It is in this surrender to the thing made, to the creation taking over the creators, that we find the pathos of the real as really made up.

*Perhaps Truth Is a Child?*

The camera flies onto the snow. The magician grasps the throat. The man who would unmask is unmasked. And the ethnographer has become a ritual extension of that which he studies, as has this very text I labor to write. Perhaps we too feel those hands. Feats of great daring litter the field, death threats flying over the heads of women outmasking masking by knowing what not to know. "To be good at *not* knowing," counsels Nietzsche. "Perhaps truth is a woman."

Perhaps truth is a child? For it has indeed transpired that a kid, but not, of course, a woman, will recognize and denounce a spirit as a disguised human—from the way it walks, for instance. (Spirits, you understand, walk quite differently than men.) Young people in fact are dangerous because, unlike adults, they can't keep a secret, and certainly not a public secret—although you don't exactly "keep" a public secret so much as know how to be kept by it. Adolescent boys have even tried to kill men disguised as spirits, which is why men keep an extra-special eye on them. Whether this is because of an uncontrollable anger consequent to seeing through their disguise, or whether it's something like the opposite, an anger stemming from too strong a belief in the reality of these spirits emerging from the Big Hut, I cannot tell. And this is my point. You cannot tell because of the cunning with which the public secret plays with revelation and concealment, by turns confusing and soothing. It is this that catches people off balance and thus do children, in the particulars of their blend of innocence and astuteness, slide either side of the public secret, graceful for all of that, but unable as yet to achieve the performative maturity required to modulate the claims reality makes on illusion.

Why would they get so steamed up that they'd want to kill a spirit? Well, Tenenesk told the story of a marvelously adept Shoort who was shot by his younger brother, who was anxious and angry at the prolonged absence of his brother in the Big Hut, not realizing that in fact the Shoort was the very brother he was looking for. The Shoort died, but not before, summoning his formidable strength and acting ability, he'd made it back to the Big Hut without appearing to have been wounded. (Spirits do not get wounded.)[38] The men then held counsel in the Big Hut, buried the corpse right there, and sent a close relative of the dead man late that night to the dead man's home, where he lay down for a brief period and then left, taking the dead man's bow and arrows so as to leave the impression that the dead man was not dead and had in fact spent the night there with his wife. They were making an alibi, you see, so that it would seem as if the dead man, who played the Shoort, was still alive. On the next day a group of men assembled for hunting and invited the dead man's younger brother, the one who had inadvertently killed him, to go hunting with them. They found a herd of guanaco and told the lad to go around them. As he set off, they shot and killed him. His own father had agreed to this. Just as they released their arrows they "unmasked" the dead Shoort, crying, "Why did you fire against the Shoort yesterday? He was your brother!" When the hunters returned to camp they told the people there that the two brothers had been hunting with them, gotten into a fight, killed each other, and that they had buried them there and then.

## Do the Women Believe?

I keep asking myself whether the women really believe, even though I spent an entire section on not-knowing about not-knowing in the previous chapter. Maybe the women are just acting as if they believe? Mightn't that mean they still had the secret after all, practicing the ultimate deceit, pretending not to notice the men's deceit? Could that be why the men are always worried, always on the lookout for revelation?

At one point, where Gusinde emphatically reasserts that the Selk'nam women know nothing of what he calls the "hoax," he refers to a letter he received from Lucas Bridges in 1928 describing how, during an initiation of men in the Big Hut around 1909, a rumor circulated that women on the northern end of the island "suspected something of the great deceit" and so a group of men smeared their faces and heads with ashes, stood in front of the Big Hut, and made faces with their lips protruding, their eyes squinting, and their teeth bared. They exhaled strange whistling noises as other men performed obscene gestures against the women of the camp. All this, said

Bridges, was to demonstrate the determination of the men to defend their se-cret, and the men were relieved to see that the women then stayed in their hut as this indicated that they would not attempt an uprising.[39]

An uprising!

And could anything be more calculated to undermine the men's secret than this performance?

Of all the outsiders who expressed themselves concerning the secret among the Selk'nam, Martin Gusinde seems to have had the clearest picture, and an elegant scheme it was too, the engagement of a crisp negation: the men don't believe; the women do. Case closed. Anne Chapman said that he believed the men put on this greatest show on earth so as to control the women with fake spirits hauling themselves out from the fiery bowels of the earth, others, clad in lichen and feathers, swooping down from the heavens to gather inside the Big Hut with the menfolk from the camp, shoulder to shoulder, each in his own sky, under the command of Xalpen down there yelping and wanting, the earth vibrating and shooting fire.

But, in fact, Gusinde himself was mystified about the function of the se-cret, and he took pains to deny it existed so as to control the women.[40] Yet he was in no doubt about one thing: "I express my firmest conviction," he wrote, "when I assert that not one of the Selk'nam women has discovered the men's hoax, and that the entire female population lives today in the firm conviction that the spirits of the Big Hut are a reality."[41]

But Lucas Bridges leaves the question of women's belief hanging. Heavy, but hanging. He is certain, here, that the men would kill them, but as to women's belief, he wavers.[42]

This wavering becomes still more curious when he observes that the ini-tiates, "who had lived constantly with their mothers for the twelve or thirteen years prior to the initiation and would surely have heard any careless word had it been spoken, were undoubtedly terrified when they came face to face with Shoort for the first time."[43] Elsewhere he wrote that in the "early stages of their instruction, before their initiation into the Big Hut, these lads im-plicitly believed in supernatural monsters, having, as children, often watched them from the encampment and joined in the stampede when Xalpen or Shoort approached too near."[44]

Could such conviction coexist with a wavering mom?

Fifty years later, Anne Chapman came and copied down what some of the surviving Selk'nam said.[45]

*Esteban*: "If a woman thought something of the truth about the Big Hut, she wouldn't let on because if she did a shaman would kill her."

*Lola*: " . . . told me that that she had never gone near the places where she knew a Big Hut had once stood. It is my impression that even during the last year of her life, when we lived together, she still firmly believed in the spirits of the Big Hut, even though she knew that those which appeared in the ceremony were only men in disguise."

*Anne Chapman*: "I never queried her directly on the subject because I thought I might offend her if I did."

Whatever belief is, conceptually, in these matters, it is inseparable from danger and beyond our or anybody else's determination of its realness or its fakeness—as Bridges pithily pointed out: "Maybe the women suspected; if they did, they kept their suspicions to themselves." Bridges doesn't know if they know. And the women will never tell. Or, in Anne Chapman's case, "I never queried her directly on the subject because I thought I might offend her if I did." In Bridge's formulation it's the threat of death that "contaminates" the purity of knowledge. In Anne Chapman's formulation there is this other intimately related but different danger of causing offense, as if the act of questioning may rupture something elusive and delicate, bound to the constitution of the Other's being. (And this despite or because of living together for a year!)

"Angela did confide in me that she had never believed at all in the spirits of the Big Hut, but this belief notwithstanding she never approached a site where a ceremonial hut was known to have existed."

Once, when participating as spectator for the Big Hut, she whispered to a woman friend that one of the spirits looked human.

A man overheard her comment and he repeated it to the men in the Big Hut.

"In old times a shaman would have killed me," said Angela.[46]

## Do the Men Believe?

If in this circle of danger the men believe that the women believe, then what do the men actually believe as regards the reality of the spirits they incarnate with their painted bodies and great masks?

For in "no way do the men believe that they are dealing with true beings from other spheres," wrote Gusinde. Yet it is curious that he goes on to point out, as further evidence of this, that what glows with living force in the men's consciousness is their memory of the women's originary deceit as something that truly happened. And it is those very same originary spirit-enactments, supposed by the men to have been performed by the women in secret in that Other time, that the men now, in our time, self-consciously imitate.[47] For example, when the men paint their bodies to look like the spirits, they may well say to each other that this is how the women did it. "We do exactly the same as they did anciently." Thus the men may not believe they are "dealing with true beings from other spheres," as Gusinde relates, but they believe that there was a once upon a time, that Other time, and in that time women had the secret as prelude to the great disillusionment with its shattering consequences.

Something else to consider is the dense symbolic power in the form and materials of the Big Hut. It stood for the four wombs situated in the four skies of infinity, the most treacherous of which was the (imaginary) great cordillera of the east, womb of the east wind, surrounded by a sea of boiling water. In the four "skies" lived different ancestor-shamans—Sun, Wind, Owl, Snow, Moon, Rain—and these mythic skies beyond the world were the sources of their shamanic power. Moon was married to Sun and Rain was married to Snow. Different colors were thus associated; red with sunset and with the west, white with snow and with the south, black with the sea and with the north. The seven supporting posts of the Big Hut were associated with the way Isla Grande was divided into these mythic skies, such that when the men took their places they did so in accordance with their skies.[48]

A deep crevice running east to west from the entrance though the fire divided the hut lengthwise. Based on her conversations with her informants in the 1960's, Anne Chapman relates that this

> line was considered very dangerous for it indicated a vastly profound crevice or chasm, which eventually led to a sea far below, which was called, according to Frederico, *chali koxain*. Upon entering the Hain [or Big Hut] a man took great care not step on or across the "crevice." If he entered on the right side, toward the north, he could not walk to the south of the hut except by leaving and re-entering on the left side.[49]

And this is why there was a double entrance to the Big Hut, one for each side of that fearsome crevice, so that men no less than spirits could take the side corresponding to their sky.

The notion of a hoax seems far away.

I might also note in this regard that when a shaman entered the Big Hut, he had to "switch off" his powers; otherwise a woman shaman's power might connect up with his and discern the secret occurring inside.[50]

And here in the semidarkness is a man about to emerge as spirit, as the spirit Shoort, no less. He is being dressed, having the mask put over his head by his sky-companion, the same man who made the mask.

"Are you the same being as you were?" he is asked.

"Come!" they say. "Sit here! You are the same as me. We are grandsons of the Big Hut. You are now transformed. The ancestor shaman Owl has penetrated you and you are now the image of him." Shoort listens but cannot reply because he is no longer human.[51]

If it was a hoax it surely took over the hoaxers too. All the more peculiar, then, and all the more wonderful, the actual hoaxing and the ritual focus on unmasking, the "real hoax," we might say.

Along with two young Selk'nam men, Gusinde was himself initiated by the Selk'nam in 1923, and he published some 260 pages on this experience alone, including the apocalyptic moment of unmasking of spirit with which the initiation began, immediately following which the history of the massacre of the women and appropriation of their secret was told, and the initiates sworn to secrecy on threat of death.

It seems obvious from his account that this masked theater of men guarding their secret from women and children owes its impact and ongoing energy to unmasking, and that unmasking is not only an elaborated art form, but that in so dramatically revealing the trick to the initiates—for *trick* it most decidedly is—the initiated men recharge the universe with mystery and heightened sacredness. Such a curious outcome suggests a source of weakness in current scholarly theorization of religion, ritual, and symbol. For instead of finding equivalents for symbols and signs, instead of abandoning "meaning" for the "viscerality" of the "body" in the "habitus" and "embodiment," and instead of pilfering "theories" of drama or of "rites of passage" with their emphasis on catharsis via "liminality," the evidence here suggests we look first and foremost at the trick and the complicated ways it configures faith with skepticism, and presence with representation.[52]

Here is how Gusinde described the initiation.[53] (And let us not forget the "ethnographic present" and presence here involved, for it would seem that the Indians had put this on specially for our ethnographer. Initiation, let alone the population, was in sad decline, and Gusinde's enthusiasm, not to mention his purse, seems to have played a part in bringing this 1923 initiation to fruition.)

There were three candidates, including Gusinde, and when they were led into the Big Hut, specially made for this occasion, measuring eighteen feet high at the center and twenty-four feet in diameter, they found a circle of men surrounding a fire in the center, silent in the darkness. Suddenly there was an extremely loud chant, *hohohohoho*, for some three minutes and the men in the circle fixed their gaze on the initiates who were led to the end of the hut opposite the door and thus forced to form a line of three, their bodies rigid, and to stare into the fire. Behind each initiate stood a guide. Two shamans knelt on either side of this line. (Anne Chapman notes that when the women in the camp hear this chant, "they know that the rite of passage has begun and they run into their huts to hide."[54])

The fur clothing of the two Selk'nam initiates was removed, but not, so it would seem, the clothing of our ethnographer. The two stood naked but for their red body paint. "Look up!" one of the shamans ordered, and each guide grabbed the head of an initiate and violently forced their gaze up. The shamans gazed at them "with irresistible power."

Suddenly two Shoort spirits leaped out of the fire amidst great noise and knelt down by each of the two Indian candidates, legs slightly astride, buttocks resting on their ankles. The bodies of these Shoorts must have been completely naked, if the photographs are any guide, painted red with white spots, their head hidden behind a mask covering the entire head.

"An icy terror" gripped the initiates as the Shoorts grasped their legs and began to breathe deeply as if, says Gusinde, crazy with sexual lust, stretching and twisting their bodies lasciviously for two minutes. Up to this time the initiates had had to stand still with their arms crossed against their bodies. Now they had to place their hands on the crowns of their heads with their elbows out to the sides.

Then, without warning, a Shoort seized the genitals of one of the initiates and squeezed hard. The breathing of the Shoort grew ever deeper. This playing with the genitals lasted fifteen minutes and was concluded by an extra heavy pull with both hands as the Shoort let out a heavy whistle.

There was a respite for five minutes and then began the struggle between the initiate and the Shoort, it being expressly forbidden to remove the Shoort's mask. The men in the circle grew more excited, yelling at the now exhausted initiate, who was allowed to use his arms freely to defend himself and grab the spirit. If an initiate, so Gusinde was told, ever looked like getting the better of a spirit, the guide would step in to subdue him or the spirit itself would swing burning wood or bite hard into the initiate's arms, legs, or penis. As the fight went on the men kept on with the resonant sound around the fire, *hohohohoho* . . .

After thirty minutes the spirit suddenly stopped and knelt down, which only made the initiates even more scared. The moment was still and quiet.

"The fight is over," said the guides. They pointed to the mask on the spirit.

"Touch it!" they ordered.

Trembling with fear the initiate dared only to place the tip of his finger on the shoulder of the spirit. Just the slightest touch. Upon further encouragement, he palpitated the chest and the neck with his index finger. Finally he gathered the courage to actually touch the mask itself.

Threatened by the other men, he finally placed his hand on the upper part of the mask. There was nothing else to do but grab it. "Terrorized he slowly raised it. His gaze hardened. It was the face of someone he knew well . . . and this face was smiling at him, while remaining completely still."

The young man had no idea what was going on. He seemed totally perplexed, while the men around him smiled and laughed.

"This is a game of men. It is we who represent all this. What's just happened to you just now that made you fear so much, all this is nothing more than something made by men!" Then they threaten him. "Never reveal any of this to women or children. Your death will immediately follow if you do."

And Anne Chapman's description goes like this.

When the naked initiate is in a state of frantic despair, the contest is stopped short and the supervisor, pointing to Shoort's head, gives the startling command.

"Grasp it!"

Another man shouts, "Touch Shoort! Is he rock or is he flesh?"

Encouraged, the initiate passes his fingers over Shoort's head and neck. With further urging he grasps the head, feels the mask, and starts to pull it off as Shoort covers his face with his hands.

A guide orders the initiate to pull Shoort's hands away from his face.

He stares with amazement at the unmasked face.

"Who is he? Could he be an ancestor?" shouts an elder.

"Who could he be? Maybe an Airu? Or a Woo?" (These are the names of neighboring people.) "Perhaps a Joshe?" (This is the name of a killer spirit.)

Others break in with their questions.

"Don't you know him?"

"Name him!"

"Don't you recognize the face?"

Minutes usually pass before the young man identifies the face—in part because it is blackened and the muscles are contracted and the eyes tightly closed.

He calls out the man's name.

"Push him!," someone yells, and the spirit tumbles to the ground. The men roar with laughter.[55]

At which point the initiate relaxes, but in Lucas Bridges's account of the ceremony to which he was invited years before, at the turn of the century, something different occurred. "He attacked him with such fury," said Bridges of the initiate, "that he had to be dragged off, to the accompaniment of roars of laughter in which Shoort joined heartily."[56]

Obviously, un-masking is crucial. First there is the exposure of the genitalia, squeezed and played with, causing excruciating pain for some fifteen minutes while the other tabooed area—the face of the spirit—is made even more taboo with severe warnings against touching it. The more the penis or testicles are squeezed, the more the face of the spirit must be avoided. This is the first field of transgression set up, the first field of dialectically opposed negations, holding face and genitalia at arm's length. Then comes the second transgression, negating the first.

"Touch it!" "Grasp it."

The tip of the finger cautiously ascends to the face, palpitating the chest and neck. . . . The touching becomes a grasping and then a removing of the mask, succeeded by looking and then:

"Name him!"

"Don't you recognize him?"

It must have been an intense, even beautiful, scene; the leaping shadows of the fire against the silhouettes of the men, some masked as spirits, the drumming on the ground and the chanting as well, the slow yet violent crescendo leading to the ultimate revelation . . . succeeded ineluctably by the massing of mystery. And beyond, the early winter snow covering the land, the women hiding in their huts with their children.

### The Power of Unmasking Lies in the Riddle of Childhood Memory of Maternal Speech

*And the women? They know they must not know.* They know they have to keep right away from the Big Hut, go far over, that way, for water, and far over that other way for firewood, and never come close by. They know there's someone guarding the place. They know they're being watched. And when the Shoort spirits come out in their fury, they'll take it out on any of the women who've been seen lifting their eyes above the furs they're meant to cover their faces with, lying on the ground, the epitome of unseeing.

Yet despite the draconian restrictions on their movements and on what they must and must not see, Gusinde stressed the active nature of the women's nonparticipation. Indeed it is the women's complicity with their "blindness," one might venture to say, that allows the spiritual reality to assert itself. And have you ever thought how hard it must be to be the unknowing part of that which you're meant not to know, coupled with threats of death if you so much as appear to know you must not know? And in that case, surely the greatest performance is that of the women? Don't they have the task of being choreographed into the performance of the secret without being told what it is they are doing? And they perform beautifully. On again. Off again. Hiding their eyes one moment. Watching intently at others.

Then there's the women's song so that the Big Hut can function. It is the mother of the eldest initiate, for instance, who sings the midnight song those first eight nights in that deep voice the women have, a voice of men, this sad and frightening song taken up by the other women of the camp. "It would awaken me from dreaming, as if threatening me," wrote Gusinde. With this song, the women wanted the initiates over there in the Big Hut to know they were not alone, that the darkness of night shall dissipate.

With dawn the mother of the eldest initiate emerged once again from her hut. She had slept little or not at all, worrying about her boy. The women sat in front of their huts singing a salute to the sun, happy the night had passed and anxious to communicate that to the initiates. At midday they sang a different song, a homage to Xalpen and her husband Shoort, so as to calm them and put them in a good mood. Each woman sang the song particular to the part of Isla Grande from which she came. When this was insufficient, there was another song they sang late in the afternoon and in the early evening.[57]

This was accompanied by a wondrous sympathy exuding from the mother of the eldest initiate, usually with her singing to the dawn, during which she would mimic her boy, especially as a tiny child. Early in the morning she tripped out of her hut as if learning to walk, at times on all fours. She not only imitated the particularities of her boy; she also imitated his imitating.[58]

What's more, she would slip in and out of this enactment by commenting on it.

"My son is now an initiate," she declared. "When he was little he played happily around my home. He was always happy and loved to visit other homes to play with the children there. How happy his life was then!"

She smiled, clapped her hands and jumped like a child for joy. She became adult and serious and began to wail. "But now my son is an initiate sitting over there in the Big Hut! Oh! How he suffers!" In between sobs she cried, "He is gone and I'm alone! How will he fare in his suffering?"

And just as suddenly, her mood switched and she was happy and a child again.

"And so in truth are children all over," comments Gusinde, as if it was not the mother mimicking the child, but the child mimicking the mother mimicking the child.

She feels real and terrible pain, he added, and that is why her acting is "more than acting." What's more, this is a collective pain felt viscerally by the other women in the camp.[59]

Perhaps, with poetic license, we could imagine this pain visually, like a cloud, wafting slowly toward the Big Hut to envelop it, such that the "more than acting" of the women engages with and boosts the "less than acting" of the men making men from boys with the magic of the secret the women know they must not know. This logic would seem to dictate—insofar as logic dictates anything—that thanks to song the mother is here in the fastness of the Big Hut without being here, because it is she from whom the secret must be kept and from whom the break must be made, she who knows so well that she must not know. This is why it is fitting she is here in disembodied form, singing in the dawn in intermittent maternity-acts of remembrance and separation, registering mimetic fusion with the child's history of bodily form, with the child's history of imitating and hence discovering if not mocking the world, this child separating from its mother to definitively break with the world of woman, this child become man on learning the secret whose overweening feature is that it must never, on pain of death, be revealed to woman. And in this we are witness to her gift in the general economy of gift giving, of which mimesis is but a part, mimesis itself being that faculty of becoming other in the trade in secrets.

And has not this woman been here before?

*Hotex*: "When I was still a boy my mother told me all that was going on in the Big Hut. Later when I was admitted as an initiate I could see it just like she said. . . . But how would my mother and other women know?"

*Gusinde*: "On further discussion I concluded that his mother had only told him about events external to the Big Hut, and that what had happened was that after being initiated he had read back into his mother's words what was going on inside!"[60]

*Lucas Bridges*: "To me it seemed impossible that the women were utterly deceived, yet the initiates, who lived constantly with their mothers for the twelve or thirteen years prior to their initiation and would surely have heard any careless word had it been spoken, were undoubtedly terrified when they came face to face with Shoort for the first time."[61]

*Reading Back*: Secrecy secretes itself into the obliqueness of language and riddling—in the implicit as much as with the complicit—nowhere more so than when it takes the form of public secrecy. When a man remembers his mother telling him as a boy what really went on inside there, he's probably reading back into her speech *what was in fact already there*, and Gusinde is thus both right and wrong; right in that there is a process of reinterpretation of the mother's speech, wrong in that the boy is not "making it up" that the mother told him what was going on inside. The inside was there all the time and Lucas Bridges is wrong insofar as he directs our attention to a "careless word," as if the secret was something that could be sprung by a mistake when all along it was hiding in the light.

The "undoubted terror" on the face of the initiate that Lucas Bridges refers us to as evidence of the depth of the mother's belief in the reality of the spirit-forms, would thus be the Tierra del Fuegian equivalent of what Marcel Proust so famously called *involuntary memory*. For it was all there in the active unknowing of the mother's speech, and what surfaces in the wake of the mother tongue for the boy becoming a man with the staging of the unmasking of spirit in the Big Hut is definitely not a question of retrieval of "information" from the archive of conscious memory. On the contrary, what emerges with the unmasking of spirit in the Big Hut is a type of shock in which the "reading back" through the all too open doors of the maze of the secreted secret whiplashes time into an overpowering instant of flooding recall, dripping with possibilities, theatrical and otherwise, for transformation. It is not that something previously unknown is gloriously unveiled for the first time as the very acme of secrecy. Nor is it the return of the repressed. For with unmasking, discovery gives way to recovery, and what is recovered by this reading back through the disclosures of the public secret is not so much an item of remembrance but *something new* that emerges from the charged juxtaposition of present with past, creating (as the young Samuel Beckett remarks in his dazzling essay on Proust) a mystical fusion of the *imaginary* with the *real*.[62] And it is of course just such a fusion that ensures that a new mystery surfaces as the secret is unmasked.

How spectral this experience can be is the subject of Proust's work in search of lost time, its tenacious labor testimony, thought Walter Benjamin, to the erosion in modernity of our capacity for experience, and therefore of memory itself. Recording the shudder running through his body at the first shock of remembrance of the *taste* of the *madeleine* pastry, Proust tells us that in vain he searched for any object or event that could account for the all-consuming joy overwhelming him. The memory evoked by the accident of the taste of the pastry is itself like a visceral process, starting as a wave of inchoate feeling, clawing for definition that will not come. As the attempt at conscious recall gets Proust nowhere, as his frustration with the blockage to memory increases, all he can finally do is to surrender to the sensation itself, this stirring in the thickets of the past. There and then he felt start within him, he says, some force embedded like an anchor at great depth. This *movement* is also the *moment* of what he would come to call *la mémoire involontaire*, and I retain here the foreign phrasing for emphasis, "*the* involuntary memory," so as to set it apart as an epiphany of everyday life, something which

hitherto seems to have received little attention whenever people discussed the
mysteries of memory (including Freud). Proust forces us to make room for
the microseconds of hauling in the past as so many unfolding images. He
conveys to us an immense panorama condensed in minutiae, the "echo," as he
puts it, of great spaces traversed in the vast structure of recollection. He refers
us to a Japanese game in which one dips into water formless bits of paper
that, the instant they are wet, "stretch and twist and take on colour and dis-
tinctive shape, become flowers or houses or people, solid and recognisable."[63]
This is more than remembering things; it is the process of remembrance itself, as substantialized through things such that time and its manifestations in-
terlock in determinate Being.

Small wonder, then, that Samuel Beckett regarded the *mémoire involontaire*
as "sacred action," intellectualized *animism* as the mark of the fetish, while for
Benjamin the *mémoire involontaire* was the subject of a spiritual presence, as
found in premodern ritual where voluntary and involuntary elements of
memory fused together.[64]

Such "sacred action" of remembrance would account for the mystical consequences of unmasking in the Tierra del Fuegian ethnography. To the auratic rupture and subsequent stimulation of the *mémoire involontaire*, we need
to add the truly complex yet marvelous notions of time compression and time
expansion thereby involved in the events and material objects that occupy the
memory as the past careens into the shocked present-time, such that time itself is suspended out of time. This will occupy enormously critical dimensions in Benjamin's philosophy of history as well as of memory, while for
Beckett it amounts not only to a first approximation, if not "solution," to age-
old questions about symbolism and the nature of the connection between a
symbol and what it stands for, but also establishes a "new reality." And of
course it is precisely this new reality to which I wish to draw attention as the
mystical surplus spilling over from unmasking. In his first extended discussion of the *mémoire involontaire* Beckett puts it like this:

> The identification of immediate with past experience, the recurrence of
> past action or reaction in the present, amounts to a participation between
> the ideal and the real, imagination and direct apprehension, symbol and
> substance. Such participation frees the essential reality that is denied to
> the contemplative as to the active life. What is common to present and
> past is more essential than either taken separately. . . . Thanks to this

reduplication [achieved by such a memory] the experience is at once imaginative and empirical, at once an evocation and a direct perception, real without being merely actual, ideal without being merely abstract, the ideal real, the essential, the extratemporal. But if this mystical experience communicates an extratemporal essence, *it follows that the communicant is for the moment an extratemporal being.*[65] (emphasis added)

Repetition is essential for this fetish-surge. But this does not mean that the second time, the time of recovery, is only a carbon copy of the first. Far from it. Something powerful emerges with the repetition, from repetition itself, so to speak, and not just from what it is that is repeated. In remembering his mother telling him as a child about the secret, for which she could be killed, a man being initiated is not simply confirming her disclosure, but its memorable history of having being withheld from the child—only to be later revealed as the centerpiece of initiation into society, initiation of men here being, if not the source, then at least the drama by which society reproduces itself through the medium of persons. Everything depends on the withholding. For it is this that allows the adult's imagination of the child's imagination, magnified by the secret, to fully blossom and engage with the extraordinary retroactive force of the *mémoire involontaire* sprung by the ritual of unmasking.

> Spirit is this power only by looking the negative in the face, and tarry-
> ing with it. This tarrying with the negative is the magical power that
> converts it into being.
>
> H E G E L, *Phenomenology of Spirit*[66]

The unmasking I describe endorses this passage from Hegel's *Phenomenology*
to the letter, step by step, a march of negativity through the face building up
a head of magical power until the "being" of spirit as presence is attained,
surging forth with unmasking. This is why it is presence and presencing that
preoccupies me, here, with Martin Gusinde's description of unmasking
among the Yamana, coastal neighbors of the Selk'nam; and I want to begin
by pointing out that Gusinde talks much of *illusions*, magnificent theatrical illusions, which intensified the spiritual plenitude of the Yamana universe. Yet
the notion of illusion runs the risk of getting us off on the wrong track, because it has an unpleasing suggestion of gullibility, simplistic and even offensive, which can make you want to appeal to the more dignified notions of the
*symbol* and *representation*. Instead of saying, for example, that the theatrical
representation of the fearsome spirit Yetaita, in reality a masked and painted
man, is an illusion that the initiates fall for, gullible creatures that they are,
many of us may feel the urge to move to occupy the intellectual and moral
high ground by declaring that the presentation of Yetaita should be understood as a symbolic representation of the real Yetaita, who for complex or
even inexplicable reasons is then believed in all the more firmly when the
mask is removed to reveal a mere man. For, as is so often the case with ritual,
and what is indeed the most difficult thing to understand, the symbolic character of the symbol erases itself, and what the symbol stands for is experi-

enced as real and no longer a mere symbol of it. The symbol passes, so to speak, into that which it otherwise merely represents. However, as we shall see, because everything in the initiation hinges on unmasking the representation and carefully explaining to the initiates how it has been contrived, and *because effectiveness depends on negating the illusion*, neither the notion of representation nor that of symbol seems adequate.

## The Labor of the Negative

Gusinde describes the scene of Yamana unmasking. The first thing to notice is that the initiate has his eyes covered and is pushed blindfolded into the Big Hut, where there is what he called an indescribable howling. Fists drum on the smooth ground and the framework of the hut shakes. "The helpless chap is in an awful state," he wrote, "for he has a foreboding of dreadful things and knows that he is completely defenceless."[67]

Some time before, several men had stealthily prepared for the entrance of Yetaita. In the underbrush near the Big Hut a younger man had taken off his clothing and smeared his body with white paint, on which he applied short vertical lines about two inches long and as wide as a finger. He did not wear a mask, but his face was covered with thick red paint and many delicate white lines, like rays, extended in all directions from the corners of his mouth. From one shoulder to the other, forming an arc across his chest, hung a feather ornament the same as the forehead decoration signifying a *yekamus* (or shaman). His hair was ruffled up with *imi* powder rubbed into it. This man is now Yetaita.

He moves imperceptibly toward the blindfolded initiate and at the precise moment that the blindfold is removed, Yetaita leaps in front of the initiate and two other men stir the embers in such a way that it looks like the spirit has come out of the ground or even the flames. Immediately a struggle begins (but not if the initiate is female; the Yamana initiation of the *Ciexaus*, unlike the Selk'nam, included young women and girls). Yetaita "shakes him vigorously, bends him angrily from side to side, presses him against the ground, and tortures him until beads of cold sweat appear on the boy's body."[68] Yetaita is silent and careful to keep his face averted so that it is impossible for the young man to recognize him. The yelling and howling increase, together with the stamping and drumming on the ground. The young man is helpless and, like a doll, is lifted and shoved. . . .

After ten minutes the noise suddenly stops as Yetaita crouches down stock-still, directly in front of the initiate, who has to get up on his knees. The boy is made now to look his tormentor full in the face, and then he recognizes him!

"Look closely" says the man besides him. "That is your kinsman, not Yetaita! The true Yetaita looks like your kinsman here, who is painted like Yetaita. Watch out for Yetaita! Pay careful attention to what will be demanded here of you in the *Ciexaus*. . . . Keep strict silence about what you will experience here. Now you know that Yetaita is much rougher than your kinsman. This man is not Yetaita himself, but you should know now to watch out for him." (The man says specifically this is your uncle, this is your father. Following the general custom of the Yamana he does not mention his given name.)[69] The man disguised as Yetaita now becomes the boy's sponsor for the duration of the ritual, lasting weeks or months.

Sometimes this unmasking is done more simply. Yetaita is revealed to be a human being behind a curtain to the assembled initiates. Then the curtain closes back over him and each initiate is asked "Whom did you see?" Timidly each replies "Yetaita." Then the adults say, "That was not Yetaita himself. He is much more dangerous."[70]

Let us ask how such unmasking might contribute to the sense of realness of invisible beings, how belief is sustained not despite, but because of unmasking. Gusinde has some pretty heavy-handed suggestions as to the impact of fear and of brainwashing. But I think the testimony points in other directions, to what I will call the labor of the negative.

One of his close informants was Chris, who told him about his initiation many years before. His blindfold was lifted every now and again during the struggle with Yetaita so that he could see the spirit. When the unmasking occurred, said Chris, "My sponsor placed himself before me and regarded me seriously. I trembled with fear. He said, 'Now I shall tell you how you must sit here in the Great Hut! Your eyes must always be cast on the ground, on the place where my feet are. . . . Keep your inquisitive eyes in check and sit still.'" Squatting beside Chris, his sponsor asked, "Did you see the one there who leaped out of the fire?"

"Yes."

"And do you know who it was?"

Chris replied, "He rose up out of the earth!" Then the sponsor assured Chris: "Yes, indeed, that was Yetaita who lives down in the earth. He came here!" "Again," Chris said, "I was seized with terror."[71]

*Gusinde interrupts*: "With this false assertion he wishes to make the candidate believe that the apparition had really come out of the interior of the earth. By doing so he intends to fill him with terror. Once he has achieved his goal, he finally tells the candidate the truth."[72]

*Chris continues*: "After a time my sponsor again asked me: 'Do you believe that this was really Yetaita?' Completely terrified, I replied 'Yes!' Then he smiled and said: 'It was I myself! I behaved just like Yetaita who lives down in the earth. Watch out for him! He keeps a sharp eye on whether you are scrupulously living up to everything that you are told here. But not everything that goes on here in the Great Hut is an illusion!' . . . After that my sponsor was constantly by my side.

"Later my godfather warned me. . . . 'Do not talk in the dwellings about what goes on here. All this is very serious and secret. Outside you must be silent about it. But you will quietly think about it by yourself. Talking a great deal about these things will cause you to die prematurely. Know that not everything that takes place in this house is an illusion! Think of him who lives down here in the earth. Above you is the sun. Both these see you and watch you closely. So be on your guard!'"[73]

Despite the labored efforts at revelation, elaborate make-believe persists as the days pass, as if the secret is no sooner exposed than once more concealed. Take the question of food. The initiates get very little. They are told that Yetaita is partaking in the meals and that initiated adults eat nothing at all. The blindfold is placed on the initiates so that they are supposed not to know that an adult, while secretly eating, will throw a piece of meat into the fire saying this is for Yetaita. "This, too, is supposed to encourage the candidates' false belief in this spirit," advises Gusinde.[74]

Or, again. Gusinde tells us how the old people make Yetaita's voice. A man places himself flat on the ground and leans his face against his hands, which rest on his little fingers and encircle his mouth. This creates a small hollow space into which he yells a long, drawn-out, howling sound. At a slight distance this sound seems to come from the interior of the earth.

What happens when the initiates discover this trick?

*Chris*: "Later they plainly see that such calls come only from the men. . . . This realization does not destroy anything for them now, for they are already on the right path."

*Gusinde*: "This is supposed to mean that the fear and terror implanted earlier in the candidate through the appearance of this evil spirit were not without effect, but put him so firmly on the right path that he will not deviate from it even when he recognizes the true nature of this scary device."[75]

Here I think the "even when" gives the game away. For is not the trick all the more effective upon exposure?

### Transgression

At the outset, then, let me assert that the issue seems to me not one of affirmation but of *negation* in which the spirit in question emerges with compelling force precisely because it is unmasked not as a symbol, not as a sign, not as a substitute, but as a deliberately contrived fake. Such presencing through negation is tantamount to what I now want to focus upon as transgression.

In this I am following Bataille's idea that transgression, the breaking of a prohibition, is not a rejection of rules that give human culture much of its form and density, and is most certainly not a regression to some sort of pre-cultured, animal-like, instinctual state. On the contrary, the transgressed rule is brought into ever greater relief, its power more fulsome as there is created, by means of its violation, an unresolvable negation of the negation whose sole aim and destiny is not resolution of contradiction but its exacerbation.

Surely something crucial to this is to be found in Nietzsche's *The Birth of Tragedy out of the Spirit of Music*, which traces a similar plenitude arising from negation? Nietzsche described the Dionysian immersion in music and dance as a sustained ritual of rule breaking in ancient Greece. And rule breaking is most certainly what this Dionysian thing was all about, as we see most clearly when Nietzsche discusses the rites of the barbarians with their "extravagant sexual licentiousness, whose waves overwhelmed all family life and its venerable traditions."[76] It is the "horrible mixture of sensuality and cruelty," he points us to, and we sense his curiosity as to how pain and pleasure could be so passionately, even magically, bound to *becoming Other*—which in the final analysis is what this Dionysian attitude is all about, the merging, if you will, of magical transformation with the breaking of prohibitions.

Uncongenial as these terms may be for contemporary ethnology, they speak eloquently to Yamana unmasking as a sustained and passionate meditation on secrecy *and its annulment*, on what it means to break the rule as an artistic and sacred act, and how therefore to harvest a fulsome spiritual plenitude from sacrilege, the sacrilege of unmasking.

The striking emotional atmosphere generated by unmasking, and hence transgression of the rule about keeping the secret, is achieved, so it seems to me, *through a curious doubling back of the rule on itself*, which we could describe as a sort of *ghostly haunting by the spirit of the rule of its transgressed form*. And it is precisely this haunting, in my opinion, which accounts for the augmented presencing of spirit subsequent to its unmasking and exposure as fake.

This haunting would explain the emphasis that Bataille gives to things sacred as marked by an intense ambivalence, which is how I understand the play of presence too, being at once very real, but very ephemeral. Transgression *suspends* the taboo without suppressing it, says Bataille, adding that here in this suspension lies the mainspring of eroticism and religion.[77] Insofar as it captures the magical lightness together with the hanging weight of the waiting, "suspension" gets a good part of this complicated—yet familiar—state right.

*Sacrifice: Spending the Secret*

This figure of "suspension" can be thought of in overlapping ways, including the repetition haunting the second negation by the first, a theme I have tried to address in at least two ways with regard to Selk'nam unmasking; namely, the haunting of patriarchy by the "memory" of matriarchy (a phrase of Anne Chapman's) due to the massacre of women that (I argue) congealed the previous transformative flux of Being in the universe, and second, the *mémoire involontaire* fusing the real with the imaginary as provoked by unmasking in relation to the triangular relationship over time and through memory between the mother, her young child, and the latter grown up as initiate brought face-to-face with the dramatically unmasked spirit Shoort.

But now I want to draw attention not to these two types of hauntings by the ghost of the first negation in the body of the second, but to the haunting created by the transgression involved in *sacrificing the secret by spending it*. Sacrifice consecrates that which it destroys, says Bataille, and in this he follows a long-established tradition in French ethnology. "The suddenness of the blow that strikes it," noted Hubert and Mauss in 1898, with regard to the bullock, in their analysis of the ancient Greek sacrifice of the Bouphonia, "demonstrates that, like a lightning flash, consecration has passed over it. . . . It becomes that spirit, so much that its slaughter is a sacrilege."[78] With regard to the *victim* (which for me, by analogy, is *the secret* itself), they assert that sacrifice in itself "effects an exaltation of the victims, which renders them directly divine."[79]

Drawing upon Vedic, biblical, and Greek and Roman texts, Hubert and Mauss are at pains to distinguish sacrifice from other forms of *gift-giving* to a deity, precisely on the basis of the *destruction* by which "consecration destroys the object offered up; if an animal is offered on the altar, the desired end is reached only when its throat has been cut, or it is cut to pieces or consumed by fire, in short sacrificed." And they further emphasize *how much stronger* sacrifice is than other forms of offering, and how its effect is one of *perturbation.* "The religious energy released is stronger," they note, and "from this arises the havoc it *causes*."[80]

On the basis of his fieldwork among the Nuer in the southern Sudan in 1936, E. E. Evans-Pritchard saw their sacrifice of cattle to God *not as the gift of flesh* but as *the taking of the gift of life.* They "say that they are giving God a thing, a gift. But it is a gift which is immolated . . . and the gift must be a life or something which stands for a life."[81] Clearly the intelligence is here focused on a puzzle, even an opacity resistant to analysis, on what we could call *the gift of the negative* and what Evans-Pritchard calls *the taking of the gift of life*, to rephrase the formula of sacrifice as that which consecrates what it destroys. Evans-Pritchard emphasizes giving for the sake of giving, *despite* the existence of a giftlike economy binding the sacrificer and God into a set of obligations of taking and giving, such that one might at first assume reciprocal expectations of a return on one's gift, making sacrifice similar to some sort of business deal or contract with God, as argued by E. B. Tylor in his influential *Primitive Culture* (1871). But there are problems with this balance-of-trade argument. After all, what is it that God gets? He is royally cheated with some scrap of fat or smoke. And anyway, it was all his to begin with—life, that is. The answer is that he gets nothing—nothing doubled! *What he gets is the loss.*

And this is Bataille's point over and over again. "The emphasis is not on the receiving but on the giving," Evans-Pritchard tells us. "It is a question, Nuer say, of the heart . . . and in this sense one can only give oneself; there is no other kind of giving."[82]

Thus through twists and turns the exchange-theory of sacrifice is examined and, if not rejected, then at least radically modified. In the end it is the *immolation of the gift* that stands out as being the significant feature of Nuer sacrifice, and the hardest thing to understand about it. What is rejected is not so much the gift-theory of sacrifice, but the theory of the gift, which, like Hegel's dialectic, in its usual form, insists on a triad of obligations to give, to receive, and to pay back. But what sacrifice demands in light of the aforementioned texts is that we try to understand the nature of a giving that involves destruction—precisely the terms of the revelation of the secret and its subsequent etherealization as some sort of spiritual presence.

In thus drawing an analogy between sacrifice and revelation, between sacred victim and the secret, I am led to the question of the immolated gift, to loss, and hence to that special but by no means unique form of sacrifice, experienced throughout world history and subject of much discussion in the history of religions, in which *the victim* is not an ox or other intermediary but is *the god* and . . . what is more, much more, *is sacrificing itself.*

In the sacrifice of the god, claim Hubert and Mauss, lies the very essence of the mechanism of sacrifice. It is, moreover, because the god submits himself to destruction by sacrifice, that "his own origins lie in the sacrifice itself."[83] Substituting the secret for the god, this effervescent circularity yields the notion that the origins of the secret lie in its sacrifice—its revelation. Such a substitution is easy enough, given Canetti's feverish figure of the secret as a process rather than a thing, a process which ineluctably bestows upon the secret a godly status, prior to its terrible self-destruction. Indeed, the parallel here between the secret and the self-sacrificing god is uncanny. If we make a further substitution, that of the public secret for the secret proper, then we move the parallel even closer to the self-sacrifice of the god as the prime mechanism for the origin not only of the god, but, as I see it, as the origin of Being itself, because with the public secret—knowing what not to know—there is a decidedly repetitive if irregular pulse, a sort of trembling between revelation and concealment by an infinitude of what we could call mini-self-sacrifices from which springs a life no less constant than death. The outstanding feature of Selk'nam and Yamana unmasking is to have harnessed and given magnificent ritual-form to exactly this wavelike sacrificial energy of revelation and concealment.

Hence we are, I believe, in a better position to understand the spiritual consequences of unmasking and the way it can institute presence. We should also note that what is reborn with the self-sacrifice of the secret is the secret, paralleling Foucault's hugely important (to him) point, regarding transgression and "the repressive hypothesis," in his *History of Sexuality*, that the secret (of sex) in the modern West is in fact constantly revealed, so as to be exploited as *the* secret.[84] Hence his poetic figuration of transgression as a wavelike energy-form oscillating at the extremes of language, foam sinking into the sand.

*Sacrilege*

In their 1898 book on sacrifice, Hubert and Mauss hinted in several places that sacrifice involved a crime, and they used the word *sacrilege* to convey this. In their step-by-step description of the consecration of the victim and of the persons for whom the sacrifice is being performed, they eventually reach the climactic moment of immolation. "That which now begins," they write, "is a crime, a kind of sacrilege." Referring to sacrifice in the four religious traditions they know well, they draw our attention to the use of ritual expiations at the moment of slaughter, how excuses are made for the killing, the weeping, and the begging for forgiveness. And they point out that the instigator of the slaughter might be punished by beating or by exile, and that the purifications that the sacrificer had to undergo after the sacrifice resembled (according to an example from Frazer's *Golden Bough*), the expiation of a criminal.[85]

It is sacrilege they invoke also where they strive to insert us into the shock of the immolation, as in their depiction of the killing of the bullock in the Athenian Bouphonia. "The suddenness of the blow that strikes it demonstrates that, like a lightning flash, consecration has passed over it. It has embodied the divine spirit immanent in the first fruits it has eaten. It becomes that spirit, so much so that its slaughter is a sacrilege."[86] This last sentence is especially curious, this "so much so . . . ." Sacrilege is important to sacrifice as the "crime" within the sacred act that makes it sacred, just as the *lightning flash*

and the *shock* seek to acknowledge the instantaneous opening *and* closing of
the limit suspended by transgression, the dynamic both Bataille and Foucault
wrestle with in their writing on transgression. This sacred or quasi-sacred
quality given to transgression and implicit in it, emerges in yet another way in
a wildly creative contribution by Claude Lévi-Strauss in *The Savage Mind*,
where he would have us see these two things as opposites. *Sacrifice*, through
immolation of the victim, creates an empty but charged space in the great
chain of being, the space previously occupied by the victim now filled in its
nothingness by divinity seeking a compensatory connection between person
and god; while on the other hand, *sacrilege* is the inverse of this, bringing the
two ends of such a chain of being too close together, as with incest or bes-
tiality, thereby creating an emphatic no-space, emptier than empty, charged
with a completely different type of nothingness than the space opened up by
sacrifice, with its own and very special brand of holiness, as this curious image of a space imploded into itself might suggest. Sacrifice, for Lévi-Strauss,
would then be a semiotic version of Hegel's recuperation of the labor of the
negative, while sacrilege would, I believe, serve to take up the "waste prod-
ucts" and mad excesses of such labor, excesses, incidentally, which in the "savage mind" provide a most useful arsenal for healing and for hunting—a point
that Durkheim raised in his *Elementary Forms of Religious Life* in 1912, with his
idea of the "impure" or "negative" sacred, which fascinated Bataille all his
life's work, and which Lévi-Strauss alludes to in his discussion of the role of
pollution and of menstrual blood in Hidatsa eagle-hunting rites.[87]

But to my mind this inspired distinction between sacrifice and sacrilege can
be misleading. For what it obscures is that sacrifice *contains its inverse* as sacrilege *within itself*, and this is precisely what makes sacrifice holy and powerful,
and possessed, as Hubert and Mauss say, with "havoc." The death-space created by the killing of the victim is then also a no-space of extremes facing
each other, the no-space impossibility of the immolated "gift of the taking of
life," the "space" of the limit, a timeless space of de-facement overflowing with
proliferating presencing as I have discussed at some length, at the beginning of
this book, in reference to the way statues come "alive" precisely when they are
destroyed and put to "death"—defaced, as if their "secret" emerges from deep
within so as to displace their status as representation—and by magic become
instead that which they represented. It was no longer just the statue of the

queen that was defaced. It was no longer simply muscular force exerted with a sledgehammer and a hacksaw against cement fondue. It was violence against a *person*. Her death as a statue brought her to life as a person. And what is more, this "presencing" spread in waves through the media, via corgi dogs, photographs, TV, cartoons, and letters to the editor. In this form, therefore, transgression is a variation on an old story, the story of a vicious and at times joyful sympathetic magic in which impaling or tearing apart, or otherwise destroying an image, brings that image to life, even as it dies.

I wish to propose, in other words, that we think of unmasking as transgression, defying the prohibition against revelation of the public secret so fearsomely teased, so obsessively prohibited, according to these stories the ethnographers bring us from Isla Grande. Unmasking is tantamount to sacrifice. It consecrates that which it so spectacularly destroys, namely the illusion regarding contrived spiritual performance.

Indeed it is more than sacrifice. It is sacrilege. And the peculiarly empty space charged with expectant presence is doubly pertinent. Let me repeat my allusion to my earlier analysis of desecration of statues, where I characterized the labor of the negative there as embodying a sense of proliferating presence because something akin to hidden mystery bellows forth, *exacerbating and dissipating presence itself*, for it is this combined, doubling and canceling action that I wish to draw attention to with unmasking.

As an aside, we might note that if *secrecy magnifies reality*, in Simmel's phrase, then this magnification is due to the secret generating *invisible presence*, indeed the *presence of presence itself*, all the more complicated, all the more "absent" or invisible or phantomlike, and therefore powerful, when what's at stake is not so much secrecy as public secrecy. It is thus my contention that it is this presenceful presence, this hollowness within, that floods forth with sacred force at the moment of unmasking. What this amounts to, in a formula, is ritualized exposure, but not destruction, of the secret, vindicating Benjamin's statement that "truth is not a matter of exposure which destroys the secret, but a revelation which does justice to it."[88]

Here speed is as crucial as is unexpectedness and swift changes in pacing, for transgression inhabits secret spaces and tabooed desires, which, in a rupturing moment, it both renders and renders momentarily visible. This moment is akin to that flash of exposure of Canetti's animal, striking like lightning prior to swallowing its prey. Yet it is no less elemental that what makes the secret a public secret is that this rupturing moment involves endless rep-etition, eternal return to the scene of the crime, and that in this endlessness of the momentary, it expresses a sublime degree of effervescent instability.

This zigzagging incandescence of transgression is corollary, as it were, of the public secret as that which is permanently partial in its exposure. There is no end to unmasking. The term is a contradiction, drawing attention away from the continuous yet arbitrary sequencing of revelations and concealments of face, crossed and recrossed by a wave of proliferating presence—of a life, we could say, a life born of negation, even as it dies.

I hope by now it is clear why notions of *illusion* or of *representation* seem to me not only inadequate but may actually mystify the task of understanding how unmasking can have an effect quite opposite to what one might generally assume; that instead of dissipating the reality suggested by the mask, that its wearer is not a man but a spirit, unmasking instead adds to what we might call "the reality" of the spirit or of the nether realms of which the spirit is an element. I have therefore foregrounded what to me is the salient fact, namely the revelation of a deliberate deceit, and I have come to define such a revelation as a form of defacement, violent and transgressive in its own way, being first and foremost the transgression of a secret—an "artificial" secret, we might say—that is held to be of the utmost and most compelling importance by the society, as if it were the ultimate test of worldly loyalty. What makes this strange and exciting, both for the analyst like myself, as well as for the participants on Isla Grande, is that it's not really a secret that is transgressed but a pseudo-secret, a public secret (knowing what not to know) which, like all public secrets, cannot in the final analysis be exposed yet insists we keep trying, thereby provoking a storm of theatricality in which the unmasking of deliberate deception stokes the fires of spiritual plenitude.

Here I want to draw attention, however, not to the great drama of unmasking but to the "background noise," the taken-for-granted hum of daily activity in the Big Hut with its atmosphere of meditation that follows the drama of unmasking and that should be seen as a vital part of it as well, what Gusinde so rightly refers to as "an extraordinary state of mind." This atmosphere fascinates me for its ability to *presence* spirit, achieved in ways exceedingly strange, between concentration and dreamy distraction, between *absorption into* the world combined with a *dreamy floating above it*. I call this "double consciousness," aware that the term does scant justice to the sort of cutting and splicing entailed as phenomenological corollary to the logic of defacement.

This antithetical and doubled-over action is where person and spirit coalesce through *meditation* combined with *dance*, collective, drawn-out, orchestrated dance, mimicry, and a quiet humming passing from person to person each dawn, gathering into a discordant multitude by the time evening comes. Such doubling refers to what Walter Benjamin seems to have had in mind when he discussed the mental atmosphere of the scene of storytelling, the listener rocking back and forth in repetitive labor, spinning and weaving, lost in self-forgetfulness. Rhythm of work is the key idea here, having the repetitive movement of the body split the mind into a state of half-attentiveness as the body interacts with the materials of labor, dishes in the sink, the thread being spun, whatever, thereby releasing the mind for strange destinies that, for Benjamin, involved the fusing of experience with both voluntary and involuntary memory in the (declining, if not lost) art of the storyteller.[89] It seems to me that what Gusinde calls "the extraordinary *Ciexaus* state of mind," referring to Yamana initiation, corresponds to this same doubling-over of contemplation in distraction, which, try as he might, Benjamin was never able to successfully separate and use as a criterion for distinguishing painting from cinema or sacred art-forms from art in the age of mechanical reproduction.[90]

As regards storytelling, and its dialectical relation to "listening," Benjamin put it like this: "Boredom is the dream bird that hatches the egg of experience. A rustling in the leaves drives him away. . . . The more self-forgetful the listener is, the more deeply is what he listens to impressed upon his memory. When the rhythm of work has seized him, he listens to the tales in such a way that the gift of retelling them comes all by itself."[91]

This is one form of combining distraction with concentration, and it is important to note that it involves the body in both relaxation and movement, as if this were the body's and not just the mind's mode of distraction and concentration, too. Body and memory, body and story, combine so that, finally, the story tells itself.

As for film, very much the product of the forces of modernity that were driving out the storyteller, it was Benjamin's argument that something quite specific, which he labeled *Zerstreuung*, "distraction," was a primary feature, and this he considered to be the very opposite of the "contemplative immersion" demanded, so he thought, by a painting and—we could add, following his train of thought—by a story. Shock effects were crucial to this, as with the jerky montage of film, which, in dovetailing different images, allowed the spectator little time for contemplative immersion. The difference also amounted to this: with contemplation, the individual spectator is absorbed into the painting, while with film a distracted mass of people absorbs the work of art.[92]

On this account, then, we are encouraged to think of the storyteller and the storyteller's audience as taken out of themselves, so to speak, into some other realm beyond both mind and body, to where the story exists in its own time and space, just as Benjamin describes the body of the viewer becoming absorbed by the picture. He described this type of absorption earlier in some of his short essays on children's books. "The objects do not come to meet the picturing child from the pages of the book; instead the gazing child enters into those pages, becoming suffused, like a cloud, with the riotous colors of the world of pictures."[93] Such a "gaze" is implicated in a type of mental short-circuiting of the mental, Benjamin making the point that this child of his imagination is actively engaged with the illustrated text by scribbling over it, popping the pop-outs, tracing a finger over its figures, coloring it in, and so forth. Such organic interplay with a text, which we can in all justice call reading, with no metaphor intended, lets us see language in new ways, like futurist or Dada sound poems, decomposing words into rebuslike particles, as with illustrated animals for each letter, *A* is for Ass, for example. This is reading as "a total work of art" as we see vividly when the child plays with language, skipping rope and playing games while reciting the alphabet and extending old rhymes. "Prince is a word with a star tied to it, said a boy of seven."[94] Such is the perception of the moviegoer as well. Learning to read is thus the prototype of film.

Bearing in mind this eye-opening notion of reading that invites us to consider not merely the interplay of image with text, but how such an interplay becomes an extension of the human body which disappears into it in the history of reading, I cannot but be skeptical of Benjamin's arduous and often-quoted efforts to separate and even oppose "contemplation" (mystical and traditional) from "distraction" (shock, secular, and modern). Instead, distraction seems to me but a "higher" form of contemplative immersion in which the mimetic impulse can either penetrate the body of the perceiver (as Benjamin states is the case for Dada performance, film, and advertising imagery) or have the body penetrate the object of perception. A two-way street, the importance of which is not so much to fret about Benjamin, but instead appreciate what filmlike events and storylike events have in common; how magical the relationship—or should I say realization—of the image to the human body can be.

For me, it is precisely the function of unmasking, and of many ritual forms in so-called "primitive" society, to mix the different meanings of "distraction," thereby conjoining, if you will, the ancient art of storytelling with the sine qua non of modernity, the cinema. After all, in what sense is one "distracted" at the movies—but not in staring at a painting? Distracted means "scattered." And it also means "absentminded." So there seems plenty of room for antagonistic impulses and moods, focused anxiety no less than dreamy wanderings. This is also the argument of *The Birth of Tragedy*, that there is a profound and positive connection between distraction and concentration and that one is necessary for the other.

Let me begin with an observation. In his description of the first stage of Yamana initiation, the *Ciexaus*, Gusinde was moved to remark that (1) the Yamana had "no particular talent" for song or dance, but (2) did have an amazing talent for mimicry (the latter point was made eighty years earlier by Darwin and emphatically endorsed at the turn of the century by Lucas Bridges) and enjoyed "dancing and singing to the point of satiety."[95] A question thus emerges as to how these might come together and what are the implications thereof, this amazing talent for mimicry, together with this enthusiasm for singing and dancing, for which they had "no particular talent"? The question becomes more pointed if we ask how they might come together in seeing (through) illusion, and, more pointed still, if we go on to note that what Gusinde calls *meditation* plays an enormously important part—meditation accompanied by dancing, every night, and by singing, which never stops, night or day.

*First, the meditative stillness*: "The adult participants regard their stay in the

*Ciexaus* hut as a period for collecting one's thoughts and deep meditation."[96] This revives vivid memories of times long before they were initiated. What they desire is self-reflection, which can be achieved only by what Gusinde calls an "enduring silence." Long conversations in the hut are not permitted. People become annoyed if "torn from meditation." The initiates must not move. "Everyone stays in the seat he chooses for himself at the beginning, where he remains quietly and stiffly, avoids all unnecessary movement, and almost continuously stares into space in front of him. He does not turn his head in all directions nor does he move his whole body back and forth."[97]

Yet at least one person must be singing in an audible voice. It is mandatory that there must never be complete silence in the Big Hut, day or night. So, together with the "enduring silence" in terms of speech, there is this constant hum of a singer chanting, repeating a single word with a slight deviation in pitch. Instead of words spoken between people, there is one word sung again and again, interchanged with silence. In the small hours of the morning the humming passes from one person to the next, softly building in intensity and number of participants as the day stretches into afternoon. By early evening several people are singing at the same time, yet without the slightest attempt to sing in unison. It is a great hubbub, says Gusinde. "Nevertheless the ear is not offended because the individual rendering as such is low and sounds deep and hollow."

Gusinde thought this singing allowed a person "to hold fast to his thoughts about his own ego without any particular effort. The singing is so monotonous that it does not require the slightest attention," but the rhythm that carries it along prevents distraction. People say "I can reflect best when I am singing softly." "Now we realise," says Gusinde, why the singing may never entirely cease in the Big Hut."[98]

*By late afternoon* each and every day there begins a dance that Gusinde would have us understand as catharsis, letting off steam after hours of sitting still in meditation. This is the time when people's "inner agitation" reaches its climax and seeks expression in voice and body. The singing now becomes melodious, reminding our anthropologist of Gregorian chants, while spiritual emotion makes the whole body tremble.[99] A person is no longer able to remain in a squatting position and gets up, holding a dance-staff horizontally between the outstretched fingers of both hands, and glides from one end of the Big Hut to the other, through the central area where the fire is. Soon a second and third person follows. At times almost the entire group is dancing simultaneously, each person *gliding*, quiet, solemn, and graceful, the body upright, swaying slightly forward and from side to side. The steps are carefully executed, the body moves with grace, and the entire mass of crowded dancers moves more or less uniformly in this direction, then that, through the Big Hut. Sometimes a person moves faster and glides past the others. Even those who remain crouched in their places move their bodies rhythmically in time with their song and with a corresponding rolling up-and-down motion of their dance staffs. The singing does not vary but every so often a person is seized by a special excitement and moves trembling from one exit to the other, shoving aside anyone in the way. The others say, "That person has been seized by *kespix* [spirit, enthusiasm]."[100]

People sleep only two or three hours a night. They are tired, have little to eat, and enter into what seems like a dream state, a twilight zone, wherein the Big Hut becomes the meeting place, so Gusinde says, of the spirits. People do weird and unexpected things, frantic things. "They feel they are in another state of mind and believe themselves to be in another world in which their imaginings appear to them as real persons."[101]

*Face and body are subject to elaborate and beautiful painting in red and white*, renewed every night for the dancing, and a solution of white powder is smeared with both hands over the entire body. "It quickly dries by the fire and looks dazzling."[102] "Formerly a glance into the *Ciexaus* hut must have excited remarkable reactions when the white color all over the bodies of the participants squatting on the floor in two rows was lighted by the glow of the fire. These white figures seemed like creatures from another world."[103]

*Memory of the dead*: Often the face is painted as a sign of mourning. It seems that memory and death are paramount to the *Ciexaus*, no less than to the meditation essential to it. "Since every adult in the *Ciexaus* thoroughly reviews in his mind the events and experiences of recent years," notes Gusinde, "the memory of his dead relatives is quite vivid." It is not unusual for people to give repeated and open expressions of this, sometimes frenziedly crushing charcoal and rubbing it over the face as a sign of deepest mourning.

The glide-dance seems indissolubly linked to memorization as melancholy, absorbing itself ever deeper in the body of the recent past, spreading from the death of an individual to the dying of the Yamana as an identifiable people. "Ah! How poor we Yamana are today!" cried Mary as the dancers moved around her. "Only a few of our people are still living. This makes me incredibly sad. In my memory I see the many who were with me in the *Ciexaus* for the first time."[104]

The *Ciexaus* thus seems like a storehouse of collective memory, the key to which lies with an altered state of consciousness achieved by an artfully elaborated diurnal form of meditation, thanks first to silence and stillness permeated by soft humming, and then to the body set in motion, humming and gliding through space in changing group formation and reformation. And remember, the *Ciexaus* used to last several months!

*Interruptions*: There is a lot of formality, to be sure, but also a lot of free play and interruptions, so much so that Gusinde has a long section entitled "Free Interjections." It is as if the form provides the wherewithal, we could say, for its breakup, its transgression. Here is what he says at the beginning of this section:

> Proof of the complete freedom with which each participant in the Great Hut may express his innermost feelings is given by the impromptu words which he scatters through his singing. He is permitted to do this any time of day. Usually he contents himself with a few short sentences. The words of one will sometimes stimulate his neighbours to carry on the same thought or to supplement it. When almost all the people take part in the common singing in the evening, the various interjections not only follow one another directly, but also are given simultaneously. They enliven the already excited movement still more.[105]

Such interjections included anxious exclamations concerning the Chilean government's intentions regarding land the Yamana were occupying at Puerto Mejillones, on the north shore of Navarino Island.[106]

And as for speech as interruption, so for other registers such as the communal games, the play-acting of the Guard breaking up the routine, and so forth. It seems as if the point is to confuse boundaries separating visible and invisible realms, so as to cut up and splice fragments from them in the charged space provided by the secret expanding itself in the stops and starts of its unmasking.

The evening is usually concluded with the *taxer* song begun by someone who gets up and strides through the hut dancing, staff outstretched as sign of asking for something. Berries, pieces of meat, and fungi, are given. The person dances off and gives some away and eats. The singing and movements become increasingly lively, for this is farewell to the day and to the spirits who now leave the Big Hut for their own home. The arm movements indicate the work of rowing as one glides over the waves, and this same song is sung at the end of the entire rite. The purpose of this end-of-day song is "to attend to the spirits who have come from afar to the initiation ceremony, to calm them down after their lively participation and make them find their way back to where they belong."[107]

*Gusinde comments*: "In referring to these 'spirits' our Yamana mean in particular the memory-pictures and fantasies which take tangible form in their vivid imagination, with whom they associate in their thoughts and also converse in audible words."[108] Now they can turn back to the everyday world, "shaking off the extraordinary *Ciexaus* state of mind."[109]

Yet as the interruptions indicate, not only the spirits but the everyday world is itself vividly presenced by this extraordinary state of mind. Take for instance the politics of land claims at Puerto Mejillones, or the fact this could be the last *Ciexaus*. It would seem in fact that the world of spirit, too, is enhanced by this articulation of the ordinary with the nonordinary interrupting the meditative flow. The presencing of spirits, which Gusinde understands as the consequence of fatigue, lack of food, and "suggestibility," is also the consequence of crashing through the magic circle that the art of the secret—knowing what not to know—otherwise creates. This must be why, at the conclusion of the *taxer* song, you summoned back your own spirit by making a wide sweeping movement with your arm, pulling it back again quickly and at the same time closing your outstretched hand in a tight fist, inside of which, may we surmise, lay the entire secret?

Authentic mystery must *remain* mysterious, and we should approach it only by letting it be what it is in truth—veiled, withdrawn, dissimulated. Authentic dissimulation is inauthentically dissimulated by the violence of unveiling.

JACQUES DERRIDA, *The Gift of Death*[110]

Despite his modesty, Gusinde could not restrain his sense of triumph at being, so he thought, the first outsider allowed into the secret of the Indians. There is something so familiar with this elation at being first, as with "first contact," something so absurdly pleasurable at breaking through the skin of the secret, that it must be the outcome of some profound merging of dream with reality, as if the glowing image of the formalized secret of the primitives had come for the European to stand for the ultimate secret of existence itself, for the steadfast Otherness of the Unknown. And how much more is this magnified by being not merely *first*, but also *last*, as it was Gusinde's fate, he said, to participate in the last initiations ever held by the Indians. Only the secret, we might say, remains, as an exposure, as its creators pass away into death and the pages of ethnography. Yet how fragile the whole phenomenon! For like the dreariness that fills native artifacts once they are taken to the ethnographic museum, there may be nothing more dissatisfying than the exposed secret, the triumph of exposure giving way to some vague sense of being cheated. *There was nothing there, after all.* This I take to be emblematic of Enlightenment, bringing light to dark places, most ethnographies being the verbal form of the museum exhibit, which, no matter how transparent the glass or bright the light, reflects an increasingly opaque display, ever more turned in on itself.

First there is the exaltation of the secret. "The Yamana guard their secret youth initiation with extreme vigilance," Gusinde wrote with regard to the *Ciexaus*. "A stranger would never be able to surprise them in the midst of it, and it would be still more impossible for him to force his way in unobserved. From the start, therefore, it was impossible for navigators of earlier times to find out anything about it from direct observation."[111] "There is no other institution," he later wrote,

> about which our Indians are as strictly silent as they are about youth initiation. Their reticence in this matter could be compared only with their habit of never repeating the name of a deceased person. In their daily life there is actually almost no occasion to speak of it, and if it should be necessary, they regularly resort to circumlocution which they are also fond of using on other occasions.[112]

Gusinde's friend Fred Lawrence had been married to a Yamana woman, Nelly Lawrence, for twenty years, and had learned many Yamana customs and was a keen observer. But he had only a few vague impressions about the *Ciexaus*.[113]

Then comes the revelation, not only of their secret, but of how it was made manifest. It is shocking to realize that there were but seventy "pure-blood" Yamana when Gusinde arrived, in 1919, at the Lawrence brothers' ranch at Punto Remolinos.[114] No initiations had been held for many years, and it seems largely on account of Gusinde's urging and supplies of food that the Yamana decided to recreate the full initiation cycle, provided he participate as an initiate with his anthropologist companion, Father Koppers. As for the Big Hut among the Selk'nam, where, if anything, the demands for secrecy were even greater, Gusinde's enthusiasm and economic support were also fundamental. He offered each Selk'nam man one Argentine peso (worth around one and one-half German marks) for every three days of ceremony. "With this you will be able to buy a lot of stuff at the hacienda." In addition, he promised much tobacco and three hundred sheep, although another sixty were eventually required.[115]

This raises many questions. Would the terrible destruction of native society have made this enactment of the secret more, or less, significant to its participants, even if instigated by the anthropologist? What distorting effect, if any, would Gusinde have had upon the execution of the rites and on native exegesis? Could his presence have coarsened the secret or could the opposite have occurred? Lucas Bridges had some devastating comments about the effect of the whites on the Selk'nam in this regard: "I did not sufficiently realise," he wrote, "that these rites would shortly cease for ever. The advance of civilization soon laid bare the secrets of the Lodge, so jealously guarded for countless generations. They became common knowledge and the women were well aware of the hoax. Indians were induced for a few dollars, to en-act some of their plays before scientific audiences."[116]

But I want to ask, not only Gusinde but myself as well: having gotten the secret, what next? What does one do with it? Or, more to the point, what does it do to one? And of course this is a funny way of talking, because sim-ply in saying one has "gotten it," like catching a fish in a net, is to augment and make it truly real when all along the realness of the secret had a great deal to do with its unrealness and consequent mystery, and even more with its questioning of reality. *In other words, is not the secret something that, once got-ten, disappears?* And in that case, what does it disappear into, if anything? This is why, when Kees W. Bolle asserts that there is no religion without secrecy, he is concerned to nourish a self-reflexive and antipositivist view of such se-crecy and its exposure, as when he evokes limits, special mystery, caution, and self-restraint. "How do we become fully aware of it without distorting it?" he asks.[117] It sounds like the framework for a fairy tale. To which we might want to add that "having" the secret is likely to be a dangerous thing, too.

Which would take us to Canetti's apotheosis of the secret as a fetish with powers over the people who construct it, powers that include the fear of the secret's exploding. Here, instead of disappearing as its realness is solidified, and instead of being out-maneuvered and trapped, the secret has assumed command over persons and sets the rules of the game. Instead of being trans-formed, once it has become caught, into a something-that-becomes-nothing, in this account the secret transforms a reality kept in considerable creative tension on account of the very fear of the secret's eventual self-destruction. *Here the secret may "disappear," but in that case its mystery lives on in the violence of its self-destruction.*

Enlightenment, as I use the term, is like a first-strike strategy aimed at pitting these two types of disappearance of the secret against one another, using the violence of the about-to-explode secret to expose itself in such a way that its mystery is transformed into something no longer mysterious but held captive so that it cannot disappear. *This is what demystification is all about; wanting the power of the mystery but without the mystery.*

In this sense Kees Bolle, in the quotation I provide from his work, perhaps underestimates the problem of exposure of the secret (which he claims to exist in all religions). It is not only a problem of *distorting* the secret's inner content, but also of appropriating its energy, intact, without, as Benjamin advises, undertaking a revelation which does justice to it. Indeed the whole problem lies in the ease with which the secret invites injustice, an invitation which Enlightenment cannot easily resist in its unappeasable hunger for the raw energy provided by demystification (rather than Benjamin's reenchantment). Moreover we have to ask if Enlightenment can in fact carry out its mandate. To what extent, in recruiting the fetish power of the secret, can Enlightenment actually shed that convoluted mystery, a mystery all too easily made more convoluted by apparent "exposure"?

To recall the fetish here, as with the fetish power of the secret, means taking note of Freud's fetish, a telling instance of charged knowledge locked in the public secrecy of concealment and revelation. This state of affairs has been famously evoked by Jacques Lacan, drawing upon the scene of Freud's eighteen-month-old grandson in *Beyond the Pleasure Principle* playing the *Fort! Da!* game when his mother was absent, throwing a wooden reel, with a string attached, over the rail and into his curtained cot so that it would disappear into it, giving vent to a loud *o-o-o*, at which point he would then pull on the string so as to retrieve the reel, hailing it with *da*, and then throw it so that it would disappear again. *Fort! Da! Fort* (as in *o-o-o*) meaning "gone," *da* meaning "there," the joyful sigh of retrieval, which could also be interpreted, looking at the "game" as a whole, as a certain joy of loss, a certain joy of concealment, and a certain joy of repetition of the same.[118]

With Freud we could interpret this game as registering a significant stage in the dawning of negation, what Freud describes as the "child's great cultural achievement—the instinctual renunciation (that is the renunciation of instinctual satisfaction) which he had made in allowing his mother to go away without protesting," a renunciation achieved in good measure by the illusion or game of taking one's life into one's own hands by recreating the scene of loss in which the passive victim now becomes author of the plot.[119]

With Lacan this game becomes also the mythic event underlying the symbol as that which, *in signifying its object, simultaneously signifies its absence*; hence the somewhat overused and trivialized, but nonetheless highly significant expression *absent-presence*, which I myself think of, in connection with unmask-

ing in the Big Hut, as enormously relevant, in good part because of the intense pressure it brings to bear on one's thinking about the density of nothingness and hence possibilities for an overwhelming realness, an overwhelming presencing, of absence itself.

What I want to suggest, then, is that it is just this realness and just this
presencing of an absent-presence that unmasking achieves when it reveals the
masked spirit as a most deliberate work of fakery, shrouded, what's more, in
layer after layer of public secrecy masked as secrecy (beginning with the remembrance of things past in the mother's speech so long ago). "Thus the
symbol manifests itself," writes Lacan, "in the murder of the thing, and this
death constitutes in the subject the eternalization of his desire."[120] This then
is how we might understand the paradoxical effect of unmasking in aug-
menting the mask, reenchanting the world through disenchantment, flooding
the world with "that which takes on body only by being the trace of a nothingness," as Lacan puts it.[121]

Indeed my understanding of what is important in Freud's concept of the
fetish—a term laden with spiritual no less than sexual meaning—is that it is
the epitome of the nervous energy locked into the negation of the negation,
as with Hegel's scene of Spirit in its sojourn with death, "looking the negative in the face," locked in the magic thereof, such that the fetish is a token of
recognition—recognition not of something but of its absence, combined with
disavowal of that absence. Thus does Canetti's notion of the fetish quality of
the secret leap to mind, shimmering in the expectation of its self-ordained
apocalypse as it condenses into a thinglike entity, "the secret," at the same
time an evocative and powerful no-thing, an elusive power lying, as he states,
at the very core of power and continuously on the point of self-combustion
and disintegration.

Demystification, like its inverse, deliberate mystification, falls afoul of the
dialectical subtlety of this no-thing. "We penetrate the mystery," commented
Benjamin with regard to surrealism, "only to the degree that we recognize it
in the everyday world, by virtue of a dialectical optic that perceives the
everyday as impenetrable, the impenetrable as everyday."[122] As a formula for
his method of "profane illumination," this observation by Benjamin instructs
us all as to how we might play with the play of the public secret if we are to
do justice to society's ways of explaining itself to itself, revealing and concealing at one and the same time. As such, I believe the profane illumination

refers us to the same issues as does James Joyce's idea of epiphany in everyday conversations and street encounters in Dublin. *Ulysses*, a big book, an ethnographic book, with many secrets and one big public secret about Molly, can be read as bulging to burst with just such epiphanies, "as the gropings of a spiritual eye which seeks to adjust its vision to an exact focus. The moment the focus is reached the object is epiphanised."[123] The point is the contradiction, or apparent contradiction, in the encounter between the extraordinary and the ordinary in everydayness right where secrets mesh with their public nature and their public nature meshes with what we might call a "sociology," but one, admittedly, like no other sociology named as such heretofore. What Joyce pulls off, as the magical realists like Alejo Carpentier or Gabriel García Márquez long after him did not, is to keep the epiphany grounded, continuously rumbling, so to speak, within the pulsing mix of revelation and concealment demanded by sociology, another name for the public secret.

There is a comical aspect lying in wait for those who, at their peril, ignore this mix of impenetrability and everydayness that constitutes the public secret— as when the anthropologist undertakes to reveal the secret of the Big Hut, *yet all along revelation was part of the secret's secret*, part of its secret. From this perspective, then, the demystifications practiced by Enlightenment are already long included in a more inclusive script in which demystification is not only a preliminary step, but is itself mystified, blind to the child getting ready to hurl the wooden reel once again into the obscurity of the crib.

Comedy, however, lies as close to sadness as presence does to absence, and while the unmasking performed by the Selk'nam or the Yamana demystifies, only to reenchant spirits, the unmasking performed by Gusinde seems to me to lead to a postinvestigatory *tristesse* at the nothingness therein—another sort of absent-presence altogether, a nothingness first defined in terms of the Big Hut as a "hoax," thus lacking a certain plenitude, and secondly, in terms of the Big Hut *not having a function* and *not fitting in*.

What is so revealing in this *unmasking* of the Indians' secret, is the need on the part of the analyst to *preserve* obscurity and mystery, *but now on terms chosen by the analyst*, displacing the energy of the mystery onto baffling questions of origin and function, which I hold to be—here as elsewhere in social inquiry—thinly disguised transcendent mysteries designed to eradicate mystery so as to all the better smuggle it back in. For there can be no mystery greater than function, unless it be origin, and the mind secures its function in the continuous deferral of the secrets therein.

If this be Enlightenment, like a mouse continuously engaged with climbing a spinning wheel that its clambering motion causes to spin, bringing light from dark places so as to all the better obscure them, doomed to deferral of the empty mystery revealed, is it any wonder that, having first made such a big deal about their Big Hut, and having then revealed its secret, Gusinde is demonically driven to then pose the question of function? Yet unlike later anthropologists—British social anthropologists and U.S. functionalists, for instance—he was intellectually honest enough, at the end of the day, to admit that he *finds himself mystified as to what function the secrecy served.* An obvious contender was male dominance. But then, he could not see any need for the men to deceive the women in order to control them through fear. *If anything, he thought, it was the other way around: that it was the men who were made afraid by the Big Hut!*[124] Nor could he for a moment understand why the men were convinced that if the women found out—if the secret were unmasked—the women would not only rebel but do so successfully, just as the men were supposed to have done so long ago at the end of that Other time.

Not to mention other, more minor, "contradictions" that worried Gusinde (especially in the case of the Selk'nam, with their male-only initiation). If the men were so rabid about the Original Deceit of the women, and this anger was continuously aroused in the Big Hut, how was it possible, he wondered, to make it a point in the instructions given to the novices in the Big Hut that they must respect and love their future wives? Or how was it possible for the men to be fulminating against women in the Big Hut, one moment, and then to return to their womenfolk and feel genuine sadness at their having been subjected to such frightening spectacles? And how was it possible for "our Indians," as Gusinde put it, "naturally so joyful and inoffensive, not really wanting to maintain a secret at all," how was it possible for them "to continuously deceive persons they loved and esteemed so greatly"? "At the bottom of his heart," he wrote "each man loved his wife too much to be able to see her suffer from the phantasmagoria of malicious spirits."[125] (Likewise, Donald Tuzin was similarly vexed at the gap between the misogynist histrionics of the men's secret society of the Tambaran in the Sepik River region of New Guinea in the 1960's, and actual male-female relationships, which were, by and large, far less conflictful and inharmonious. He confidently suggests that the "Tambaran's gender tyranny actually helped to maintain good relations between the sexes."[126])

It was these contradictions that encouraged Gusinde to complicate the functionalist anxiety driving his need to explain, and so if he couldn't find a neat functionalist fit, then he did what so many of us do, which is to find a conflict of function instead. In the case of (explaining) the Selk'nam he thus evoked what he saw as their strategic *amnesias*, and how, far from being a fit, there was instead a *sharp cleavage* between the events of the Big Hut and the routine of everyday life, so that no sooner had the Big Hut finished, than it was as if it had never occurred, and all was forgotten, including the "misogynist logic." For if any man in his everyday capacity made so bold as to apply any of the Big Hut ideas regarding women to actual women he would have been smartly dealt with by her family and by other men.

But like the men, driven by their secret, so Gusinde was driven too, by the remorseless intellectual fantasy that the social world had to fit together, in the final analysis, into a functional whole, *most especially when riddled with the energy of irreconcilable contradiction.* Although his copious and highly detailed Selk'nam ethnography—among the most extensive ever compiled and published for any group of people—provided, in fact, little that could be taken as evidence of functional interrelations, and perhaps because of his having discovered—but not always acknowledged—contradiction after contradiction and mystery within mystery, he had to find a function for the secret and have it fit into a rational whole—claiming that since there was such a "cleavage" between the Big Hut and society, then the Big Hut *must be a foreign importation* and that is why it contained so many outstanding contradictions![127] And this was compounded in his Yamana ethnography because, with greater equality between men and women, the Yamana equivalent of the Big Hut seemed to him even more incongruous, and so his conclusion was that it too was a foreign import, this time from the Selk'nam![128]

In a laudatory review of Gusinde's Yamana monograph, published in 1938 ("Altogether Gusinde has achieved a remarkable work, which merits the closest study by all Americanists"), Robert Lowie endorsed this trick of explaining contradiction in terms of an alien intrusion into an harmonious social arrangement.[129] This "outside agitator theory" is especially striking because of the clarity with which Lowie pinpoints the central issue, drawing attention to the Yamanas' "meticulous insistence on secrecy," and asks why a constabulary force is required to keep away the uninitiated, given that among the Yamana the only uninitiated were immature children, who were guarded by a few adults anyway. Why must male initiates, who go on hunting trips during the ritual period, be taken so assiduously to places hardly approached by women or children, especially if (as is the case with the Yamana), the women are initiates? Why are all remains of food carefully burnt lest outsiders, who are sporadically allowed into the Big Hut on purpose, suspect the tale that the food is destined for the spirits? Are these outsiders whose suspicions are deemed of such importance, Lowie asks plaintively, simply the immature children?

It must have been as serious a moment in U.S. anthropology as now, with little sense that people might do things for fun, or that kids might serve as a reservoir for adult fantasy life. It must have been a time when the love of sheer excess was little appreciated, either as an end in itself or as the building block of social institutions. Above all, there is a disappointing failure of imagination when compared with the "primitive" societies placed under the microscope, most especially with regard to the crucial place of secrecy and theatricality in human society.

So for Lowie, as for us, the Big Hut amounts to a Big Problem, one that can be solved by invoking a truly classic groove, namely history, origin, externality, and diffusion. The problems of Functionalism lead directly to History, where the incongruities of the present get ironed out by chronology as narrative, and the narrative is propelled by resort to an always-outside-and-beyond mysteriously driving the chronology forward—the mystery, of course, being completely unacknowledged and hence all the more effective in supplying the aura requisite for "explanation," where curiosity, if only for the moment, is put to rest.

Thus is the phenomenon, in this case the men's secret, continuously bracketed, and its magnificent contradictory excessiveness, so we are told, lies not with the world-building mischief of the public secret posing as the secret, but lies instead with the Yamana having imported it from their neighbors, the Selk'nam, who in turn had imported it from. . . . And so we keep moving, unable to stay within the secret or at its edge, unable to forgo the temptation to unmask it, yet unable to come to grips with our own desire to keep on the treadmill of the *Fort! Da!* Nor can we break with the fetish and avow—by some unimaginable magic—our disavowal of absence, our need not to see.

And so we take refuge in an unmasking that all the more effectively masks through continuous deferral.

To that end we concoct fantastic stories masked as sober histories—to wit, the Big Hut is an alien presence imported to the island from the mainland, from the Tehuelche Indians across the Narrow Ice Bridge during the last glacial age.[130] It is a serious discussion, judiciously weighing, for example, the claims of a rival theory to the Ice Bridge, as if all that mattered was determining the mode, not the fact or the logic, of an alleged cultural diffusion of the secret of the Big Hut. Hence geological evidence is provided to contest the countertheory that the Great Migration was effected not by land but by other Indians handy with canoes, this getting round the troublesome fact that the Selk'nam have never been recorded as having canoes, that they are said to be afraid of water, and therefore live as far away from the coast as possible, despite their being islanders. Be it also noted that one old Selk'nam man, Kwanyip, told Gusinde that it had been a custom of mainland Indians to hunt for guanacos in these island parts until one day there was an enormous convulsion in nature, great waves formed, and the way back was cut off by sea. "Not that I accept mythology as history," advises Gusinde, who cites geological evidence for the bridge as well.[131]

As prehistory rivaling the prehistory retold by the Indians of that Other time of matriarchy and primordial flux, the historians' Ice Bridge is a beautiful figure indeed. For it grants the notion of *system* a basis in scientific mythology, by means of the poetry of which *an always-outside-the-system* has to be invoked so as to ensure the system. Yet the attempt to invoke diffusion from an origin to account for incongruity merely displaces incongruity back into the origin. . . . And the secret becomes all the more mysterious, a deus ex machina, Canetti's fetish writ large.

But in a way Martin Gusinde was right. Having declared its status as a foreign implant in this otherwise homely world of ours, he banishes to homelessness—and therefore to each and every home—this theater of the skin of the secret stretched tight by collective archetypes of deceiving womankind forcing men to do more of the same, and bloody murder as well. This would make of our Big Hut a ghostly presence, like the rule of women whose place it takes to be actively forgotten as soon as the skin has been wrapped away, hidden like the revered masks in the drier part of the forest . . . until the next time when new men shall be made from mothers' sons.

People pack quickly and leave discreetly for their different parts of the island without even saying good-bye. "Everything happens," writes Gusinde, "without the slightest allusion to the initiation ceremony which has just finished. One gets the impression that it's as if the whole thing has been wiped suddenly and completely from memory."[132] The Big Hut is left standing as a skeleton without its guanaco-hide walls. Emptier than empty it remains, stark effigy of the great knowing what not to know. Perhaps one day it will be used again, but till then men avoid entering and women give it a wide berth because the fear of the spirits there "has a strongly dissuasive force."[133]

I myself see this skeleton as a monument, an eloquent figure of the emptiness created by defacement, now left to decompose on the edge of the forest. (What a contrast to our cathedrals!) As such it is a monument which, virtually unseen by persons, elegantly completes the cycle of active-forgetting, its masks now hidden, leaving the empty rib cage of the secret as the trace of its most deliberate revelation that nobody dares get close to.

In thinking about why I am obsessed by this haunting figure, I am reminded of a similar space that Lucas Bridges mentions when he writes, apropos of nothing much, that there is a belief among certain white men that guanaco, when old and infirm, go to lay their bones in a special place, a sort of guanaco cemetery. But, he points out, there is a more practical explanation for the masses of guanaco bones to be found in Patagonia and Tierra del Fuego. In severe winters guanaco will collect together where there is less snow and food is more plentiful. In a blizzard, they will seek the shelter of bushes which they eat, however hard or thorny, but soon, "having lost all their strength and with a white world of snow stretching for leagues in every direction, they give up hope and, one by one, lie down and die." Sheep in the same situation become covered with snow which the warmth of their bodies melts, only to have it reform around them as an insurmountable ring of ice which they cannot break through.[134]

What is so thought-provoking here is how Bridges's very matter-of-factness creates a sense of mystery far more overwhelming than the European superstition it challenges. I take this to be a fair illustration of what Benjamin deemed a profane illumination. Its sense of mystery mixed with revelation thus also directs us, I believe, to a revelation of a secret—a secret of nature—which does justice to the secret and does not destroy it through exposure.

Gusinde, on the other hand, would have us, if not his Indians, trace a path along an ice bridge as a way out of what he sees as the public secret's contradictions, a bridge to nowhere and everywhere but always beyond the perplexing truth-games, not of nature but of society, staged in front of us and which so strongly suggest, as Nietzsche would have it, that error is the fundamental condition of life, and that "this error can only be destroyed if one destroys life itself." Indeed Nietzsche would seem right at home here in this game of masks and illusions. "We must love error and tend it," he says at one point. "It is the matrix of knowledge. Art in the service of illusion—such is our form of worship."[135]

Banished to homelessness, the secret spreads its wings and has found a home across much of the globe, men miming spirits, women miming belief, men miming belief in the women's belief—all under a long shadow cast by the memory of that Other time when it was the women who ruled and had the secret, deceiving men. Why this prehistory, passing from women to men, is so necessary to the secret, will forever remain a matter for conjecture, as is the fact that the secret is now, in Our time, jealously guarded by men prepared to kill or maim any woman skeptical of it. Yet the secret of the secret is that there is none! It is "known" to all! But note how opaquely these formulations clarify. What sort of "nothingness" is one plunged into with this secret of the secret? What sort of knowing is this?

---

Christopher Crocker tells us that among the Bororo of central Amazonia, where he did fieldwork in the late 1960's, the men take elaborate precautions to conceal the bullroarers from the uninitiated, it being crucial that no woman see them, even accidentally. Were this to happen the woman's stomach would swell and she would die. Yet for the initiation of men, the bullroarers are "unmasked" and the amazing sound they make is revealed to be the work not of spirits, but of men.[136]

Bullroarers are likened to the phallus and painted black with red and white semicircles said to be vaginas. When alone, men treat them and their associated ceremonies as a bawdy joke whose very obscenity necessitates their concealment. With insight Crocker identifies the secret here with (what Emile Durkheim) called "the sacred," in that it is mystically potent, set aside, hidden, and opposed to mundane secularity. Yet, as Crocker goes on to note with admirable understatement, the obscenity and associated ribald attitude "is not what Durkheim had in mind,"[137] reminding me of Bataille's complaint that, in Hegel, Spirit is all work and death—to the neglect of the no less "negating" practices of sex and laughter.

The sound of the bullroarers announces the invasion of the supernatural into the villages during the last phase of a funeral. Of principal importance are the water monsters, known as *aije*, whose arrival inaugurates three days and nights of ritual. After midnight young men sneak out to the river and return covered with mud, swinging the bullroarers and attacking the houses, imitating the cries and sounds of the companions of the *aije*—howler monkey, *capibara*, alligator, tiger, bittern, great-horned screamer, rhea, turkey, pygmy owl, anaconda, wild pig, otter, maned wolf, and still others, each with its own cry.

The actors impersonating the *aije* are coated with white, smelly river mud, and black lines are painted on their faces in imitation of the jaguar. Their main activity is to wield the bullroarers that are shaped like their own tails and whose sound is supposed to be that of the *aije*'s call. "So monstrously sacred are these creatures," writes Crocker, "that it would be lethal for the uninformed and unprotected even to look upon them." Yet the actual truth, that men simply dress as spirits, is well known to all—as is "the further truth, that the women know and make a pretense of belief." This, Crocker calls a "public secret," which he neatly defines as something "privately known but collectively denied."[138]

"To experience the *aije*'s visit inside one of the huts, as I have three times," he writes,

> is most disturbing, even terrifying [and] there is some evidence that Bororo men intend to cause this terror and interpret the *aije*'s attacks as a violent intrusion of nature's most lethal agents into culture's very home. But I have never seen any other Bororo, except very small children, manifest any fear of the *aije*, and women, the explicit focus of their attack, regard the whole affair as a sham.[139]

Once, Crocker's wife nervously inquired what was going on. "Oh nothing much," responded an older woman. "It's just a silly man's game." She went on to describe the bullroarers and various details of the ceremony, all supposed to be masculine secrets. Nor were the children particularly impressed, except that the older boys were eager to join in the fun. But, emphasizes Crocker, "all honored the injunction not to spy on the proceedings, *neither was there, at any time, any skepticism about the mystical powers of the bullroarers*" (emphasis added).[140]

And in contrast to the overall impression one gets from Gusinde's Selk'nam analysis of the men's Big Hut, here it is clear that women do not believe in the "hoax," as Gusinde called it. Instead, as Crocker so elegantly puts it in a string of negativities including both men and women, "persons act as if something they know to be false were true, so true that certain grave dangers await those who do not act falsely."[141]

What is so intensely curious, therefore, is that such rites, in seeming to defy ritual itself, in ritualizing pretense as if for pretense's sake, can be so evocative of presence, as when Crocker notes how "when the men bear impossible loads upon their heads, or when the *aije* come thundering out of the blackness, the human imagination does something more than demonstrate its fertility: it makes the masks into what they represent rather than what they are."[142]

Close-by Thomas Gregor reports on the bullroarer in the men's house of the Mehinaku along the Xingu River: "Any woman," he writes, "who enters the men's house, or who so much as glances at the sacred flutes stored inside, will be gang raped by all the Mehinaku men other than the closest kin."[143] It is the spirit of the flute which rapes if seen by a woman, and if this spirit did not rape, then "all the men would die," an informant is quoted as saying. "It must happen."[144]

"Mehinaku women live with the threat of rape," Gregor tells us. "The fear follows them into their dream life where they are haunted by nightmares of male violence." At the same time, women are "the main conduits for malicious speculation that some of their sisters have spied on the sacred flutes."[145] Yet like Gusinde, Gregor is puzzled by this unbridled misogyny, given "the evident affection of Mehinaku men for their wives, parents, and children." What's more, the secret, according to Gregor, is strangely disappointing, "neither 'dark,' hiding damaging information, nor 'strategic,' concealing valuable facts," for it is "little more than the nature and appearance of the sacred flutes and other cult objects and the identity of the participants in the men's rituals."[146]

"Little more"?

In the late fall when the pequi fruit were in season, bullroarers were included in these cult objects. They were given, one and all, a spiritual name and identity, and the women were warned to get into their houses when this spirit entered the village. There were fifteen bullroarers roaring in the plaza when the anthropologist was there, and it was loud, very loud, like an airplane revving up its motors in your living room, he said. The women were told that it was the voice of the spirit and that to see it is to incur supernatural punishment, but they peered through the walls of their houses and, "incidentally, [saw] through the men and their pretensions." Moreover, "the men are fully aware that the women are party to the secret of the bullroarer."[147] But in that Other time long ago at the beginning of time, it was the other way around. It was the women who dominated the men. It was they who had what is today the men's house and the secret that could be heard but not seen.

---

In "The Myth of Matriarchy: Why Men Rule in Primitive Society," Joan Bamberger tells us that the most complete myths of the rule of women in that Other time in South America come from Tierra del Fuego, from central Brazil, where she did fieldwork in 1962, and from the northwest Amazon, where the Yurupari trumpets are, like the central Amazonian flutes, the core of the secret and the secret is the core of much else besides. Stephen Hugh-Jones reminds us of this when he writes that the Yurupari rites "provide the context" for male initiation, but that "these rites are much more than simply rites of initiation" and their focus is the concept of *He*, referring first to the sacred musical instruments *and the ancestors they embody*, and second to the *state of being that existed in that Other time*, prior to this time, but *"that now exists as another dimension of everyday reality"* (emphasis added).

This *He* state is known through myth and story but also through dangerous circumstance, both uncontrolled, as with dreams, illness, menstruation, childbirth, and death, and in a controlled form through ritual and shamanism involving drugs such as coca leaf and the hallucinogenic *yagé*.[148] From this we are reminded, if such reminder be necessary, that the taboo and transgression involved in the play of the secret is of cosmic dimensions, including what seems like the very life of society itself.

In his early 1940's study of the Cubeo of the northwest Amazon, Irving Goldman was told that "at the beginning" it was the women who played the flutes and trumpets and that they spent all their time doing so until the flutes were taken away and given to the men by Kuwai, the "tribal culture-hero." These instruments are taboo to women, and men are cautioned not to speak of the ancestors lest they drive the women crazy and they die. If a woman sees the instruments, "it is felt she should be put to death by sorcery so that the secret will be kept from other women."[149]

"It is not clear from the published reports whether the women actually believe the tales told them by men," Bamberger wrote in 1974 with regard to the Yuripari trumpets, "although the penalties brought to bear on women and children for infractions of the ceremonial injunctions seem to be real enough."[150] She held that throughout the vast forests of the northwest Amazon, south into central Brazil, and at the very tip of the continent in Tierra del Fuego, over these huge distances and at these widely separate locations, men "rule through the terror of the well-kept secret." What principles, she asks, could explain this enormous distribution?[151]

And as regards what I take to be so crucial and so puzzling—namely, why it is frequently stated that, in that Other time, it was the women who had the secret—Bamberger suggests that this exists on account of its *ideological function*, what she calls its "ideological thrust," in providing (as if such were necessary) justification for male dominance, the myth of matriarchy being the story of women's inability to handle power, that they did not know how to handle power when they had it.[152] This is seen as close to another piece of ideology, that woman *represents* "chaos and misrule through trickery and unbridled sexuality."[153] Inadvertently this brings things into what I believe is a more accurate and more thought-provoking perspective, for, at the risk of my belaboring the point, it is simply untrue that the men rule, as she says, "through the terror of the well-kept secret." It is most definitely *not* a secret but a public secret—and the fallout from this is that our entire analysis is therefore pivoted away from "ideological thrusts" and ideas per se to their mischief instead, to prohibitions that give reality its necessary if not sublime tension, to deceit, trickery, and the never-ending play of the labor of the negative, knowing what not to know, turning the very nature of reality inside out, continually begging the question. Thus we turn also from Being to the never-ending play of interpretation.

---

"*Churinga*," wrote the biology professor from Melbourne and the Alice Springs postman at the end of last century in a book that virtually launched modern ethnographic theory of religion, "*Churinga* is the name given by Arunta natives to certain sacred objects which, on penalty of death or very severe punishment, such as blinding by means of a fire-stick, are never allowed to be seen by women or uninitiated men."[154] (Yet the page opposite displays ten of these secret-sacred objects in black and white.) "Why," asks Lester Hiatt in 1971, do Australian aboriginal men "enact their reproductive pantomimes secretly, excluding women and children on pain of death?"; and, "given that men and women are jointly responsible for the everyday production of food, why is it that men exclude women from magical production?"[155]

Here again we encounter the problem of the analyst displacing the problem of the *secret* by the problem of the *symbol*, the problem of the *public secret* by the *ideational content of idea and image*, mischief by the sweet drug of Being and deep meaning. It is a tour de force of Hiatt, for instance, to draw attention to the role of female symbolism in the men's secret rites, subincised penis = vagina, and so on, men "taking over" female reproduction, but at the end he can (only) say as regards secrecy—his basic question—that it exists so as to "mystify and intimidate the women."[156] The inadequacy of this is inadvertently made manifest in a footnote he manfully supplies from Annette Hamilton's fieldwork in Maningrida where she was told by women that such men's ceremonies were rubbish, the women adding that "men make secret ceremonies, women make babies."[157]

In this analysis of what he calls "uterine rites," Hiatt summarizes Spencer and Gillen's description of the fourth and most impressive stage of Arunta male initiation, the *Inkura*, which lasted some four months and had as its climax the "amnion rite," in which an object likened to the amnion or placental sack was the object of extraordinary attention, being raised and lowered all night long in the secrecy of the male-only ceremonial grounds by an elder man, surrounded by silent and immobile novices. If the strength of the man failed during this "weight-lifting marathon," it was said the novices would die. At dawn the three men followed by "the novices in a solid block proceed in silence towards the assembled women until about five yards away. Then they suddenly throw themselves headlong on the ground, *hiding the sacred object from view* [emphasis added]. Immediately afterwards the novices fall on top of them." When two minutes had passed, the novices then formed a square in the midst of which they hustled away the three leaders with the amniotic sack, at which point the months' long ceremony came to an end.[158]

It is worth noting the size and some of the character of this amniotic sack. It is described by Spencer and Gillen as a special sacred object made of two *churingas* (sacred-secret things), each about three feet long, bound together by human hair so as to be completely concealed, and then carefully covered once again with rings of white down, creating a double yet highly visible concealment. Furthermore, the top was "ornamented" with a tuft of owl feathers.[159] All in all, this eye-catching package would seem not all that easy to hide with the human body. On the contrary, its obvious and highly aestheticized concealment—like the wrapping on a present—suggests ritual perfection of the play with concealment and revelation.

It is as if the wrapping vibrates with the very energy of the prohibition not to see the insides, and W. Lloyd Warner makes much the same observation on the basis of his 1926–1929 fieldwork with the Murngin in Arnhem Land in northern Australia concerning the sacred nature of the corpse and the magical power—*dal* or *mana*—that can be appropriated from the dead. "Women can no longer look at the corpse," he observes, "which is immediately wrapped with paper bark and completely covered like some totemic object. The paper bark is now 'outside' and something the women can look at, while the dead with the sacred emblem upon it, is now 'inside' and *dal*."[160]

These Murngin categories of "inside" and "outside" seem bursting with sacred import. "Inside" encompasses secret or special names, as opposed to ordinary names and everyday language-use that are "outside." The men's sacred camp or site for ritual is described as "inside," the common camp as "outside." The water in the clan well is "outside," whereas the subterranean water down below, where the totems and the ancient ancestors live is "inside."[161] Yet what I want to draw attention to is not the binary distinction and patterns an observer could meticulously generate from such, but rather the pulsating magical power of the play of presence and absence implicated in "concealing" the inside from the eyes of women as with the paper bark wrapping the corpse.

The point is that this skin not only conceals, but in its concealing, reveals, and it is this that manifests the magical force of what Lloyd Warner chooses to call *mana*—a term of Melanesian and Polynesian origin that entered early ethnology to convey, as Marcel Mauss put it in 1902–1903, a sort of magical key to magic in general, *mana* being an extraneous substance that "is invisible, marvellous, and spiritual—in fact it is the spirit which contains all efficacy and all life. It cannot be experienced," he adds with a manic twinkle in his eye, I'm sure, "since it truly absorbs all experience."[162]

In this regard it is worth noting what I can only call "the display of display" in Hiatt's example of the Arunta the night before the men approach the women and children with the secret. The men take sticks glowing with fire and, as one body, approach the riverbed, which they cross running toward the women's camp.

> When they were twenty yards away from where the women stood, and still running on, all, at a given signal, hurled their fire-sticks in rapid succession over the heads of the women and children; hundreds of them whizzed like rockets through the darkness; the loud shouting of the men, the screaming of the women and children, and the howling of scores of dogs produced a scene of indescribable confusion. Suddenly all once more became dark, the men turned back, and, running as rapidly as they could, crossed the river and reached the *Parra* [sacred mound], where they once again laid themselves down, and once more there was perfect silence in the camp.[163]

Hiatt sees in this the young men signaling their separation from their mothers. While I myself am intrigued by the *spectacularity* per se; all that fire, all that commotion, all those dogs barking and humans screaming, the utter chaos leaving nothing but pure light, pure sound, pure confusion. Indescribable. Precisely.

In other words, the anthropologist provides symbolic explanations for the different phases, $X$ = a more basic, more essential $Y$, sort of thing, as in the following equations: "(1) in attacking the women, the novices are breaking with maternal ties; (2) seated all night raising and lowering the 'womb,' the men are giving birth to the stock-still novices by their side; and (3) 'the male mothers' in the company of their 'new-born' sons *flaunt the instrument of birth in full view (almost) of real mothers*" (emphasis added).[164]

But to me what's crucial is the "(almost)," the flaunting, with Hiatt's "(almost)" both hiding and revealing with its bracketing the very same *Fort! Da!*

action that to my mind energizes the ritual. I feel it would be mistaken, therefore, to "read off" this as though it were a set of symbols or even a text with a deep symbolic meaning, because the more pervasive "meaning" is that there is none—the men themselves say they are mystified—other than the secret itself, the whole point of which is to reveal concealment, men approaching women with a more than three-foot-long, heavily and beautifully "concealed" sacred object topped with owls' feathers, throwing themselves on the ground when within five yards of the front rank of the women, "hiding the sacred object from view."[165]

I thus find most welcome that maverick theorist W. E. H. Stanner who, in his *Oceania* monograph, *On Aboriginal Religion*, published between 1959 and 1963, based on his fieldwork with the Murinbata in the northwest of the Northern Territory, emphasizes the mysterious nature of the religion even to the most knowledgeable of old men. Discussing the revelation of the bull-roarer as the voice of the Mother in the final stage of male initiation, which he characterizes as "extremely sacred and secret," Stanner remarks that ceremonies of this kind are well known in the Australian literature. Some of them have been called fertility cults, but, he continues, "I prefer to describe them as cults of mystery. There is some warrant for such a description in the way in which the aborigines themselves speak of them as things they do not really understand but believe in deeply."[166]

And he lays down as the two cardinal principles of this religion (1) the notion that at the beginning, things took on their character because of marvelous events that took place in the once-for-all, and (2) living men must memorialize what happened then and somehow keeps on happening. Note here the absence of allusion to purpose. Simply, living men must memorialize . . . and *somehow* what happened, keeps on happening. And if the *must* here is demanding, then perhaps one can take comfort in Stanner's proto-poststructuralist fulminations against "structuralist anthropology," citing his informants' characterization of their religion as a joyous thing with maggots at the center. "It takes considerable temerity," he points out, "to try to improve on this imagery."[167]

As with that Other time in Tierra del Fuego, or *He* among the Barasana of the northwest Amazon involving not only the secret flutes and trumpets, and the ancestors embodied in them, but also the state of being that existed in that Other time, which can burst through into the present with danger or ritual, so in Australia this Other time of prehistory, this "dreamtime," speaks to an extraordinary division of time in Being itself, a division demanding theatricalized repetition of the highly gendered figure of the secret.

As I read Stanner, unmasking is the key moment of this eternal return so basic to the society. The young men have been told that they will be swallowed alive by the Mother and then vomited out. (Shades of Canetti's secret!) She is a fearsome creature and the buildup of events during the days leading up to her "unmasking" add to this fear, as the novices are moved into a secluded space away from the women and children. The day begins with singing accompanying sexual horseplay between the moieties or "clans" of initiated men, grabbing at each others genitals and shouting things which would normally be thought of as obscene, hurtful, or embarrassing, as the novices watch. This is a clearly marked event. It has a name, *Tjirmumuk*, and is repeated the following mornings.[168]

The novices are stripped naked and their personal names are no longer used. Instead they are "wild dogs." They are frightened. The initiated men crouch down, kneeling, in a circular excavation, their bodies covered with ochre and down and fire-dried leaves, forming a circle facing inward, alternately bending down until their heads touch, then straightening to sit up with their shoulders quivering, uttering a low hum. There are singers also, to the side, keeping time with tapping-sticks. When the dancers rise to their feet, the violence of their movements shakes off a small cloud of dried ochre and fragments of their decorations. . . . This is the mime of the blowfly that is attracted to rotting flesh. It is performed each day after the *Tjirmumuk*.

Now the naked novices are covered with blood drawn from their (potential) wive's brothers, but they are told it is the blood of the Mother and they are smeared with it from head to foot, the face being subject to special attention. The blood is allowed to dry in the smoke of the fire while the initiated men break into a rhythmic chorus of animal sounds and bird songs.

As the sun sets they return to the main camp where the women and children are. While the novices are kept at a distance, the initiated men leap over the heads of people at the center, where the fires are, and act out the *Tjirmumuk* again. Later at night "when the women and children are asleep or at least pretend to be," the novices are brought into the center of the main camp where the initiated men sing over them. With the morning star they are led back to the ceremonial ground.

On the third day, when the time comes again for the anointing with blood, men hiding nearby make the bullroarers whir, sign of the imminent arrival of the Mother. At this point, it is not unknown for novices to piss or shit themselves through fear.

Suddenly the sound is "unmasked," as the men with the bullroarers spring to view. Now the novices are told the true origin of the blood. Then each one is given a new bullroarer as a gift by the man whose blood has been smeared over their body, and the donor rubs the bullroarer across the novice's chest and loins, leaving it thrust upright between his thighs.

Full knowledge brought immense relief to the novices, notes the ethnographer with regard to the unmasking, "but I saw no signs of the cynicism one might have expected. Evidently the interior life is so deepened that the inculcation of fear comes to seem to them just and wise."[169]

---

"There is certainly nothing more characteristic of Melanesian life than the presence of Societies which celebrate Mysteries strictly concealed from the uninitiated and from all females" wrote the missionary-ethnographer R. H. Codrington in 1891, on the basis of twenty-fours years of service in the Melanesian Mission.[170] So all-encompassing were these societies that they obscured the power of the chiefs, and they were to be found from New Guinea through the New Hebrides and Solomon Islands to Fiji, and as far south as New Caledonia. In all these societies, the ghosts of the dead were said to be present and formed the focus of the mysteries, in which sound and visual spectacle were paramount. Indeed, in Codrington's account sound and sight play off against one another. In the light of day, the secret was clothed and presented by means of elaborate masks and sometimes by lavish edifices as well. By night, you became aware of the presence of the secret by its strange cries. Sound and mask amounted to the same thing, concealing yet presencing the secret.

Everything depended on display involving dedicated artistry. The society in the Solomon Islands known as the Matambala, for instance, presented a screen ten feet long by nine feet high, painted and ornamented, and carried by several men behind it into the open, "where it could be seen by the women, children, and uninitiated, who firmly believed it to be not so much the handiwork of ghosts as an appearance of the ghosts themselves."[171] But that was nothing as compared with another device so large that eighty to one hundred men got inside and carried it down to the beach where the outside population gazed at it.

As for origins, there was a story on the Banks Islands that it all began (as we might expect) with a woman who was given the gift of an image by a ghost, an image displaying the mask and cloak of what was to become the standard costume of the ghostly apparitions manufactured by the secret society. She kept this image hidden behind a partition in her house. (First instantiation of the secret.) Then "it became known that she had something wonderful concealed, and she admitted men on payment to a private view." (Second instantiation of the secret, now verging on the public secret. Watch it grow and metamorphose, textbook model of Freud's fetish, the fantasy of the mother's phallus that was made absent, hence also the model for splitting belief into all manner of contradictory combinations of disbelief and affirmation, of real and unreal.) For when the number of men was large enough, they took it out of the woman's hands and "*were taught by the image, which was all the while itself a ghost*" (emphasis added), how to make the masks and establish the first secret society, with the strictest exclusion of all women ever afterward.[172] Disarmingly, Codrington adds that "From this story nothing can be learnt concerning the origin of so widely spread an institution."[173] What sort of "origin" was he seeking?

Apart from the wonderful masks, many reminiscent of the cocked hats of European naval officers, our missionary-ethnologist felt disappointed when inside the lodge of a Banks Islands secret society because there was nothing unusual there at all—except for one thing, and this was the curious apparatus for making sound, believed by outsiders to be the cry of ghosts. It consisted of a flat stone on which the butt end of the stalk of a frond of palm was rubbed. The vibration made extraordinary sounds which, moreover, could be modulated at will as to volume and tone. It is told that its discovery was the result of two men of the major secret society of the Banks Islands coming across an old woman sitting on the beach rasping shells on a stone in order to make them into money, using a palm frond umbrella as the stick to hold the shell. Hearing the sound and realizing how useful it could be for their lodge, they killed the woman and ran off with her implements.[174]

And what special knowledge did the initiates learn in their ordeals and removal from the society at large? Other than what was well known and practiced in the society, *there was no special religious or magical knowledge*, says Codrington. Only one secret was imparted and that was that the fantastic images and sounds were fake—that "whatever was done was the work of men and not of ghosts, which was no doubt a surprising revelation."[175]

The fact that our ethnographer feels inclined to add that this "was no doubt a surprising revelation," suggests something more lies in store than exposure of fact. Indeed the fakeness of the fake and its inauthenticity turn out to be not so easily settled, because we may be sure, he advises, that members of the secret society, new no less than old, firmly believed that the art of making the images and sounds, as well as the elaborate spectacle formed around them, had been taught by the ghosts of those who originated the secret society and the ghosts of subsequent members of it. In other words, these are "authentic fakes," supernaturally authenticated illusions with a ghostly pedigree, a true untruth. . . . There is a great deal more to this, therefore, than claiming the secret of the secret is that there is none. *For the deceit as to the work of the ghosts is itself the work of the ghosts.*

Yet for all that pride in deceit, that power which rests on the equation of the lie with art, outsmarting reality by mastering truth through its manipulation, for all of that there is what seems to be an inexplicable fragility and a built-in capacity for dramatic self-destruction and sudden collapse of the entire, magnificent display—as when Codrington tells us as regards the secret societies of the Banks Islands, that the "downfall of this superstition and imposture has been complete" since all the young men came to know "what ghost mysteries really were." Bullroarers became the "playthings of the boys, and the old men sat and wept over the profanation and their loss of power and privilege."[176]

As for *mana*, the Joker in the pack and the true secret of magic and hence the secret of all secrets, let us return to Marcel Mauss and the Murngin of northern Australia, as evoked by Lloyd Warner. The point was that the bark concealing the corpse not only concealed but, in its concealing, revealed all the more intensely the presence of the thing within. It is this combination (made manifest in separate and opposed rights of men and women) that would seem to be what generates the magical force of *dal* or of what Lloyd Warner, following the ethnological convention of his time, chose to call *mana*—an extraneous substance, wrote Mauss three decades earlier, that "is invisible, mar-

velous, and spiritual [and] cannot be experienced since it truly absorbs all experience."[177] Seeing it as a force, yet also a substance, as a power, yet also a
milieu, Mauss vainly tries to describe this elusive thing, *mana*, which thus
seems to me the exquisite distillation of the public secret, of its knowing what
not to know. Like quicksilver it is no sooner caught than it disappears, one
interpretation passing into another. It is a "glory," Mauss writes, but also a
"destruction." Very much of this world, it is also of another world. It is not
only concealed, but as with the *nahual* of Mexico, it may be the disguise itself
and hence the force of both transformation and self-transformation, mobile
and spreading. . . . And if these forms and transforms threaten to escape us
and even our comprehension, what then? At least they lie there, contained, in
the maggot-riddled center that is joyous. Joyous it be and joyous it stays in its
being, if not exactly centerless, then at least both more and less than it once
was, haunted by a rich mulch of secrets truly, as it has been said of the secret,
"magnifying reality."

Sound has a privileged function in stoking the dialectic of Being and Nothingness in the public secret. Recalling the eerie sounds of the *molimo* in the Ituri forest among the Mbuti pygmies of central Africa in the 1950's, "when the women shut themselves up, pretending they were afraid to see 'the animal of the forest,'" Colin Turnbull sat entranced every evening for a full month listening to the secret, enmeshed in its pretense. "Every evening," he says—in terms that must by now be as forbiddingly familiar as they are continuously intriguing and shocking in their clarity—"Every evening when the men gathered around the fire, pretending they thought that the women thought the drainpipes were animals; every evening, when the trumpet drainpipes imitated leopards and elephants and buffaloes—every evening when all this make-believe was going on, I felt that something very real and very great was going on beneath it."[178]

When times are bad, the forest sings like this, and we are told in countless ways how beautiful and stirring this mysterious singing is. Indeed what pours out of this ethnography is the forest—the forest as music made by men playing their *molimo*, pretending they think the women think the sounds they make with their hidden trumpet are the cries of animals. And as we have learnt from other manifestations of the secret, it was said here that if women were to see the *molimo*, they would die, and yet long ago in some quintessentially Other time, it was the women who owned it, only to have the men steal it from them.

We can of course be skeptical and wonder if the anthropologist has been able to separate his own enthusiasm for the music of the forest from that of his hosts. But then his text is unique and remarkable for its spotlighting not only the play of pretense, but the interwoven pretense as to the Other's pretense—within an all-encompassing reality-shaping experience. Indeed, to question the anthropologist's sincerity and accuracy here is to enter a quagmire of forbidding depths, a never-ending series of reflections as to the pretense of pretense . . . such that "pretense" acquires a vast and exhilarating mimetic potential for entering into the experience of the Other. This is no small point, and it is also what Nietzsche claims throughout his life's work for Dionysian pathos, its music and dance, from *The Birth of Tragedy* to *Twilight of the Idols*, it being this music that allows, or indeed makes, a person "enter into every skin."[179] Here therefore we would do well to consider the implications of all that imitating, of leopards, elephants, and buffaloes, for instance, let alone of all that goes under the heading of "pretense" and, of course, pretense as to the Other's pretense.

---

Some ten years earlier, in 1948, another Englishman, K. L. Little, wrote of the secrecy of secret societies of Sierra Leone as "something more than an institution," constituting "the hard core of culture," it being secret societies in this region that had, long prior to British colonial rule, administered law, regulated trading practice, fixed prices, and continued to exert much power thereafter, including initiation of the young into society.[180] Undoubtedly the real power of the secret society, he wrote, "resides in the spiritual force it personalises and professes to possess"—and this spiritual power, characterized by masked figures, involved in the case of the most important secret society, the Poro, "the prohibition of the sacred bush to all non-members, including especially the women and children."[181] The anthropologist was told that "originally" any woman who learned one of the Poro secrets was severely punished, along with members of her family. A masked member of the society—one of its spirits—would have rushed to her house followed by a crowd of members who razed it, leaving no trace of the dwelling, and the legs of the victim would have been tied to two trees that had been bent towards each other so that upon their re-

lease, she was torn apart. At the time of writing in 1948 this did not occur (if
in fact it ever had) and instead the woman was forced to become a member
of the Poro, women having their own secret society, the Sande.

The anthropologist provided two accounts of the origin of the Poro society, striking for the emphasis both place on sound *combined with the prohibition
of sight*, the sound being a distorted voice emanating from a distorted human
face.

In one account, the Poro came about with the concealment of the death of
the first Mende chief, it being feared that knowledge of his death would dis-
rupt the society. Hence someone impersonated him and because the chief
had had an impediment that made him speak in a nasal tone, the impersonator had to be a suitably voice-impaired person, duly sworn to secrecy with
the appropriate magical medicine.

In the other account, an influential old man contracted the first known
case of cancer of the nose and his voice became harsh but musical. (Note that
an important medicine among the Mende is *Tilei*, medicine that eats away at
a person's nose.[182]) He was made to live away from human settlement, and
women and young people were forbidden to visit him. The other big men of
the district decided to kill him but maintain his fictive presence by means of
a curious instrument, a hollow stick with skin stretched over it, that would
produce the same tremulous sounds as his voice. Returning to town, the
killers announced that the old man had turned into a devil. Thereafter they
would bring him to town for a feast, at which point women and children
would rush into their houses in both appreciation and fear.[183]

---

In his 1949 discussion of the secret societies of the Kpelle in Liberia, William
Welmers tells us that each form of sale, or medicine, is secret, and that the
word is also applied to the mask of the spirit central to the main secret society, the Poro of the men, the Sande of the women, "into which every member
of the tribe is expected to be initiated. Initiation is the entrance into full priv-
ileges of the tribe."[184] Great secrecy surrounds these societies, the woman's including clitoridectomy as its essential secret.[185] Noting in 1980 that the threat
of physical punishment and even death from the mysterious powers of the secret societies is a major source of the authority of elders, William Murphy
similarly understood Kpelle society as providing an ideal case study of secrecy,

"because the institutionalisation of secrecy is a paramount and pervasive feature of social life."[186] On the strength of fieldwork among the Kpelle of Liberia extending over thirteen years, beginning around 1970, Beryl Bellman says that there existed from ten to fourteen secret societies at the local level. In the village in which he lived, with a population of only fifteen hundred, there were twelve active secret associations.[187]

The secrecy *centers around* what Welmers calls "the forest thing," or *namu*, referred to as the "bush devil" in Liberian English. But the secret presents a confusing problem, for although it is something, it is also a no-thing. The "forest thing" more accurately designates an idea, writes Welmers, than it does a personal or impersonal being.[188] Indeed, he goes on to say, "*the various phenomena cannot be assigned to a single cause which can be called a 'being.'*"[189]

The forest thing can appear as a "grotesquely costumed being" wearing a gown of blue cotton, a sleeveless leopard-skin jacket, a raffia skirt over raffia trousers, and the wool of sheep's throats over its hands and arms. The head is covered by an intricately carved wooden mask, and the man assigned to make the mask, says Welmers, "works in complete isolation and secrecy, and when his job is finished he is fatally poisoned[!]"[190] This manifestation may be seen by anyone and speaks in a distorted voice that Welmers interprets as a way of concealing the identity of the impersonator and maintaining the fiction that this not a human being.

A second manifestation of the forest thing is a *special kind of music* heard only at night. Welmers flatly states that this "*is universal and is basic to the mystery*" (emphasis added). This music is sometimes referred to as *namu*'s wife or as the female *namu*. Unlike the first manifestation, no noninitiate is allowed to set eyes on this alleged being (as Welmers calls it), the offense being referred to by the Kpelle expression "to meet namu's voice." The penalty for an uninitiated boy, so it is said, is initiation, and for a woman, death by poison. There are actually five musicians that comprise this manifestation, which is, however, said to be just one being.

With reference to the mystery and the place of the invisible presence of sound in the mystery, note the conflicting reports by *initiates* who, as Welmers says, are in fact "revealing no secrets at all." While some say they "saw" the forest thing and spoke with him, others speak vaguely of "seeing" him but insist that it is impossible to describe it, while still others say they heard the sound but saw nothing.

"No one is lying," notes the anthropologist, taking us into an archipelago of negations, because the first person is referring to another of the several manifestations that this being can assume, the second person who "sees" it but cannot describe it, sees the origin of the sound but "cannot describe it in terms of the single being that it is supposed to be for the ears of non-initiates," and finally, those who claim they see nothing "are not blind," but they "do not see any single being who might be called the forest thing in this manifestation for the simple and obvious reason that it is not a single being but some five people."[191]

And the equivalent center of the women's mystery is a hollow noise produced by using a pot as a resonator.

Yet again, as we have seen from Tierra del Fuego across the Pacific to parts of Australia, it is women who in a prehistorical Other time discovered and had the secret. It was a Kpelle woman who discovered the forest thing, but the men took it from her, conceding, however, the women's right to "rule the forest alternately with the men."[192]

---

Bellman cites George Harley's 1941 account of what was *supposed* to happen to a woman who accidentally found out what happens in Poro initiation and refused to keep the secret. She would be killed and eaten in a great feast in the Poro, said Harley, or, if she came from a wealthy family, her life might be spared on further payment in cattle, but she could never speak again as long as she lived. She was given a medicine that paralyzed her organs of speech or, "more scientifically speaking, she was probably hypnotized." She could not even talk in her sleep.[193]

Bellman uses this alarming description as a foil for introducing his own approach to the (public) secret as *speech-play* in which what he calls the "not sayable" stimulates an enormity of roundabout talk, metaphorization, and different degrees of directness of reference according to the particular "speech environment," all of which seems an eminently sensible thing to point out; obliquity is the name of the game, and Linguistic Science is herewith validated in its framing and mastery of such.

Harley's ingenuous account is therefore ripe for a scalding critique, insensitive to nuance and context. Yet is there not a counter-risk here of being overly subtle, using Linguistic Science so as to bleach out all that is crazy and wild in the story conveyed by Harley? Is not Harley's account notable precisely because it is so extreme, and isn't it therefore incumbent on us, at the receiving end of the story, to honor that as, in all likelihood, also a quintessential characteristic of secrecy and secret societies?

My fear is that once you categorize play (as "speech-play," for instance), you've taken away all the play. To name here is to destroy. Naming it is to break the rules of the game (of knowing what not to know, for instance) and hence channels the game's energy and playfulness into quite other pursuits— an explanation, for instance. So much about these secret societies seems not just "make-believe" but mock-real, and as forms mocking reality they demand a response that can also burlesque Being, allowing the material of raw description, for example, to creep up and disarm one before one can disarm it. Otherwise we lose sight of what extremity and hyperbole imply for magic, dream-realities, sorcery, and the medicines, which supply the drama of secrecy and public secrecy in everyday life.

---

In this regard it is noteworthy that Bellman frequently refers to his making videotapes of village life, including certain manifestations of the Poro. Yet he analyzes only the speech, never the tricks intrinsic to the mise-en-scène of the staging of the speakers (tricks, we might note, that are by no means restricted to the Poro, but are intrinsic to both the watching and making of film and video, second-order representations of representations). When he resorts to the videos, it is merely to extract the speech and publish many pages thereof, so as to demonstrate with such acoustic realism how the unsayable exists as "speech-play." There is, in other words, a sort of active negation of the filmic representation, a virtual concealment of the visual so as to all the better reveal the oral. And what is more, this bears an uncanny resemblance to the art of the secret societies themselves, presencing sound while prohibiting sight!

But what an opportunity lost! Indeed what violence! And what an indictment of the tunnel vision of Linguistic Science! For surely it is the visualization by film of the paraphernalia and processions, tableaux and ribaldry, of the public presentations of the public secret that presents the possibility for the most wonderful epistemological breakthrough for a Gay Science continuous with its subject. I surely do not mean that one should film secrets, but rather that one should dwell on what it means to strip film of its visual component.

The point is not that one's analysis becomes more "complete" by adding the mise-en-scène of performance, as if "completeness" is in itself a necessary or good thing. The point is rather that, in adding film language to verbal language, one is exposed to a powerhouse of representational trickery, including, first and foremost, revelation and concealment. Walter Benjamin posited an "optical unconscious" present in reality yet hidden from the naked eye and habits of perception until the advent of photography and cinema. But he failed to include in this unconscious made manifest by film the fact that film is in itself a "secret society," a tool as much of revelation (of the optical unconscious) as it is an inherently deceptive medium playing the full range of tricks beloved by shamans and their patients the world over. And because film is the modern medium of magic, it would, I imagine, present fascinating new opportunities much appreciated by the stage directors at work in west African secret societies today—a point not lost on producers of fast-selling feature videos in contemporary Ghana, for instance, with their visualization of sorcery, an activity previously restricted to words, hearsay, and secretive ritual.[194]

If I want to equate the language of film with secret societies, I must also consider dreaming as an interior "equivalent" to the film. For instance, Bellman presents the case of a young woman who died abruptly of "natural" causes the day after a Poro initiation was begun in her village. He was told she had been killed by Poro medicine because she had followed the proceedings too closely and had even gone into the Poro precinct. But Bellman, too, had been closely following with his video camera and had not seen her there.

Then someone told him the problem was that she had seen the secret Poro initiation *in a dream* (and confessed to the Poro medicine too late). Bellman emphasizes that for the Kpelle, dreams are accorded a facticity analogous to everyday reality, together with the power to divine and to alter the nondreaming world,[195] a phenomenon found in Tierra del Fuego and in Australia, if not in all the societies I have so far drawn attention to in my anarchic survey of secret societies.

For me, this terrible story is a reminder that the play of the public secret is embedded not only in a secret society, spectacle, or men's house, but as Rosalind Shaw points out, has a far wider domain in magical and oneiric realities that are inherently mysterious and often used to create more of the same, notably in life-and-death power struggles.[196] We should also be reminded that visualization is itself a mystery-mongering process whose main source of mystery is its being taken so for granted, thus providing the raw material for the trick, so brilliantly exploited through the language of film, no less than on the flickering screen of both dreaming and the unmasking of spirit entities.

---

As for the moment of unmasking, Welmers writes with regard to the Poro that, having sworn never to reveal the secrets, the novice is then masked, his head being covered with a heavy cloth while the *namu*, the devil, a mere man now, stripped of his wonderful regalia, comes out of a house to announce his true self, while the cloths are removed from the heads of the candidates so that at last they see the unseeable and discover it to be not a spirit but a man. The other manifestations of the *namu* are explained (i.e., "unmasked") as impersonations by men, and the essence of the initiation is thus complete.[197]

Yet is the mystery dissipated by unmasking? It does not seem so. It merely changes and, perhaps, becomes even deeper, certainly more complex, on account of its revelation. Welmers forestalls the predictable reaction when he adds that one "would presume [wrongly] that there would be general disappointment when the fabled forest thing turns out to be nothing more than one's next door neighbor," and on this point, some 35 years after Welmers, Beryl Bellman goes further.[198] Unmasking does not destroy a new member's belief in Kpelle cosmology, he says, with reference to a closely related secret society in which what is faked is the return of the ancestors. "Rather, new initiates have an even stronger sense of responsibility for maintaining the public belief system by referring to the spirit apparitions as real." He notes, moreover, that when the Guinean government declared the Poro illegal and had the membership display their instruments of deception before the women, this did not destroy the hold of the Poro, which at the time of his writing was vigorous as an underground association in Guinea, with young men crossing the border into Liberia to be initiated in the Poro there.[199]

But to talk of "belief" as in the "public belief system," may put too much stress on "belief" as plenitude. For as Bellman informs us, in one of those marvelously simple strokes with which ethnography wipes the slate clean, despite the enormous importance of secret societies to "virtually every aspect of daily life," the Kpelle have no single word for secrecy. Instead they use the phrase *ifa mo*, literally translated as "you cannot talk it."[200] The indigenous for-mulation of the public secret (that which is generally known, but cannot be articulated) is here striking in its emphasis on negation. Rather than "belief" as in the "public belief system," this would seem to me to be a *public unbelief system*, whose salutary feature is to capture and emphasize not only the great rituals and formalized expressions of deceit, as in the initiation rituals held every sixteen years or so, but, more to the point, to give dramatic force to the role of the half-lie, half-truth, in everyday life—in Liberia, I venture to say, as much as in my hometown of New York or in even more open-faced and honest burgs such as Washington, D.C., or Middletown on the rolling prairie.

"The whole enterprise is riddled with puzzle and paradox," lovingly com-plains John Picton in his joyous essay, "What's in a Mask?," concerning mas-querade by Ebira men in Nigeria in which "faith and deceit are disconcert-ingly combined."[201] His experience makes him take a lot of modern Western assumptions about masking to task, and he does this by distinguishing distinct types of masking. In his opinion, the type of mask at issue in these masquer-ades is that which denies human agency and in which secrecy is essential be-cause the masked person is no mere animator or actor. Instead the masked being has *entered a space that belongs to and is held to be, in itself, something other* (emphasis added), and this procedure is held to be *dangerous*, such that it is likely to be preceded or succeeded by rites of purification or sacrifice. He in-sists that the masker "in some sense becomes whatever it is that the mask hides, sometimes in a state of possession by that metaphysical presence, some-times not, though invariably with the authority to speak as its oracle."[202] It is thanks to the elaborate deception of women, however, that the masked dead are thus brought back into this world as dangerous beings, in which "faith and deceit are disconcertingly combined."

Men like to tell stories of how they outwitted women bent on discover-ing how their deceased husbands or fathers could come alive as masked be-ings. The confusion for the anthropologist is that, while these stories reinforce the idea of *trickery*, at the very same time they present the masquerade as con-veying *real ancestral presence*, the point being that *women are not to be trusted* with the knowledge of how this is achieved. In this regard Picton has his own good stories concerning this particular category of masking, involving, as it does, the public secret and the presencing of sacred beings. He was with his assistant, Andrew, outside a house in which one of the masked performers called an *ekuecci* was dressing himself, and while talking with the performer's sister was witness to the following brilliant, if unintended, unmasking.

> Suddenly there was her brother at the window having chased everyone out, wearing nothing but some magical medicines around his neck and trousers made of the particular indigo and white cloth used only for shrouds and masquerades. The sister averted her gaze and I, thinking to seize the chance for some cross-gender discussion said (in English, which she did not speak) to Andrew, "Let's ask her what she saw?," but he replied, "No! You cannot ask her that: she will say she saw nothing."[203]

We who come long after and from far away might want to ask a further question; What moved the brother to unmask himself so beautifully in the full frame of the window in such dramatic state of undress? Just medicines and indigo pants.

---

Medicines: the "hard core of culture." It was Kenneth Little who in 1948 characterized the secret societies of Sierra Leone as something more than just an institution, amounting instead to the "hard core of culture," and now, having dedicated so many pages to the intangible power of music and strange sounds in these societies, I should, in conclusion, draw attention to what he has to tell us concerning that very tangible and "hard" element that seems equally if not more important, namely magical charms and substances.

I take "hardness" here to be useful, metaphysically. It not merely echoes the rhetoric of Little's metaphor of "the hard core of culture" (contrast with Stanner's "a joyous thing with maggots at the center"), but connects that hard-core way of understanding things to modalities of secrecy that thrive on metaphysical dualities such as matter and spirit, appearance and essence—in short the whole staging of reality that in turn depends upon the notion of a secret, a truth, within.

In his 1951 account of secret societies among the Mende of Sierra Leone, Little informs us there are many spirit beings, such as (1) the remote Supreme Being who made the world, (2) those of the ancestors, often a little too close for comfort, and (3) various genii such as water spirits in the form of mermaids who can come to one while dreaming. But it is (4) the spirits of the secret societies that are in his opinion by far the most important, and here we should take note that each secret society spirit is intimately connected to its magical medicine (i.e., supernaturally charged charm, substance, or liquid).[204] Indeed "medicine is at the very foundation of each of the Freetown [Freetown being the capital of Sierra Leone] secret societies," comments John Nunley in *Moving with the Face of the Devil*. "To know the medicine of each group is to share its secret."[205]

What is fascinating is that it is precisely these, the "most important" spirits, that, unlike the other three categories, are *materialized*, as with masks, gorgeous costumes, weird sounds, and all the mischief, pomp, and drama, of which the secret societies are capable—including the indispensable medicine. Now Little says all this "signifies, perhaps, that although materalisation of the society spirit is necessary for social action, there is nothing lost thereby in supernatural content."[206] I find this a strange comment in that it so disarmingly assumes a contradiction between spirit and matter. But why not assume some other relationship, that for instance spiritual reality might be simply an extension of whatever it is that makes matter matter? We see the same dualism, I believe, when Little states that the Mende word *hale*, usually translated as medicine, "in common parlance . . . denotes any physical object or instrument employed to secure certain ends by supernatural means." Then he adds: "Such a reading, however, tends to conceal the fact that the object concerned is impregnated with a supernatural force which is external to the object itself."[207] Thus, for the anthropologist, this would seem to amount to a double concealment; the impregnated object conceals supernaturalness within itself, and common parlance tends to conceal the concealment! But what would happen if we took common parlance at face value?

I am very taken with this picture of an object impregnated by a supernatural force. For one thing it is certainly paradigmatic of the secret and the two-layered reality the secret fosters, let alone the magnification of reality to which Simmel points us. For another it seems marvelously Christian and Platonic. But what if we perform the defacing maneuver and translate the secret into a public secret and understand the two layers as a fiction, even a handy fiction, necessary for thought and life to magically speed on its way? This would be Nietzsche's advice, I'm sure, in which case the concealment Little refers us to lies with the secret of the secret society or with the sorcerer, and is, if I dare put it this way, probably a good deal more physical than metaphysical. It is physical in the sense of the trick and elaborated deceits involving pretense as to the pretense of the Other, and it is physical in the sense that E. E. Evans-Pritchard reiterated more than a decade earlier in his classic study of Zande magical medicines, where he emphasizes that the mysticism or super/naturalism at issue was not to be understood in terms of a metaphysical dualism. "Magical action is *sui generis*," he wrote, "and is not explained by the presence of spirits residing in medicines nor by the attribution to them of personality and will."[208] Like Little, he grants central importance to magical medicines and substances; indeed they seem to sum up most everything that is important in this culture, beginning with witchcraft substance itself, *mangu*, but he firmly resists the attractions of the supernatural impregnation thesis, noting that the "efficacy of magic lies in the medicines and in the rite and not in any power outside these. . . . When making magic a man addresses the medicines and not the ghosts, for the power is in the medicine."[209]

Indeed what makes the Zande book so enduring is its resolute attachment to "surface," stylistically as well as philosophically. Secrecy, in many senses of the word, abounds in Zande society as here recorded, and the passionate attachment to the poison oracle is merely one manifestation of this, albeit a dazzling illustration of what Benjamin has in mind when he urges upon us a form of revelation that does not expose and hence destroy the secret, but instead does justice to it. The magical power of these wonderful medicines lies not in their having been impregnated with supernatural force external to the medicine itself. Instead, like Gertrude Stein's rose, a medicine is a medicine is a medicine.

In conclusion it would be hard to overestimate the importance of medicines in relation to secrecy here, as in much of Africa, and we should note in passing that among the Mende practitioners of magical medicines in Sierra Leone, "first and foremost . . . come the officials and senior graduates of the secret societies."[210] We might also note that the intricately ritualized public secrecy of the secret societies stands as a glorious counterpoint to the illicit secrets of the sorcerer who has medicines so horrific that they in themselves double and redouble secrecy. Little mentions the possibility of killing persons so as to use their fat, genitals, or liver as medicine. In Bellman's more recent study among the Kpelle in Liberia this seems an undoubted fact.[211] And this is a common enough story elsewhere in Africa, serving as an indigenous world-picture of the sinister workings of politics and of the modern, post-colonial state as well.[212] When we take into account this wider context, then we can appreciate the pomp and circumstance of secret societies as merely carefully crafted caricatures of the skill essential to being a person, a social person, no less than a storyteller or poet—knowing what not to know.

If secrets are made to be transgressed, Canetti's explosion of the secret is only half the story, the other being slow-release maintenance of the plateau in that impossible place between knowing and not knowing, with its exhausting tendency to excess. Crossing and recrossing, we return, strange as it may seem, to Schopenhauer's beard, thanks to the Andalusian secret of the South recycled through Pitt-Rivers's Andalusians and Thomas Mann's death in Venice, it being a common enough story in the eastern highlands of Papua New Guinea that it was the women who, in that Other time, were owners of the flutes, "repositories of all cosmic power," which the men then stole from them and made into the focal point of a secrecy so all-encompassing as to be virtually resonant with culture itself. Not just ordinary women, in that Other time, but *kore badaha*, in Gimi language, "wild women, spirit women," living beyond the village in the forest which, after the theft of the flutes, became accessible only to men. Thereafter, the forest formed a reservoir of life force for new generations, saturated with the spirits of transmogrified dead men, ascendant from their furry possum, femalelike form at the base of the tree mass, to become beautiful birds singing high in an arboreal landscape.[213]

In so many ways, then, the life force of the forest is derived from its being not only taboo to women, on account of their immense powers of pollution, but in its being the privileged zone of purgation thereof ("purgation," of course, being a singularly fraught concept when applied to the power arising not only from "cleansing," but from the "pollution" itself ). According "to Gimi of both sexes, the threat to male purity and superiority created by the proximity of women emanates from a particular feature of female sexuality—the regular occurrence of menstruation."[214] When men stole the flutes, they inflicted on the women "a wound (literally 'a mouth') which some informants likened to castration," and thus women began to menstruate.[215]

But why do I invoke "Schopenhauer's beard"? Is it because it was he who claimed for music that uniquely privileged position of being a true and faithful representation of will, and that legend has it that, despite his philosophy of pessimism, he affirmed morality and played the flute—every day, after dinner?[216] Or is it because here in the highlands of New Guinea women had plugged the mouth of the flute with their pubic hair so that when the first man to seize the flute tried to blow it, a beard grew around his mouth, "so that today," states Gillian Gillison, "all men have beards which are really, so the men say, female pubic hair transferred."[217] Leonard Glick's earlier version is slightly different. In order to exact revenge for the theft, the Gimi women removed some of their pubic hairs, singed them to ashes, and secretly smeared them around the mouthpieces of the flutes, so that when the men next blew on them, the ashes blackened the lower parts of their faces, and therefore they have had mustaches and beards ever since.[218] This is a common enough story throughout these highlands.[219]

Yet dangerous as it is, men find menstrual blood intensely erotic, no less than the quintessence of pollution. "Although Gimi men genuinely fear menstrual blood, speak of women with contempt and go to great lengths to avoid them," Gillison tells us,

> they are also attracted to women's dangerousness. Sitting around the fire inside a hunting lodge, men discuss the delights of heterosexual sex. Their songs celebrate the eroticism of menstrual blood: 'I follow the River—to its source. As I climb along its course I see blood staining the rocks. As I round the bend I see you standing naked in the water, beautiful blood streaming down your shiny black legs. When shall we have sex?'[220]

Indeed, before missionaries prohibited menstruation huts, built to isolate women at their time of (what the anthropologist refers to as) greatest danger to the community, sexual intercourse routinely occurred in menstrual huts, and women said they could not convince their husbands or lovers to stay away when they were menstruating.[221]

Even stranger: the anthropologist understands men's sexual attraction to danger and to pollution to be nothing more than "the often wide gap between stated and practiced norms."[222] It is as if she's caught them out—all of us, really, engaged as we are so constantly in our acts of untruth, our double-dealing and hypocrisies that speed the world on its weary course. But instead of referring us to tropes of "stating versus practicing," which have the effect of closing down analysis in the name of analysis, diverting attention from the power of the contradiction—instead of this stating versus practicing, is it not the inexhaustible power of attraction and repulsion that creates and then fills to overflowing, the "often wide gap," the wide gap of secrecy, specifically public secrecy, with its all too dramatic, all too fearsome, injunctions against women's seeing? And is not this *gap*, like the bleeding wound, also *the beard itself*, as the gap that sutures over as elaborate deception the ghost of the phallus of phantom matriarchies?

What the beard as public secret sutures is surely the play of active not-seeing, the avowal *and* disavowal of the wounded whole. For nothing is more pronounced in this study of Gimi thought than its concern with the labor of the negative, creating identities through splitting wholes and curiously mirroring as *alter* the objects thereby separated in a restless, interminable process. If it is the nature of Gimi *woman* to reproduce and nurture nature by bodily *incorporation*, then it is the nature of *man* to *split* Being itself from such an all-consuming wholeness—spectacularly so with the stealing of the flutes and the creation of the bleeding wound, or with forcing the women to release the spirit of men whose corpse they have eaten so that it can then enter the world of the forest.[223]

It is the genital wound splitting female wholeness, so dramatically expressed in this New Guinea society, that is constitutive of the human subject and human culture. The parallels with Lacanian logic are too obvious. "To the degree that the object has been lost," Kaja Silverman informs us, "the subject has been found."[224] Or as Lacan put it with reference to the *Fort! Da!* game of absenting presence: "Thus the symbol manifests itself first of all as the murder of the thing, and this death constitutes in the subject the eternalisation of his desire."[225]

Schopenhauer's beard, you may remember, is a biologically guaranteed mask for the benefit of men in their unequal relation with women, women being innately talented in the arts of mimicry and two-facedness. However, the salient point is that in serving as a mask for men, the beard achieves its function not simply as a shield or cover, like a sheet of paper over the face, but does so by enacting a tension between the face and the genitalia, the uncovered and the covered, the open and the secreted, transposing, so to speak, not only the pubic hair of woman to the face of man, but its ghostly phallus as well, the figure within the figure of the absent-presence, also rendered by the "mouth" that is the wound the wild spirit women received at that moment of transition of the flutes from women to men, as Other time passed over the patriarchal line into present time.

The Lacanian resonance of absent-presence with Gimi thought is graphic, dramatic, and inescapable, at least with what Gillison calls "largely unconscious" thought, the myth of the stolen flute being, in her opinion, "an organizational idea upon which Gimi culture as a whole is constructed and which its members (both male and female) accept as axiomatic."[226] "My interpretation," she writes, "of the Gimi flute myth and rites of male initiation which are supposedly kept secret from the women implies that men view the female both as 'phallic' and as 'castrated,' as once having possessed the penis (flute), as having now lost it, but as retaining the rights of original possession."[227]

Being both phallic and castrated: it is surely of some moment that the "organizational idea" upon which the culture as a whole is constructed is embodied not only in the flutes, and not only in secrecy, but in *curious games of occultation* of the public secret proper. Indeed the anthropologist lets drop in a strategic footnote (the appropriate place for secretion?), that in discussing

> and enacting their rites of initiation, Gimi men and women *continually refer* to the secrecy of particular myths or ritual sequences. Women conscientiously post guards during portions of their night-time celebrations to ensure that no male is lurking in the bushes to spy on them. Yet my interviews with informants of both sexes indicate that adults have intellectual (*if not visual*) knowledge of *the entire range* of so-called "secrets" (emphasis added).[228]

It's the seeing, not the knowing, that's critical, says Ronald Berndt. What he refers us to is—how to put this?—a special sort of seeing, a seeing that doesn't see, a not-seeing, that activates the rites at the heart of the Fore society he studied between 1951 and 1953 in these same eastern highlands of Papua New Guinea. He relates an incident in which a woman was said to have been killed for transgressing this visual boundary. She had the misfortune to see two men playing the flutes in the forest and, after discussing the matter with her father and brother, the flute players decided that she must die. Her father and brother dragged her into the forest as she protested, by means of song, that she had not seen the flutes. It is customary, we are told, for people to sing at times of stress because people feel they can better express themselves through song than through speech, and songs have a better chance of being remembered.[229]

I
I did not see the flute playing
I did not see . . .

Men gathered around her and, drawing their bows, shot her dead as she sang. So it is said.[230]

Yet women are said to risk death by offering to have sex with men for a look at the flutes which they can hear, but not see.

"Yes! I will show you!" the men say. "It's just like a woman, with the same skin as you, wearing a skirt; but it has a hole under each armpit, no eyes, although it has a mouth. The cry comes from the armpit holes; it holds its hand over one armpit and cries from the other; then it does the same with the other side."[231]

But when the time comes, he reneges on his promise and never shows her.

Thus, weaving in and out of fear of murder and bodily pleasures, as if cheating like mad on the secret, the flute is verbally drawn in the shape of woman, eyeless but mouthed, arms moving like windmills from one armpit to the other, exuding music that must never be seen.

When *he* tells it, that's how it is, but when *she* tells it, it's like this, in song:

The flute sounds
Copulate with me
He goes on playing
The music is like the tiaga bird.[232]

Again and again it seems like we are being told to listen but not look, that it is at the point where the world is presenced through unsighted sound that the labor of the negative exerts its extremity, as with the "voice," which emblematizes Donald Tuzin's study of what he calls "the secret men's cult" in the East

Sepik region of Papua New Guinea, neatly conveyed in his title, *The Voice of the Tambaran: Truth and Illusion in Ilahita Arapesh Religion*.[233] We take note of the "truth and illusion" in relation to voice here, anticipating his remark early on concerning those "recurrent moments of religious skepticism, in which men verge close on the overt realization that the compelling truth of the Tambaran is, when all is said and done, an illusion created by themselves."[234]

And as we ponder, like these men, what "compelling truth" lies in illusion, we take further note of the *verging* to which Tuzin refers us, coming close to realizing the illusory nature of this compelling truth, but never actually getting there . . . And we dare to ask, for this is our world too: When is it, that *"all is said and done"? When will that be? What will then happen?* And what would it "mean" to realize that one lived according to an illusion created by oneself (the question Marx and Freud ask us to ask of the fetish, the question Nietzsche continuously poses regarding the need life has for error)? And how close is "close"? To be more pertinent, what is it like in there, in this space of closeness suspended between this and that in this movement, this "verging" that is neither one thing nor the other?

At one point, discussing the second of the five elaborate stages of male initiation, the stage in which the bullroarers are unmasked, Tuzin describes this voice in a particularly pertinent way. Emphasizing the "impenetrable mystery" and unknowability of the Tambaran, this protean force that is everywhere and nowhere, he nevertheless allows that "to the extent it can be known, [it] is conceived by men to reside in its voice. Like Yahweh of the ancient Hebrews, the Tambaran *speaks* creation, *speaks* destruction, *speaks* existence itself."[235]

"And yet," he continues, "despite its omnicompetence, the Tambaran cannot speak unaided. Secret sound-making devices such as bullroarers and flutes are not mere imitations of its voice, they *are* its voice, the concrete instrument of Tambaran power. This is why operating these devices in a ritual setting is a supremely sacred act."[236] Secret stories told by the men relate how women and children (and in one story, dogs) discovered or invented important cult objects. Usually these were sound-making devices which terrified the men until they stumbled upon the secret, killed the original owners, and appropriated them.[237]

Let me emphasize, therefore, that sanctity here depends upon deception, that the god—if I can use this term, not only needs mortal men to express the being of its invisible being as sonic presence, and not only needs this to be performed *in* secret, but this must be done as the performance *of* a secret as well. It is, then, a massive trick—*and all the more marvelous for so being.* "It is a moment," writes Tuzin, "when the power of the Tambaran is made manifest (created, in fact) through the agency of men, who, by the same token, become godlike by virtue of the power they momentarily command."[238] With every good reason, therefore, does Andrew Lattas, another anthropologist of New Guinea, cite Nietzsche's shrewd assessment of the sacred power of the trick.[239] Referring to the Christian god as an example of the optimism demanded by life, Nietzsche writes: "In those moments in which man was deceived, in which he duped himself, in which he believes in life; oh how enraptured he feels! What delight. What feeling of power! How much artists triumph in the feeling of power! Man has once again become master of '*material*'—master of truth!"[240] In the background we see an old man with a beard looking quizzically at his eighteen-month-old grandson throwing a reel of cotton thread into his crib. *Fort! Da! Fort! Da!* the little chap seems to be saying, although he has a long way to go before he can really speak and, in the words of another Master, master the symbolic realm where one thing stands in for something else. It is a game, a game of repetition, the old man said, adding that it aimed at achieving mastery over a beleaguered state of affairs, a game that could go and indeed will go on forever, presencing the absence, verging, merging, only to let it slide away once more. When all is said and done, a wonder.

---

The bullroarers of the Tambaran came into the world through the inventiveness of women and were taken from them by men through murder and kept secret thereafter.[241] Their sound is "altogether remarkable" to the ear of the ethnologist, and upon their being revealed to the novices, the latter witness further unmaskings—of paintings, statues, and flutes, all secreted in the Spirit House—as prelude to the ordeal of penis-cutting by men portrayed as pigs. Into the stream running below the floor, the blood flows in torrents from boys standing in a row. The noise is loud, the scene one of confusion. Men dance and shout as the flutes play, in part to drown out the screams of the boys.

But then there is a second unmasking, that of the secret drums, a sort of meta-unmasking unmasking the first unmasking, as the boys are told the first unmasking was a *trick—and all the more marvelous, on that account,* we might say. The items that were first revealed are now said to be a sham or of only secondary importance. Now it is the drums that are the real secret.[242] Concealment is followed by revelation, and revelation itself turns out to have been concealment. "Each level is organised so as to obscure the next level," wrote Fredrik Barth in his book on secrecy as religion among the Baktaman of the mountain rain forest in central New Guinea. As a man ascends in knowledge he is taught that what he had learned of earlier levels had been purposely distorted. "He realises the existence of veil behind veil," writes Barth.[243] Yet I imagine there's more to it than a realization of endless veiling. More important and certainly more strange is the effervescence intrinsic to the trickery and the mimesis therein—"becoming master of 'material,' master of truth."

We hear this voice of the Tambaran in many other ways too. Before the posts are cut for the giant Spirit House, for example, the Tambaran is presenced at night with the music of a large bamboo pipe capped by a drumlike resonator that amplifies and distorts the voice of the man secretly singing, so that his song acquires "an eerie, preternatural quality." The bamboo must be "filled with sound," as one man put it. Accompanied by a loud thumping on the ground, the men advance from all points of the compass up the ridges onto the sleeping village, a monster passing in the night. The chorus is grand with voices and pipes audible for miles around, continuing until early dawn.[244]

---

The question keeps recurring as to who knows what and how much, and what the heck is "belief" anyway in this maze of deceit in the decades-long ritual cycle dedicated to making men from boys while their moms act dumb and nobody knows, including the ethnographers, whether they "know" or not. Only much later, a year after the Tambaran had been revealed to the women in the Christian church as a trick, was the ethnographer close to knowing the extent of the women's knowing. Yet the picture that emerges is still obscure. It seemed that far from being surprised at the men's confession in church in 1984, the women had been "yawningly indifferent," and now they, too, could confess that they "had always assumed that the men were lying." But for Tuzin the even more important point is that even if they did not know, they "did not particularly care, what the truth was behind the men's fictions"—although they were mad at having been duped.[245] If this seems

contradictory—not caring particularly about the truth, but being mad at being duped—then so be it, for after all, it is precisely such a combination that
provides the public secret with both its torpor and its incandescence.

This leaves the kids who, as Tuzin points out, here as everywhere, are "father
of the man," and about whom I have speculated earlier, in my Tierra del Fuegian effort, to better understand the mystical impact of unmasking.

"Not surprisingly," writes Tuzin with regard to the children's attitudes toward the various manifestations of the Tambaran, "their general feeling is one
of undiluted terror. Theirs is the purest image of the giant ogre, the tower-
ing monster whose bloody, toothy, maw waits hungrily for naughty or un-
wary children and whose great feet and legs (the latter are likened in girth to
six-gallon drums) crush young bodes to a pulp." And he urges us to attend
more to the role of the child as "culture bearer."[246]

Yet insofar as this implies that the credulity of the child sustains the adults'
secret, it is perhaps misleading, and certainly insufficient. For it fails to recognize that the secret's power as sacred force depends even more on its revelation and on the oscillation between concealment and revelation in the twilight zone of the "half-known." The crucial quality is *not* that the religion is
made of tricks and disguises, *but that these are unmasked. The whole point of the
trick, as I follow the ethnography, here as elsewhere, is that it be revealed.*

Moreover, what is the relation here between child and adult, and what
does it mean to consider the child as "culture bearer"? If the notion of the
"child as father to the man" is meant to suggest that the formative "work" of
culture occurs in childhood, as, for example, with learning the language, then
I think we lose insight into the way by which it is the back-and-forth between child culture and adult culture that constitutes the sense of the real
and its various shadings. More pointedly, I would claim that it is not the child
but the adults' imagination of the child's imagination that is the "culture
bearer," and it is precisely this self-serving loop spinning off into referentless
world that gives the secret its sheen.

What this loop also suggests is that a "prehistoric tone" is necessary for a
society's fantastic infrastructure—as with the "prehistoric" children, women,
or dogs, who, in pre-patriarchal time, discovered or invented the tricks later
appropriated by murderous men. Furthermore, this element of prehistoricity
with its Other sense of time and identity, substance and transformation,

makes of origin myths, such as that of the Cassowary underlying the men's secret society, something rather different from that envisaged in "codes" and "charters," as if these myths were something like legal documents to be read for information, contradiction, or as semiotic crossword puzzles. Instead, "mythic reality" recruits "childishness" in the same way that adults in a movie theater sink into the screen as imaginary signifiers take over their bodies. This is not a semiotic issue but a mimetic one. The "child" is preeminently the unreality ensuring reality's punch.

How strange, given its importance to these sacred secrets, that so little attention has been paid to sound and music by ethnologists! How devastating,
therefore, to come across the beauty and power of music in Kenneth Read's
description of the sacred flutes that must never, on pain of immediate death,
be seen by women or children, but are very much to be heard by them as the
call of the mythic *nama* bird, especially and magnificently at times of male
initiation. It is sound, glorious, floating, mysterious, sexual sound—sound of
absent-presence if ever there was—that comes leaping from Read's pages as
he tries to confront the fact that the secret is not a secret but what he repeatedly calls an "elaborate deception" and a "charade." A particularly poignant
example is the special privilege granted *aged* women. As a sign of their ac-
ceptance the men allowed them to stand in front of their houses, instead of
being closed within, whenever men paraded through the villages with the sacred flutes.

In parentheses is added, "with closed eyes, however."[247]

And note that these flutes are something more than a symbol, a thing
standing in for some other thing. What's at issue is deception and the evacu-
ation of meaning in place of "the breath of empty space." Meaning itself is a
decoy. For what's at issue is the trick. Indeed, in Read's opinion, it is the concealment *and* revelation of sound as invisible presence that was as close as you
could imagine God among the Gahuku-Gama with whom he lived for two

years in the early 1950's. He makes the point that in their religion there were no gods, yet "the world and everything within it depend on supernatural force, an impersonal power operating as the force of life, having no name nor any specific location, vaguely ancestral in character, and ultimately the source of all success, indispensable for everything men hope to achieve."[248] *And this "impersonal power," in his understanding, is the sound of the secret flutes.* Special food is prepared and placed inside the mouthpiece of each flute, and when not in use the flutes are laid in pairs on beds of leaves in the men's house. "These beliefs are not formulated precisely, but native statements and the manner in which the flutes are treated lead one to conclude that the tune is the important sacred element."[249] Tuzin says exactly the same for the Tambaran in the Sepik; the flutes are not imitations of its voice, they are its voice, the instrument of Tambaran power.[250]

But surely it's not the tune so much, as the pretense it stands for, which floods the world with sacred presence? The tune would therefore be, in the precise sense of the word, a *fetish*, an object sexually and supernaturally charged with the power of the phantom presence of the known-unknown, of dis/avowal, as we discern so remarkably in the aesthetic power of Read's description, the way the tune, as he calls it, threads its way obsessively and beautifully through his 1965 narrative of male initiation in *The High Valley*, holding the ritual together, giving it life force and aura, duplicating, as the sheen to ethnographic description, the fetish power the tune would seem to have for the Asaro Valley people themselves.

As befits the fetish, this exquisite evocation of the flow of music across a landscape of hills and rustling grasses is a sacred resolution that maintains the sexual energy of the "half seen" and disavowed. It is a resolution, as I see it, in which we discern both the hand of the author and that of his hosts, as with Turnbull's rendition of the *molimo*-trumpet music of the Mbuti pygmies in central Africa, a deliberately unstated blurring by the author of these two components: the writing and the phenomenon being written about. It is in my opinion every inch an aesthetic resolution of the turmoil of unproductive anxiety we find in Read's earlier, 1952, publication in the academic journal *Oceania*, when, like anthropologists before and after him, he is painfully agitated by the ruse that is the secret that is God.[251]

In this first formulation of the ruse, the writer is continuously drawn to an irresolute formula of indecision, illustrating the intractability of the central problem of the split in belief and coexistence of contraries, believing and not believing, seeing and not seeing, simultaneously. No sooner does he point out that the secret is a charade, than an immediate corrective is applied, as when he states that the women know the explanation of the flutes offered them by the men is designed to mislead them, yet they respect the secret, and although the element of deceit has a function in sustaining the superiority of men, "but"—and this "but" will be as constant as the mystery of the secret—"but when it is so obvious that deception is being practised," he insists, "we must seek an additional explanation."[252]

Yet it is an endless seeking, starting and stopping, no sooner announced than abruptly terminated with the pronouncement that "conscious falsification is the least important element within the cult, and that it in no way affects the essential belief as to the nature of the *nama* [flutes]."[253] Thus we zigzag between essential belief and charade, pitting them one against the other, not knowing how to deal with the disturbing sensation that maybe they are the same thing. How could that be? What does it mean that "essential belief" could also be based on a "charade"? And again: "But to conclude that the flutes are merely the central objects of a charade designed for the glorification of a particular sex is to be very wide of the mark. Such a conclusion, moreover, does not accord with the emotion with which they are regarded and the manner in which they are treated."[254] This is my idea of mental torture. Whatever position we adopt cancels itself out. Clearly the "labor of the negative" in high gear. And imagine! A whole society erected on that!

But as he came to describe it later in 1965, for Read the power of the sound of the flutes seemed intimately associated with its being everywhere yet nowhere in the delicate ephemera of its being, subject to elaborately controlled concealment and revelation. In the weeks preceding the moment when the novices were shown the flutes and told their secret, the very light of dawn and the massive space of the valley was, as far as he was concerned, made luminous through sonic mystery. "I awakened one morning," he wrote, "with the feeling that something new had been added to a familiar situation. The village was completely silent, yet the air seemed to vibrate uneasily against my ear, prompting me to recall the unidentified sound that had broken into my sleep. . . . I started to dismiss it as imagined when suddenly it came again, lifting me up to my elbows with a sense of shock."[255]

This is not a sound with a fixed point of origin. It seeps into everything and seems constitutive of Being itself. "In later months the same notes came at many times of day, but they always carried the quality of that first encounter," the anthropologist continues—

> the predawn air chilling my arms and shoulders, the glimmer of light in the empty street, and the whole valley lying exposed and unsuspecting as it slept. Their sound eludes description. . . . The clear air offered it no resistance, and the notes coming from a distance, seemed to wind at will through an echoing void, tracing such a capricious path that their origin was successfully concealed.[256]

The sound spread to occupy the entire valley and time itself.

> In the following weeks the sound of the *nama* [flutes] were threaded through the background of every day [and] on any morning the calls seemed to speak to each other from a dozen different places, harshly insistent from the grasslands to the south, thin and troubled like the last notes of an echo, from the hanging valleys in the western mountains. . . . Their inaudible vibration hung upon the intervening hours, pulsing in the sunlight.[257]

Yet as he accompanied the initiated men playing the flutes, Read was "struck by the thought that they may have wanted to be seen."[258] For they were on a barren ridge high above the women working in their gardens, such that anyone moving on the ridge would be clearly visible from the gardens as figures silhouetted against the "breathless arch of sky." And as each man played on the flutes, someone handed him a bunch of leaves as a "trivial subterfuge" with which to cover himself.[259] When they got back to the house and laid down the flutes, the men were "almost drunk with excitement" and could not stop talking. Hunehune "gestured helplessly with his hands" and said to Bihore that his flute playing had so deranged him that he wanted him sexually.[260]

Some "charade"!

A Nietzschean moment: Through artistry, which means lying, man masters truth (whose name is woman). The sense of achievement of such mastery is intensely erotic. We poor writers should take heart!

And another: secrecy is intertwined with taboo, and hence with transgression, so as to create a powerful yet invisible presence; indeed, the presence of presence itself, essential to religion.

Sound, as phantom presence *has* to be transgressed by its "unmasking," and here is where the bullroarers, sacred flutes, and singing become crucial, because unlike the prohibition on the *visual manifestation* of the secret, the sound, whose whole purpose is to be public, evokes the secret's presence without otherwise manifesting it, such that sound provides a perfect vehicle for *absent-presence*. Freud, and after him Lacan, speculated brilliantly on the play of concealment and revelation of the wooden reel in the *Fort! Da!* game created by Freud's grandson, but omitted to take into account the acoustic plenitude of absent-presence this game has come so steadfastly to signify, staring them in the face, so to speak, *o/a, o/a*, rather imaginatively transmogrified into German words by Freud as *Fort! Da!, Fort! Da!*, the alternating "music" of the secret, the being of its nothingness, the *Fort!* or "gone" presencing the in-visibility identified by both Freud and Lacan as the sign of the absent mother, no less than the absence that is the mother and sign of separation and signification per se, the *Da!* its unmasking, swelling the mystery in the form of the fetish. Sound would thus be the meta-secret or the skin of the public secret thereby announcing, but concealing, its content, and it is precisely this "skin" that represents the mysterious line that has to, yet must not, be breached. Continuously.

Much has been written in the past few decades concerning the force of "Western metaphysics" attributing authenticity to speech, and artificiality to writing, the former presencing Being, the other not.[261] But it is obvious from the voice of the Tambaran and the place of sound in the examples I have cited of secret societies girdling the globe, that the nature of this sound-Being is fraught. Such "speech," like the public secret, presences presence while mocking it, and any definition of "the sacred" we may care to entertain would have to begin from this consideration. [262]

Weeks later, Read woke to a silent universe. For the first time the flutes had stopped. Men put on their finest decorations, their greased skin gleaming in the sun that flashed on mother-of-pearl and bobbing feathers as they made their way with the novices to the men's house in an adjoining village. It was completely silent. Many of the women standing there were dressed in mourning, while the mothers of the initiates had smeared their bodies with clay, their eyes "dark, sightless sockets in their masks of grey clay . . . in rigid attitudes of listening concentration."[263] Could there be a more finely focused combination of blindness and expectation of sound,

the eyes eyeless sockets,

the hearing not hearing but waiting to hear,

the face no longer a face but a defaced face,

facing "death" in the form of impending separation from the son,

in the figure of woman?

The figure of the wound rendered with terrible intensity? Unsightly and unsighted?

Thumping the ground, ululation, drumming, chest-beating, throbbing, staccato beat. . . . Sound here is made of a stark alternation, accentuating both the separation of men from women and the *Fort! Da!* phenomenon, funneling reality into itself in waves of appearance/disappearance, taking over the body beginning with an overwhelming sense of noise at this climactic stage of male initiation—the women's keening cries "stabbing into the din around me," men ululating in synchrony with their chests thumped in counterpoint to the crashing of feet on the bare ground, "and rising above it all, came the cries of the flute, which I heard at close quarters for the first time, a sound like great wings beating at the ear drums, throbbing and flapping in the hollow portions of the skull"—coinciding with the men's "ecstatic communion with an invisible force," and "apparently no less moving" for the initiates, points out the anthropologist, "because they knew of the simple deception practiced on the women."[264]

Yet this ecstasy is mere prelude to the most fantastic and fantastically violent bodily displays and auto-mutilations carried out by the men down by the river. And again it is sound that animates and directs the entire stage: As the men careened down the hillside from all points of the compass, the waist-high grass fell behind them in a lengthening wake, "the whole hillside seemed to shiver," the "different streams of sound converging in the distance, meeting, and leaping towards a turbulent climax" of initiated men standing in the brightly lit shallows of the river ostentatiously displaying their genitals and masturbating in front of hordes of other brilliantly painted and feathered men, the sacred flutes crying. One by one, the men stepped forward with rolls of razor-sharp leaves, "flourishing them like a conjurer in a spotlight," writes Read (who understands this act as motivated, in part, by a need to exorcise the polluting effects of women, no less than to imitate menstruation), the man plunging this vicious instrument up his nose so as to tear at the mucous membrane and force blood to flow, the watching men ululating while the man himself was so distraught with pain that, strong as he was, his knees were trembling and it seemed as though his legs would buckle under him.[265] It was this act that the male initiates had then to succumb to for the first time in their lives, following which they were forced to swallow large canes doubled over into a long, narrow, U shape. Read experienced it this way:

> Leaning forward from the waist, he placed the rounded section in his mouth, straightened, tilted his head, extended the line of his neck, and fed it into his stomach. My throat contracted and my stomach heaved, compelling me to look away. When I turned to him again most of the cane had disappeared, only two small sections, the open ends of the U, protruding from the corners of his mouth.
>
> I have no idea how long he held this grotesque stance, his straining abdomen and chest racked with involuntary shudders. Already sickened by the display, I stiffened with shock as he raised his hands, grasped the ends of the cane and sawed it rapidly up and down, drawing it almost free of his mouth at the peak of every upward stroke. The fervor of the crowd mounted to a clamorous pitch, breaking in wave upon wave of pulsing cries, the final surge matching my own relief when he dropped the cane, bent from the waist, and vomited into the river.[266]

It's as if the very pattern of concealment and revelation is here repeated on the body itself, as if Canetti's insides of the secret are sawed up and down by the U-shaped canes until the fetish that is the secret explodes as vomit into the river before the fervor of the crowd. And much the same could be said of the blood so painfully torn from the nasal mucosa, as eruption of insidedness.

The canes mark men off from women even more than the flutes, according to Berndt's study of the Fore, and when the use of the canes was first recorded there by white men, in 1934, it was said that women would die if they saw men using them. Read was told in the early 1950's in the Asaro Valley that the canes "were part of the secret lore of men," and that women did not know of their "significance" even though they were worn looped around their waists as a customary and relatively inconspicuous item of everyday apparel.[267] It is astonishing to realize how ingrained and everyday this is, when Berndt remarks, for instance, that "every adult male possesses and carries about with him lengths of rolled cane as a necessary part of his equipment."[268]

In Fore *mythology*, as recorded by Berndt, men were enjoined to hide their use of canes from women, and at first the canes were used straight, not U-shaped, and were passed straight down the intestinal tract from the mouth out through the anus, and vice versa, or emerged from the navel. It was a woman who sewed up the navel so as to prevent clear passage and admonished men to double the cane over and plunge it in and out from the mouth downwards. There seems an anxiety in the narrative here to impress with repetition of re-versals, with what Read called continuous "sawing" up and down through the mouth doubled-over, as opposed to straight-through cleansing.

Gilbert Herdt states that cane swallowing was spontaneously abandoned by the people he calls Sambia, without any coercion from the Australian ad-ministration, because it was too painful. "Men considered it excessively dan-gerous, and one experience," at the first-stage of initiation, "was enough to do its job." The canes, he notes, had to penetrate a foot or more inside.[269] Yet might not this way of phrasing the issue miss the point? Might it not be the "too-painfulness" that accounts for the practice in the first place?

It is emphasized, in Fore myth as much as in everyday lore, that use of the canes to induce vomiting makes men strong and attractive to women, whom, we are often told, men secretly understand to be the stronger sex. Yet we are also told in many ways that the canes' function is to purge men of the pol-luting effect of women as with the ever-present possibility of their contami-nating food with menstrual blood. Therefore, so the argument seems to run, because such purging enhances male beauty and power, the significance of the canes lies in their being instruments of purgation.

Yet could not the canes exist for their pain and violence as spectacle? Might it not be that extremity in and of itself is what makes for male attrac-tion and beauty, enmeshed in the attraction and repulsion of menstrual blood, the attraction and repulsion and above all the danger thereof that women can mean to men? Purgation seems way off the mark. It is not that women are considered by men as *unclean* when menstruating, notes Berndt, but *danger-ous*—which as we have learnt from Gillison's ethnography, is when they are also *most sexually attractive* to men.[270] Like the revealing and concealing of the insides that is the secret, this terrible play is done so as to further augment danger by what Read so appropriately calls "the Gahaku's exhausting ten-dency to seek excess."[271]

Cane swallowing could thus be thought of as a medium, like sound and music, for performing dis/avowal that is the public secret, performing it for its inherent excitement and danger. The metaphysical mystery of a concealing surface and a hidden depth, of appearance and truth, is subject to a Dionysian "eternal return"—"*to realise in oneself*," wrote Nietzsche, "the eternal joy of becoming—that joy which also encompasses joy in destruction."[272] How shallow our contemporary talk of "embodiment" seems in light of this sort of disembodiment! Grab a cane! Eat the corpse of the dead man à la the Gimi women! Then talk to me of "the body"!

When missionaries exposed and then burned the flutes in villages close to where Read lived, the entire ritual complex was abandoned, "and with it had gone the supernatural justification of the men's organization."[273] With brutal force the question thus emerges as to how a social institution—or charade, call it what you will—could be so all-consuming of a society and at the same time be so pathetically vulnerable?

Is this testimony to Canetti's apocalyptic vision of the secret as doomed to apotheosis and self-destruction, dragging down its battlements and entailments as if the very power of the secret is also its inordinate fragility? And after that, what then? What of memory? Can the secret wither away without a trace? For on his return to the High Valley in 1981, thirty years after his first visit, Read could confidently write that the "*nama* cult is not even a memory to the youngest generation of Gahuku today," and he reminds us how amazingly powerful it was when he was last there. "To the outsider who observed its rituals and heard the cries of the flutes throughout the day," he writes, "who saw the overwrought responses to them reflected in the faces and voices of men, and who passed by the closed and silent houses where women and uninitiated boys hid from their threatening calls, the final curtain had descended on an awesome event."[274]

In 1985 John Finch reported that when missionaries had gotten some of their converts in Lufa to play the secret flutes in public in front of women, this "completely ended their use in the region."[275] Among the Fore in the early 1950's, in the zone where missionary and government activity had been most focused, Ronald Berndt found that "when women have seen the flutes, all the associated rituals and ceremonies immediately collapse." The flutes are the focal point, he added. "It is the fact of observing them, not of knowing about them, which is deemed important."[276]

Yet might there not be another side to this bitter story? For surely the very act of forcing exposure of the secret, and then burning the flutes, could be interpreted as testimony to their spiritual power. Moreover, Tuzin reports that the missionaries in his area of the Sepik were no less believers in the natives' spirits than were the natives themselves, and, so it seems to me, possibly more so, if we consider that the adult men of the village had to wrestle with maddeningly complex issues of their faith's dependence on skepticism and trickery.[277]

This raises the question as to how you destroy a charade that is not a secret but a public secret (something that is known by everyone, but not easily articulable). For it would seem that such a phenomenon has built-in protection against exposure because exposure, or at least a certain modality of exposure, is what, in fact, it thrives upon. Might it not be, then, that the drama of exposure staged by the missionaries did not destroy the secret, but became instead the raw material for new myths and modernist rituals along the same lines as before? Might not my own writing wriggling itself into being here, be part of just such a ritualization, the ever-repeated final exposure of the secret that in destroying, redeems it?

This seems implicit in Gillian Gillison's larger-than-life account of a missionary going from village to village, showing the flutes to women and children. In some villages he actually entered the men's houses, took out the sacred instruments, and told the men to play them in public. Then he burnt them, threw the ashes into the river, and baptized the village. The missionary also forbade the building of the men's houses and ordered the burning of the women's menstrual huts.[278] Cecil B. DeMille, where *are* you?

That was early in the 1960's. But by the time the anthropologist got there a decade later, in 1973, there was what she calls a "revival of traditional practices" and men were erecting their cult houses and holding initiations, although the menstrual huts were not being rebuilt.

In Gregory Bateson's now famous study, *Naven*, carried out along the

Sepik River a long time ago, in the early 1930's, we are told of two incidents in which initiated men "terminated" the ceremonial life of the village by wrathfully exposing its secrets to the women and children. In Mindimbit, where the initiatory system was in sharp decline with the boys (*sic*) going away to work in white-owned plantations, a younger man's wife espied the unconcealed end of a toy flute among her husband's possessions as they were traveling on the white recruiter's schooner, and picked it up, asking "What is this?" She was seen by an older man who scolded her and reported back to the men's house. The men stormed out and collected all the small boys together, even the toddlers, and showed them everything, including the most sacred of all, the *wagan* gongs. The exposure took the form of a *public enactment of the whole initiatory cycle*, albeit abbreviated, and this was regarded as the final utter shame and destruction of the cult.[279] What the woman saw that day on the recruiter's schooner was not a sacred flute but a toy. Nevertheless this was deemed sufficient reason to expose all the secrets, as the men had decided that no flutes of any sort were to be seen by women in case they guessed the nature of the music emanating from the men's house.[280]

In another village some fifty years before Bateson got to the Sepik, so he was told, men had killed a small boy for inadvertently trespassing on the secret. It was the time when the secret *wagan* gongs were being played in the ceremonial house day and night for several months, at the end of which what Bateson calls "the final spectacle" occurs, when old men dance in front of the women, impersonating the *wagan* ancestral spirits. This involved decorating giant statues of *wagan* with croton leaves which the men had hidden outside the village in string nets. However, a shaft of elephant grass hurled by the boy while playing with other children had pierced one of the hidden bags, and therefore (!) the men chased and killed him. On their return to the village a fight ensued in which four men were killed. Then the secret gongs were hauled out and the men built a small screen around them on the dancing ground and showed them to all the women, going so far as to give them the sacred gong sticks to keep in their own houses.[281]

Yet these "terminations" of ritual life through exposure of the secret are described by Bateson as *merely temporary*, and from what he says it seems they may be even cyclical. Grappling with the curious logic, he refers us to the men's "tendency to cut off their own noses to spite the other fellow's face" whenever a situation of partial exposure occurs, sparking threats by the men to "break the screens" and expose the lot, even though this humiliating act "may cripple the ceremonial life of the village for some years."[282] But note: only for some years.

It is indeed hard to understand why a partial exposure should motivate a complete one, and even harder to understand how cutting off your nose can spite the other fellow's face, but on the surface there is a curious affinity between these dramatic exposures by the natives, and those cruelly performed by the propagators of the Word of the Christian god, and who knows who has the last laugh here, or whose face is being defaced?

Take the startling case of self-destruction recently recorded by Tuzin in which, in 1984, men stepped forth on the platform of a newly established Christian church during a Sunday service in the Sepik region of eastern New Guinea, and one by one confessed to the assembled women that the men's secret society, the Tambaran, was, in Tuzin's words, "a lie. To be exact, the secret was that there was no secret," and they explained that the visual and sonic presentations of the spirits were "illusions" and "imaginative tricks."[283]

So far, so good. But here comes the real trick. Having destroyed the secret through its revelation, the men at the same time warned that "in a truer sense the Tambaran was no hoax at all. The spirit venerated in the cult was and is real; its power was lethal in the past, and it could kill again." Known previously as this or that manifestation of the Tambaran, the men now realized that they were but manifestations of Satan! Thus it would seem that unmasking through confession, has in turn led to even greater concealment and more magnificent trickery with the devil, the arch-imitator, himself. It is as if colonialism merely added yet another stage of revelation and concealment to the preexisting five stages constituting initiation ritual. How ingenuous, therefore, indeed how masking, the notion that "by unmasking Satan and ridding themselves once and for all of his presence," the men were able to prepare the community for Christ's Second Coming.[284] We take note, also, that the Tambaran was slowly dying, anyway, without any shove from the men confessing in church. What better way therefore of reinvigorating it? The ethnographer keeps asking, indeed he claims it to be his principal issue, that if the Tambaran was on its last legs, *why kill it*?[285] The answer seems clear. Killing redeemed it in the form of Satan on account of the fact that "killing" meant revealing as the best form of concealing, and revelation thus recharged the deceptions, uncertainties, and mastery of the lie required by the truth. The trick—and here we are assuredly in the realm of inspired trickery—is to (pretend to) convert, by means of revelation, the public secret into a real or pure secret where Canetti's fireworks of the self-destructive fetish light up the darkness of the truth.

# PART FOUR

# The Face Is the Evidence That Makes Evidence Possible

> Sudden shifts of power such as are now overdue in our society can make the ability to read facial types a matter of vital importance. Whether one is of the left or right, one will have to get used to being looked at in terms of one's provenance. And one will have to look at others in the same way.
>
> WALTER BENJAMIN, "A Small History of Photography"

If secrecy is fascinating, still more so is the public secret into which all secrets secrete, whether as death in Venice or women outside the Big Hut at the "uttermost part of the earth." What might they have in common, these women and that city, for every day it sinks a little deeper into its carbolic-coated miasma, lying about its lying in order to steal a march on a north-south axis of dissimilitude. This axis is built as much into the human face, as into a mobile, evanescent, social contract, knowing what not to know in order to be. The bountiful energy therein is as irresistible as its concealment, secrecy giving way to defacing spasms crossing the border that is face, the face as fetish, the face as auratic splendor, the face limping one step behind its promise, beautiful in its status as the all-time loser we still believe in.

This fetish-effect is wrought with finesse by Emmanuel Levinas with his notion of the face as an epiphany, an event, we might say, rather than a plane tilted to the light, to which one gains access not by looking but as an ethical act. Vision gives way to presencing in the very act of a looking, eye to eye, that sunders ocular lock-in.[1] Vision melts into faciality and faciality beckons both language and truth in an astonishingly mystical movement beyond our knowledge, just as it is the basis of knowledge, beginning with sociology. In accessing the face, Levinas resorts to analogy with Descartes's statement of the infinite as an idea aimed at something "infinitely greater than the very act through which one thinks it. There is a disproportion between the act and that to which the act gives access." This is the face, the face of the Other in its purest distillation, that Other to whom one's oneness stands in debt and to whom one submits one's being as social being. This is not a question of symbols, of the face as a symbol, but of the face defacing itself as guarantor of the symbolic in a flurry of the infinite. "To seek truth," writes Levinas, "I have already established a relationship with a face which can guarantee itself, whose epiphany itself is somehow a word of honor. Every language as an exchange of verbal signs refers already to this primordial word of honor." The face is the evidence that makes evidence possible.[2]

Levinas must take Nietzsche to heart because his philosophy of the face is every inch a philosophy of defacement. No depth. But no surface either, the face of midday, moment of the shortest shadow, of sheer movement etched in black and white, "in snow and sunlight on white walls and clouds and rocks," this is the face that "moves down windy streets with blown newspapers and shreds of music and silver paper in the wind."[3] For by no means does Levinas's face depend on giving us the Other's *interiority*. On the contrary: "The Other who expresses himself precisely does not give himself," he says, and therefore the freedom to lie is maintained because "deceit and veracity already presuppose the absolute authenticity of the face—the privileged case of a presentation being foreign to the alternative of truth and nontruth, circumventing the ambiguity of the true and the false which every truth risks—an ambiguity, moreover, in which all values move."[4]

Levinas's face is clearly a fetish. And he is right, even if he doesn't see/ access it that way. After all, how does one access a fetish? Surely it's as much the Other way around? It accesses/looks at you. The fetish power with its mighty ambiguity "in which all values move" is the time of the face at midday, the defacing time when the "disproportion" that is the face as mask and the face as window to the soul, stretches to its beautiful limit and breaks into infinitude. As such, the disproportion that is the infinity that is the face is a crossing, a continuously applied defacement that is the mark of the public secret.

This coexistence in faciality of both mask and window to the soul is more than contradiction. Crossing back and forth across the face as border between mask and window to the soul is our necessary task, and it is in this "disproportion," between the act and that to which the act gives access, that we discern the presence of the "always beyond" that the fetish secretes. Either of these functions—mask, or window to the soul—is a wonder; together they make an orgy of disproportion compounded by the fact that the face never exists alone; fated in its very being to be only when faced by another face. Here is where the impossible but true coexistence of the mask and the window flares in recognition of a certain tenderness, a shyness, before the gaze of the Other with a studied incapacity to "recognize" either the masking or the windowing capacity and certainly not their coexistence. In the circle of this public secret of denial, what for Levinas is not looking but accessing, there exists Hegel's master-slave, death-in-Venice struggle for the recognition of the Other as no less necessary to social life than the coexistence of mask and window is forever bound to the unsayable. To peer into the soul of the other, no less than giving due regard to the face as mask, would be to lose face altogether. And to the (1) need to deny the mask when looking through the window, and to the (2) need to deny the window when espying the mask, try computing the added complexity when (3) it is (and has to be) not one, but at least two faces facing these reciprocating denials. Truly an orgy of disproportion, made all the more miraculous by the unthinking everydayness with which it provides the being of social being—language itself and signifying, says Levinas.

We will hold this fetishization in thrall. Or, rather, our faces will, for our fate as social beings depends on resisting the call for de-fetishization for fear of interrupting the functioning of a strategic ignorance, until the next crisis of defacement when the agreement not to know is seized by its strange energies—as when Gustav von Aschenbach, secretly in love with the forbidden object of desire, short-circuits north and south to tip over into that Other realm where face sinks into bodiedness, "tumbling and whirling down: a human and animal swarm, a raging rout, flooding the slope with bodies, with flames."[5] The disproportion of disproportion.

Here he is, busy at work preparing his treatise on physigonomy, Michel Eyquem, Seigneur de Montaigne, born in 1533, and it grieves him as he says midway that Socrates should have had so ugly a face and body, so out of keeping with the beauty of his soul. Nature did him an injustice, adds Montaigne, noting that nothing is more probable than that the body conforms and is related to the soul. In this he followed Plato's assertion that physical beauty is a sign of the beauty of the soul, no less than Cicero's story of how Socrates countered a reading of his face by one Zopyrus, an Egyptian physiognomist, who maintained that Socrates was "stupid and thick-witted because he had not got hollows on the neck above the collar-bone" and that he was "addicted to women." On hearing this, Socrates is said to have calmed his agitated pupils by claiming that he accepted this reading, it being the very force of his reason which allowed him to overcome his vices.[6]

But there is certainly a paradox here, giving rise to a treatise which keeps twisting around its seduction by physiognomy; and it is of the utmost importance, for it affects us all, this nature of nature, no less than its injustice and the possibilities for a triumph of reason over the body.

For Socrates is for Montaigne the epitome of simplicity and naturalness of expression, like the peasantry in beleaguered France—most especially when facing death—so it is doubly unjust that he of all philosophers should be disfigured when the philosophy he figures (for Montaigne) is so simple and direct.

But fortunately there is Montaigne's figure in this time of monstrous may-hem and death sweeping France, where no man can be trusted and all wear masks. For by his own admission, his own bearing "is prepossessing both in itself and in the impression it makes . . . which is the very opposite of that made by Socrates."[7] And having dealt at length with Socrates's death and the natural simplicity with which he faced it, it might not appear so strange to us how, in this treatise on physiognomy, Montaigne should spend most of his time on death and, at the end, tell us that it is to physiognomy that he owes his several escapes from death.

Nothing is what it appears to be, everything is cause for suspicion, and it is this mimetological malevolence, the drug of civil war, that underlies this trea-tise on physiognomy, motivates it, bringing out the poignant and practical point that in such circumstance—and who has not faced it?—it is impossi-ble to defend oneself through discourse. Here the plea for physiognomy strikes home.

For there is no ground on which evidence can rest secure.

Except the face—the evidence that makes evidence possible, says Levinas.

For there are propitious physiognomies. "It has often happened to me," says Montaigne, "that, solely on the strength of my presence and my looks, people who have no knowledge of me have placed great confidence in me, either in regard to their own affairs or to mine."[8] And he thereby concludes this treatise on physiognomy with the following experiences.

Wanting to assault Montaigne and his household, a neighbor feigned a great panic, arriving precipitously on horse saying he was in flight from an at-tack by an old enemy a mile away. He was anxious about his men, and Mon-taigne tried to reassure him. Then came four or five of his soldiers with the same appearance of terror, and then still more soldiers, all equipped for bat-tle and refusing to dismount, saying the enemy was at their heels. Montaigne, not given to mistrust, courteously allowed them in. The neighbor saw that he was master of the situation, and now nothing remained but to carry out his plan, but—and here's the point—"he has often said since—for he has not been ashamed to tell the story—that my face and my open-heartedness had removed his treacherous intentions. He remounted his horse and his men, whose eyes were constantly fixed on him, to see what signal he would give them, were amazed to see him ride away and abandon his advantage."[9]

Another time Montaigne was abducted by fifteen to twenty masked men, seized, dismounted, robbed, and made prisoner. They were about to kill him because he refused to pay the ransom demanded, when an altogether unexpected change came over the leader. He ordered Montaigne's goods returned and that he be set free. Montaigne comments:

> Really, I do not know even now the true cause of this sudden change of mind and of conduct, due to no apparent motive, and of this miraculous repentance, at such a time, in an enterprise that had been deliberately planned, and was such as had become sanctified by custom. For I had frankly told them at the outset to what party I belonged and where it was I was going. The most prominent among them, who took off his mask and told me his name, repeated to me several times that I owed this deliverance to my face, to my freedom and firmness of speech, which showed me to be undeserving of such a misadventure. He asked me for an assurance that he would be similarly treated in like case. It is possible that the divine goodness chose to use this insignificant instrument [of my face and voice]; it saved me again the next day from still worse ambushes. . . . If my face did not answer for me, if men did not read the innocence of my intentions in my eyes and my voice, I should not have lived so long without quarrels and without hurt.[10]

I would like to make the following comment.

Both these facial incidents conclude a long and rambling treatise on physiognomy, concerned, so it seems, more with death and civil war, artifice and authority, than with physiognomy per se. What is more, the energy in this treatise is actually directed to unmasking and its subsequent effect. Both facial incidents explored by Montaigne have as their denouement a dramatic reversal involving unmasking and the subsequent pouring forth of a physiognomic plenitude—as when Montaigne suddenly suspects his neighbor's hidden intention (sees him as if he were wearing a mask) and at the same time persists with his open-faced courtesy, which, according to his would-be aggressor, had the effect of removing his treacherous intentions. In the second incident the abductor returns, takes off his mask, tells his name, and repeats several times that Montaigne owes his life to his face and to the freedom and firmness of his speech that showed him undeserving of such misadventure. So, is this a simple morality tale, of the evils of artifice and the virtues of nature, of honesty over duplicity?

I am forced to ask this because when you think about it Montaigne is far from being open-faced and "honest." For when the mask slips, so to speak, on his neighbor, Montaigne feigns to see nothing. His disposition to courtesy (not to mention survival) leads him to dishonesty, to keep a "straight face," and it is this masking on Montaigne's part, in response to the "masking" of his would-be aggressor, which ensures the "openness" that causes his would-be assailant to demask and later wax forth on the mysterious authority of physiognomics, by which, as Montaigne puts it early on in the treatise, concerning the injustice nature has perpetrated against Socrates, "there is nothing more probable than that the body conforms to and is related to the soul."

Montaigne feigns an openness so as to conceal his suspicions of the other's concealed intention; he feigns not knowing; and both men in their seeming not to know, know that the other knows—the capsule of the public secret—until the bubble bursts in what we might, with some exaggeration, call a riot of defacement, and revelation pours forth couched as proof of physiognomy. In another terminology, Montaigne is using his own face as mask precisely so as to preserve and even empower the window to his honest soul, while in the second incident the abductor is using the window (to Montaigne's soul) to preserve his mask and way of life as an abductor.

In the end we see that there is no face without another face and that the window needs its mask no less than the mask needs the other's window. In the end, then, this is what we have: "A face is a poor guarantee; nevertheless it deserves some consideration. And had I the scourging of sinners," continues Montaigne, "I should deal hardest with those who belie and betray the promises that nature has planted on their brows."[11]

Right here with this fantasy of scourging we sense the lust for physiognomics together with a sort of postphysiognomic depression, the damning recognition of masking taking advantage of just such lust. The bursting through of physiognomic plenitude comes with a recognition of physiognomic seduction. The face is the bubble of the public secret, both window to the soul and mask—"a poor guarantee; nevertheless it deserves some consideration."

STRIKE AND ZOOMORPHIC
PHYSIOGNOMICS

Montaigne's face drifts sometimes; to voice, to firmness of speech, to bearing, and to what, at the risk of disavowing the visual field altogether, we might call "presence," the presence a person evokes, that indefinable but causative quality that Montaigne and I myself value highly—a clear case, once again, of style triumphant over ethics. What then are we to make of the fact that physiognomy, that ancient science of reading the face, of reading insides from outsides, often connected the human face to the animal so as to perform its reading?

What's more, Sergei Eisenstein pointed out—*confessed* might be more appropriate—that far from dying out as Lavater's and Aristotle's defunct science, physiognomy was boosted by modernity, thanks to the invention of the camera and the movies, as with the famous "soliloquy of the silent language of the face" discovered by the close-up.[12] Eisenstein's point was that a defunct science was not necessarily a bad art, and in any event physiognomy was the natural practice of the filmmaker. Right or wrong, reading the face was here to stay as a type of irreducible folk wisdom of popular culture. So deeply ingrained is this, a veritable "instinct" and mad ambition, that the whole visual world could be thought of as "face" to be read for its inner "soul," as Benjamin suggests in some remarks on Soviet cinema. Even milieu and landscape, he mused, "reveal themselves most readily to those photographers who succeed in capturing their anonymous physiognomy, as it were presenting them at face value."[13] Thus the realism provided by the camera, modernity's boost to the mimetic faculty, turns out to be a mimesis mysteriously dependent upon and even controlled by ancient physiognomic prejudice, now honed to ever greater skills by the arts of cinema making *and viewing*, these everyday arts of reading the face, of defining the human, the inner being, not to mention the insalubrious arts of making through such reading racial and gendered types and subtypes, in short, the great cast of characters stalking the human stage in modern times.

As if by magic in Eisenstein's first film, *The Strike* (1924), the human faces of police spies are transformed one by one in front of our eyes into animal faces and back again into human ones. It is the power and magic of film that is proudly and lovingly displayed here, no less than the power of the state and the spies. (Which is greater? you ask.) Many of these spies have animal nicknames such as, "Fox," "Bulldog," "Monkey," and "Owl," and this is how they are introduced as the first line of attack against the strikers when the police chief pulls out from his right-hand desk drawer his spy-file consisting of photographic portraits of his agents. As their names are revealed, the photographs become animated, leaping ecstatically out of the frames of the portraits in the police file, ready for action. It is a tease, and many of us laugh, secure in the darkness, as these mischief makers spring to life, ever-so-sinister smiles wide across their faces as they hang up their hats on the borders of the picture frames from which they emerge, fuller than life. There is an inspired confusion here, delight in the magic of film as it merges with the magic of the state. But plainclothes cops are no joke.

Indeed, although it might seem that the movie is motivated by the need to preach the need for workers' organization, as the film's opening quote from Lenin grandly indicates, the more fundamental issue is with secrecy and spying on the part of the police and the captains of industry, state, and capital. Eyes and seeing are paramount here, as though this neophyte filmmaker cannot let go the ambitious claims often made for the camera as a technology of surveillance, but wonders how to turn this weapon against itself. This would be the supreme revolutionary act for the filmmaker, would it not? But this is the Soviet Union in 1924. The Revolution is over. The State is not likely to wither away any day soon, despite Lenin's vision that administration by men would give way to administration by things, despite Benjamin's curious perception that things now, thanks to the camera, had a face too. A film about a strike aimed at invigorating organization after the Revolution has a difficult task. For now the rebellious impulse has to be rechanneled into one obedient to authority. The last thing we want is a strike. Another reason, then, for sneakiness in the strike, the event filmed no less than in the film itself, with its underlying current of spying, secret seeing, and human–animal transformation, as the camera surreptitiously turns on the hand that feeds it.

Thus a mysterious aura "returns" with a vengeance, the auratic field of the human face, aglow with infinite possibility. Light catches reflections in the tilted eyeglasses of the mystery figure in the dark overcoat who presides over the animal–human transformations of the police spies. And the very last image of the film is not the dead and mutilated bodies of strikers scattered across the fields, but a pair of squinting eyes filling the screen. These images are of an almost desperate, yet sinister, act of seeing, an anxious seeing of seeing, as if these particular eyes were organs stretched on stalks, eyes that are more than eyes, like Selk'nam shamans' eyes, able to see through anything and kill (or cure) at the same time.

Central to the action, and in startling opposition to the offices of the police precinct and the bureaucratic spaces of the state, is a species of pet shop, a mysterious alchemical laboratory of zoomorphosis in whose shadowy debris of animal figures and junk predominates a live monkey encircled by a hoop suspended from the ceiling. The monkey plays in the hoop. The hoop rotates slowly, back and forth. Whenever there is a facial transformation from an animal into a human spy, thanks to the dissolving and montaging capacity of film, the hoop and the monkey swim briefly into focus as if to tell us something.

This hoop is the magical circle of transformation, of secrecy and fetish powers as released by the physiognomics of film.

This hoop is the human face.

It is the face of transformation—not of animals into men but of double-men, transforming men, whose metamorphosing capacities are established through zoomorphic physiognomics.

Why *double-men*?[14] What is the significance of this? Double-men change back and forth from animals into men, and from men into animals. They are the sign of prehistory, appropriated into the modern state by an "organization of mimesis" analogous to Eisenstein's conscious practice of physiognomy and the elaborated film theory that goes along with it.[15] Double-men would therefore also be what Durkheim told us to account for and never forget, namely the *"non-contractual* elements of contract," in other words human culture as the unstated context for Hobbes's and other contract theories accounting for the origin of the state and its monopoly of violence.[16] The animal "side" of the double-men surfaces from the repression achieved by the rationality of the state. Behind every bureaucrat lurks an alchemical hot line to prehistory. Witness *The Strike.* Think once again on the alchemical pet shop, starting with its unexpectedness. Why does it so suddenly pop up, just after we see the head cop pull out his photo file of operatives? Here the animal is "all the were-wolves who exist in the darkness of history and keep alive that fear without which there can be no rule—all these men keep alive the love-hate relation-ship with the body in its crudest and most direct form."[17] Werewolf (man-wolf), epitome of *double-men.* Then of course there's the softer, gentler side, as illustrated in Part I (see page 19) with Abby, the Chesapeake Bay retriever, sniffing drugs down there in Miami by the side of the baggage carousel. "I read people's eyes," her handler says.

Writing in exile in Hollywood in the early 1940's, in the shadow of the Holocaust, Max Horkheimer and T. W. Adorno suggested an argument built on earlier work by Adorno on "the idea of natural history," to the effect that the mimetic prowess inherent to some Other "prehistorical" time, was not so much annulled by Enlightenment (read "civilization") as repressed and re-configured to become a decisive element in culture and power in the modern world.[18] We have come across something like this argument before, fittingly at the "uttermost part of the world," namely Tierra del Fuego, with the con-cept of that Other time when women had the magic, the theater, and the spe-cial effects of the mimetic flux rampant as the world. And we have seen this formative idea again and again in the chapters I have devoted to exploration of unmasking from the Amazon across the Pacific to Africa. This also pretty much sums up Nietzsche's major concepts, the Dionysian life-affirming mimetic capability, cut short historically by what he called *ressentiment,* the cunning of the "weak," denying while at the same time appropriating the mimetic facility of "prehistory" and therewith determining the course of modern world history, its mores, its institutions, and above all its attachment to reality as depth and secret. If the Dionysian state alerts and intensifies the entire emotional system so "it discharges all its powers of representation, imitation, transfiguration, transmutation, every kind of mimicry and play-acting conjointly," if the essential thing in the Dionysian state "remains the facility of metamorphosis, the incapacity *not* to react," entering into every skin, then observe how, according to Nietzsche, this capacity is hijacked and turned against itself with the advance of Western civilization, with Christianity no less than with Plato, such that the mimetic faculty now becomes an instrument of deception in the struggle for power (in academic departments as in affairs of state), notable as "foresight, patience, dissimulation, great self-control, and all that is mimicry (this last includes a great part of what is called virtue)." This world-making revolution derived from the appropriation of mimesis is the same as what William Burroughs has in mind with his contrast between the Magical Universe and the One God Universe, which we can parse in many ways; Egypt as contrasted with Christianity via Judaism, the *nahual* as contrasted with the Mexican state, and of course Nietzsche's interpretation of the pre-Socratic philosophical systems of the sixth and fifth centuries B.C. in contrast to Plato and Christianity.[19] But let not the notion here of "contrast" deceive. For the enduring point is the *appropriation*—the "*organization* of mimesis"—built on repression. Hence the surge of the state's *double-men* surging from their photographic portraits as much as from prehistory to reconfigure the Dionysian love of mimicry as police agents in *The Strike* so as to "enter into every skin."

Indeed the very magic of the cinematic image lays claim to such a notion of prehistory. Christian Metz recalls the "myths of origin" of cinema (as if cinema itself was a primitive society) in Paris in 1895, when the first audiences—*so it is said*—fled from Lumière's film, *Grand Café*, when the train hurtled from the screen, mistaking the image for what the image was an image of.[20] Metz's point is that, true *or* not, fully conscious and put into speech *or* not, these stories of credulous, primitive, first spectators, are the necessary forerunners for us who come after, and it is thanks to the naive credulity of those first people that we are able to both have our cake and eat it, be credulous, like they supposedly were, thereby engaging with the image as if real, simultaneously canceling out that mimetic illusion and seeing it for what it is—mere cinematic illusion. This continuously enacted (dis)avowal is preeminently the logic of the fetish. We retain the magic of mimesis, in other words, by entertaining *and* transcending the story of those mistaken, first people—and it is supremely telling that, so as to provide the convincing parallel, the telling "detail" without which the argument might founder, Metz invokes ethnography of secret societies, citing accounts in which informants regularly declare that "long ago we used to believe in the masks, but now we realise they were adults in disguise."

In other words, he says (and he is right), those "primitive" societies have always "believed" in the masks, but have relegated the belief to a "long ago," adding that "they still believe in them, but always in the aorist tense." The word *aorist* is defined in the *Oxford English Dictionary* as a past tense denoting an occurrence, with no limitations, however, as to completion. We have had in these pages ample opportunity to consider such "aorism" as it affects belief in the masks—equivalent, so now we see, to belief in the cinematic image—and although Metz's reference fails to distinguish men from women as regards the play of the public secret in the ethnographic record, he is undoubtedly accurate, conceptually, when he invokes childhood as a supreme instantiation of the "long ago" when one really was duped by the masks, it being that very duping that "irrigates" the unbelief of today.[21] This irrigation he also calls a "denegation," reminding us once again of the negativity redoubled in the mimetic excessivity that (dis)establishes the real. Such "denegation" however, perturbs Metz's equation of childhood with the "long ago." For the "childhood" in question is surely not the location for belief in the masks and in the imaginary signifier. Rather, what is crucial here is the adult's imagination of the child's imagination.

This is saying a good deal more than "tradition is invented." For the point is not that such prehistory with its gusting transformative flux is invented or false, but that all signification requires such a fiction so as to secure the magic connecting signs to their referents. This, then, directs us to the role of the prehistoric in the primeval chaos of late capitalism, apt terrain for the disorganization of "the organization of mimesis," as we have recently come to learn, from the mountains of southern Mexico.

> A ruler wages continuous warfare against spontaneous and
> uncontrolled transformation. The weapon he uses in this fight is
> the process of unmasking, the exact opposite of transformation. . . .
> If it is practised often, the whole world shrinks.
>
> CANETTI, *Crowds and Power*[22]

Canetti got the waging of continuous warfare right. But he couldn't have been more wrong about the *effects of unmasking*. On Saturday, February 11, 1995, for instance, a year after the Zapatista uprising in the state of Chiapas, southern Mexico, on New Year's Day, 1994, the *New York Times* reported on the front page: *Mexico's New Offensive: Erasing Rebel's Mystique*. The continuation on page 6 was headlined *Offensive To Erase a Rebel's Mystique*, and the window inserted into the article read: UNMASKED HE'S A FURNITURE SALESMAN'S SON.

Yuck! exclaimed a young acquaintance of Alma Guillermoprieto in Mexico City on seeing the unmasked face. Before that she'd swoon at mere mention of his name.[23]

"Stripped of the myth that went with his ever-present mask . . . government officials said today that they hoped the disclosure of his identity would by itself help to break a rebel movement that has never been militarily strong," began the *New York Times*. "The moment that Marcos was identified and his photo shown and everyone saw who he was, much of his importance as a symbol vanished," one official said.

"Whether he is captured or not is incidental."

"It was like a game of peekaboo," wrote Alma Guillermoprieto who as a journalist was invited to the demasking. An official took an oversized slide of a ski mask with a pair of large dark eyes, in one hand, and a black-and-white

photo of a "milk-toast"-looking young man with a beard and large dark eyes, in the other. He then slipped the slide of the masked face over the photo of the unmasked face.

*Voilà!* Subcomandante Marcos! The idol is a Clark Kent! (Worse still, the son of a furniture salesman! So what is it that makes a salesman so tawdry here? Or is it the furniture?)

He kept superimposing and separating the two images, now you see it, now you don't, until the storm of camera flashes subsided.

That was Wednesday. By Sunday demonstrations had occurred, with thousands of people wearing the same ski masks as Subcomandante Marcos chanting, "We are all Marcos . . . ," and the Mexican press had received and published the first communiqué from Marcos since the unmasking. It bore his trademark, the postscripts he attached to his letters to the press, and was signed

*The* Sup *[subcomandante]*
*rearranging his ski mask with macabre flirtatiousness,*

such that in five short paragraphs, thought Alma Guillermoprieto, "the *Sup* reestablished his credentials as an outlaw hero, brought sex into the issue, and, yanking back the mask his pursuers had torn off, donned it once more."[24]

In its lead article two years later, announcing the massacre of forty-five Indians, supporters of the Zapatistas, by other Indians, supporters of the government, the *New York Times* confirmed her assessment, describing the Zapatista National Liberation Army as "made up mostly of Indian fighters led by a mysterious and charismatic non–Indian calling himself subcomandante Marcos."[25]

So, I want to ask here whether remasking the unmasked face returns us to the status quo ante, or whether, as seems more likely, some quite other force, a proliferating magical force amounting to a sort of hypermasking, consequent to and created by unmasking, takes over? For in Marcos's case, unmasking by the state, through the deployment of the photo on a driver's license or similar document, to dramatically reveal the real Marcos to the flashing lights of the photographic equipment of the media, seems to have totally backfired—a result anticipated by no one.

What's more, this effect was achieved and enhanced because it was the state itself, seen as the most masked entity of all possible masked beings to have ever crossed the threshold of the human imagination, that was the agent of the unmasking. It was common knowledge that around the conference table up there in San Cristóbal in Chiapas the representatives of the state were distinctly uncomfortable having to negotiate with masked beings.

"It's impossible!" they said.

"But the state is always masked," was the Zapatista response.

So the negotiations proceeded between the masked rebels—whom Alma G. and they themselves see as faceless—and the faceless bureaucrats of the state, whom the Zapatistas see as masked. There is a collective portrait of some of the negotiators in the form of a black-and-white photograph by Pedro Valtierra in February 1994.[26] Seated in two rows are nine figures, visible from the waist up. It is indeed a wonderful thing, that the only *un*masked faces, those of the government representative, Manuel Camacho Solís, no less than of the friendly bishop, Samuel Ruiz, do now appear as masked, the bishop's being the mask of principled Christ-like resignation, somewhat cynical, tough, and ready for the long haul: "I have seen it all," it says, and only the shadow of his glasses across the eye signals the tiniest possibility of the miracle, while the government representative's is too smooth by half, exactly midway between murder and seduction, openness and closure, a mask composed both of maskedness and of windowing of the soul, while all around, in various shades of blackness punctuated by the vivid whiteness of their eyes, cluster the somber shapes of the faceless Zapatistas.

These eyes glowing like stars in the night remind us of the obsession with truth and lies in the subcomandante's communiqués that, to all intents and purposes, constitute this strange new guerrilla phenomenon emerging from the heart of *nahual* territory in Central America, following a mere ten days of open combat begun New Year's Eve, 1994—*nahual* as related to the word for "disguise" in the Nahuatl Indian language, *nahual* as the animal or meteorological "familiar" or "co-essence" assigned a person at birth. Ethnographic studies in the 1950's and early 1960's tell us that in some Chiapas villages a powerful person, an elder or a curer or a sorcerer, may have as many as thirteen of these *nahuales*—ranging in power from terrestrial animals such as hens, dogs, cats, rams, horses, coyotes, monkeys, and tigers, to the far more powerful creatures of the air, butterflies, sparrow hawks, eagles, and, most powerful of all, thunderbolts of different colors, lightning, and whirlwind.[27] The most powerful live in the caves in the mountains above the village, together with the ghosts of the ancestors, to function as the village's "invisible government." In the darkness of night, with the permission of this invisible government, they can kill a sleeping person, appearing first in the sleeper's dream, because when asleep, one's soul leaves the body which is in a state resembling death.[28] It is then that the *nahual* of the sorcerer is active, luminous in the victim's dream. According to figures published in the mid 1960's, the homicide rate in Indian villages in Chiapas ranged between 36 to 250 per 100,000 people, compared with 5 per 100,000 for the United States and 32 for Mexico as a whole. In the great majority of cases the victim was an alleged sorcerer, despite the fact that it takes a lot of nerve to kill such a killer.[29] (Such figures are not commonly cited in current discussions of misery and political struggle in Mexico.)

Yet a *nahual* may also be used to cure and overcome misfortune, nevertheless representing "an utterly arbitrary and capricious destiny."[30] The concept of the *nahual* is confusing and we are advised to proceed with caution and not mistake the word for reality.[31] But how could such a concept not be confusing? For surely this is its point.

And what are we to make of the nature of the *transformation* between person and animal or, to put the question more accurately, of the double figure of person-animal represented by the *nahual*? To put it bluntly, How real is the *nahual*? The question weighs unbearably on anthropological theory of symbols and metaphorical reality. It is the question posed so tantalizingly by Canetti, "transformation" being in his eyes a capacity all humans possess and use, yet take for granted, not realizing that to it they owe what is best in themselves.[32] Does this mean Canetti regards *nahualism* as the human condition—reminiscent of Walter Benjamin's scary essay on the "mimetic faculty"? Here is how that essay begins:

> Nature creates similarities. One need only think of mimicry. The
> highest capacity for producing similarities, however, is man's. His gift
> of seeing resemblances is nothing other than a rudiment of the powerful

compulsion in former times to become and behave like something else. Perhaps there is none of his higher functions in which the mimetic faculty does not play a decisive role.[33]

This could be the ur-text of Zapatista masking as expressed in the *subcomandante*'s communiqués, no less than it provides a basis for William S. Burroughs's mockery of contemporary civilization, Burroughs of gravel voice and gay science who took *yagé* with the Indians of the upper Amazon in Colombia and Peru, and went on to envision the Magical Universe of the *nahual* as pitted against the One God Universe of instituted revolutionary parties and secret services of this, our modern world.[34] The most remarkable of his *nahuales* is Margaras the White Cat, the Tracker, the Hunter, the Killer, also known as the Stone Weasel, a total albino whose body hair is snow-white, his eyes pearly white disks that luminesce from within. "Having no color, he can take all colors. He has a thousand names and a thousand faces. . . . His eyebrows and eyelashes flare out, feeling for the scent. His ass and genital hairs are wired for a stunning shock or a poison deadly as the tentacles of the Sea Wasp." He is as old as they come, and thus all the more capable of knowing the new. "Margaras can follow a trail by the signs, the little signs any creature leaves behind by his passage, and he can follow a trail through a maze of computers. All top-secret files are open to him. The rich and the powerful of the earth, those who move behind the scenes, stand in deadly fear of his light."[35]

Like Roger Caillois's 1930's notion of a pure, distilled, mimetic force— "not similar to anything, just similar"[36]—Margaras is the point zero of mimesis, just light, an invasive silver light that wipes out other programs. "He can hide in snow and sunlight on white walls and clouds and rocks, he moves down windy streets with blown newspapers and shreds of music and silver paper in the wind."[37] This is *mana*, as defined in 1903 by Marcel Mauss and Henri Hubert in their study of magic, the term *mana* being derived from Melanesian and Polynesian languages, and taken by them to designate an extraordinary substance, invisible, marvelous, and spiritual, containing all efficacy and life. *Mana* was what Mauss and Hubert resurrected and appropriated from early Melanesian ethnography as the "answer" to the multitude of confusions and omissions in Enlightenment theories of magic. Frustrated with those theories, they asked that we turn to what they called (prior to Freud) a "pre-intellectualist psychology of man as a community."[38] *Mana* amounted to nothing less than "a fourth spatial dimension, . . . mobile and fluid, without having to stir itself." "It cannot be experienced," Mauss concluded gnomically, "since it truly absorbs all experience [and] is spread throughout the tangible world where it is both heterogeneous and ever immanent."[39]

The term *nahual* in Mexico and Central America, noted Mauss, not only corresponds to *mana*, but is there more intense and systematized (a sort of super-*mana*) "applied to all systems of religion and magic by referring to the whole as nagualism. . . . The sorcerer is *naual*—he is *naulli*; *naual* is his power to transform himself, his metamorphosis and his incarnation."[40] Etymologically, claimed Mauss, *nahual* means "secret science," and its different meanings connect to an "original meaning" of "thought and spirit," while in Nahuatl texts the word expresses the idea of being hidden, enveloped, and disguised.[41] Similarly, George Foster, citing sixteenth- and seventeenth-century sources, finds the idea of something hidden, veiled, disguised, cloaked, and masqueraded.[42]

What's more, there is an intimate connection of the *nahual* to astrology and fate. Foster's seventeenth-century source, Jacinto de la Serna, for example, described how a child acquired the name of the animal corresponding in the indigenous calendar books to the day of the child's birth, and "the child is subject to him so much that he can disguise himself in his figure." Moreover, the "animals are adored by men in order to convert themselves into their form," which Foster regards as a clue for understanding the changing history of the *nahual* under Spanish colonization and for shedding light on what he discerns as the otherwise confusing relationship between the animal as sign of fate, and the animal as that into which the sorcerer transforms.[43] Today despite the fact that Christian priests long ago destroyed the calendar books, throughout much of southern Mexico the child's animal "familiar" or "co-essence," as that which both indicates and determines the child's fate, is discerned from animal (or bird) tracks in ashes from the hearth spread around the house during the night following birth.[44]

Yet far from being a confusion between (1) the animal as sign of one's fate, and (2) the animal as that into which a person can be transformed, is it not always the case with magic that one dares to blend with fate *and* mimic it so as to acquire its power, and with that the power to master fate itself? What is transformation, if not mastery over fate's mastery?

It was always this way: the struggle to find a language and a relation between language and visual image that could effectively engage with the mag-

ical force of the secret felt to lie behind the play of surfaces—whether the secret be in the horoscope or in the sorcerer's malevolence. For us who are situated outside this language, the crucial question is the nature of the relationship.
"After questioning along these lines," reports the ethnographer Esther Hermitte in Chiapas in the early 1960's, "the Indian informants looked puzzled
and, often grinning, would plainly state that there is no need for any command [between person and *nahual*]; there is no communication between man
and his animal co-essence; there is physical proximity; man IS the animal."[45]
We take note of a most amazing literalness. And they are (often) grinning.

So, how much of the play with transformation in the guerrilla presence of the
Zapatistas is owed to this transforming figure of the *nahual*? Hard to say. The
region of eastern Chiapas, stretching down into the Lacandon Rain Forest,
where the Zapatista movement slowly gestated in the 1980's, was hardly "traditional." Instead of tightly organized indigenous communities stretching
back to the Spanish conquest, if not centuries before, it was a newly established open frontier, some forty years old at the most. This zone consisted of
Indian refugees fleeing religious persecution by members of those tightly organized communities, plus non-Indian poor colonists and wealthy ranchers,
together with an active Protestant church open to women and more demo-
cratic participation. This made for a novel and unstable sociological mix in
this phenomenally racist part of Mexico. Moreover, the Mexican state in
some ways must have been a big player here. To make a land claim, for instance, twenty-two different government groups and public agencies, requiring a twenty-seven-step process over almost two years was demanded. And
that was when the claim was unopposed.[46] Then in 1992, thanks to neoliberalism and the worldwide effort to open up previously protected economies to
the world market, the jewel in the Mexican constitution, its agrarian reform
laws, were revoked by the Salinas government—now exposed as one of the
more unsavory and corrupt governing bodies in recent memory. Small wonder that the Zapatista uprising was timed to occur at exactly the same moment as NAFTA, the North American Free Trade Agreement, became law
on New Year's Day, 1994. In other words, if we want an explanation of the
Zapatista movement, there is a political history of cause and effect here that
virtually speaks for itself, *provided we know the outcome*, the flamboyant and
shrewd Zapatista movement, *in advance*.

The Zapatista communiqués, however, speak also to another historical sensibility, a less chronologically ordered, less mechanistic, mode of interpreting and writing history. Here, without my having to resort to dubious claims as to an organic connection with "traditional" indigenous life-forms, the figure of the *nahual* is indeed apposite. Here, too, the past is read with advantage of hindsight, but the magic invoked is plainly there, in the very communiqués, for all to see, along with an unquenchable humor leaving no law intact.

There is the first major statement (of the 27th of January, in the fourth week of the uprising) entitled, "Chiapas: The Southeast in Two Winds, Torment and Prophecy." Combining mockery with pathos this goes way beyond the wildest Latin American "magical realism," dovetailing the format of a sixteenth-century conquistador's chronicle, with that of a current guidebook to Chiapas describing how rich is this land in petroleum, hydroelectric energy, lumber, coffee, cattle, and maize. Yet the people are poor, their children sick, and the environment wounded. The Viceroy, imaginary figure of the colonial order, falls into a troubled sleep. He hears voices carried in the winds of above and the winds of below. He dreams his empire is in ruins. His advisers tell him the problem lies with Indian witchcraft. He needs to kill and to build prisons.[47]

His advisors tell him . . . Indian witchcraft? A joke, no doubt. Between insomnia and nightmare the dream is remorseless. The Viceroy lies dead like a dreamer in an Indian village in Chiapas, whose soul has left, leaving the inert mass that is the body for the *nahual* to enter and look into its heart to do its mischief. It is an amazing image, this appropriation of indigenous theory of sorcery and dream in the sleeping body of the Viceroy, the body that is history collapsed into the body of the nation. All this lies before us, laid out like a corpse, into whose heart we, too, may peer and, who knows, thereby be transformed? But what of the two winds, wind as in whirlwinds, thunderbolts and lightning, eagles and sparrow hawks, the most powerful *nahual*s? The story is far from complete.

In fact, states the communiqué, *the entire country* is dreaming this dream of the Viceroy. "Now is the moment to awake!"

To wake from the dream? As in a fairy-tale? As in Walter Benjamin's image of revolution, too, borrowing from the young Karl Marx? For there it stood as epigraph in Benjamin's file of notes to himself in the 1930's concerning theories of progress and theories of knowledge, the quote from Marx's letter to Arnold Ruge, September 1843:[48] "The reformation of consciousness lies solely in our waking the world . . . from its dream about itself."[49]

"Waking" was also taken by Benjamin from Proust, the reference being that magically-swift and no less unexpected restoration, visceral in tone, of a memory otherwise lost to will and consciousness, the *mémoire involontaire* which Samuel Beckett took to be an experience communicating an *extratemporal presence*. It therefore follows, thought Beckett, that "the communicant is for the moment an extratemporal being," and that the recurrence of the past here amounts to a participation between the ideal and the real, imagination and direct apprehension, symbol with substance.[50] We recall the face of the ethnologist's informants in Chiapas. Man IS the animal, they explained. The *nahual*. The participation. The smile. And we also recall that "Other time" in Tierra del Fuego, the time of matriarchy and flux between man and animal, stars and winds, like the sudden recognition and hence repetition of Metz's "long ago" of the imaginary (cinematic) signifier—*man Is the animal*—prehistoric worlds activated by current exigency harnessed to postmodern rites of electronic mail emitted from the mountains of southern Mexico.

And what is crucial to "waking" as revolutionary force in the modern world is its blending of prehistoricity with a sudden awareness as to the bizarre, unmasked face of the real, pitching one into a future. For Benjamin this sense of prehistoricity lay as commitment in the writer's crafting of what he had come to call the "dialectical image," whose goal was, precisely, to awaken the reader to that moment of recognition "in which," as he put it, "things put on their true—surrealist—face."[51] Waking *is* unmasking, revealing the surreal nature of the real. This is the writer's polar star, this, the "profane illumination."

As for unmasking, its effects were laid out early in the game, barely three weeks into the struggle, in the communiqué of January 20, when this newcomer to the scene, signing off as the "Subcomandante Insurgente Marcos," sent out a communiqué with an epilogue entitled "On Ski Masks and Other Masks." (The masks worn by the Zapatista rebels in Chiapas, you recall, are ski masks.)

"Why is there such a commotion about the ski masks?" he asked. "Isn't Mexican political culture itself a 'culture of masks'"? Yet, he warned, as if answering his own question, if Mexican society took off its mask, it would understand that the image it has been sold of itself is false, and the reality is a good deal more terrifying than was ever supposed. He warms to his theme. A veritable duel. A game like the one of peekaboo witnessed by Alma Guillermoprieto when the *Sup* was unmasked. *Unmasked he's a furniture salesman's son*, screamed the headline. But, I ask myself, is it appropriate to call these life-and-death matters a *game*?

"Let either one of us unmask," he suggests, "but the big difference is that the '*Sup* Marcos' always knew what his face was, while Mexican society will only be awakening from the long sound sleep that modernity has imposed on it at the cost of everyone and everything."

He repeats the challenge—and you can almost see him smiling behind his mask. Indeed, his mask is not unlike the smile on the informant's face explaining to the ethnologist that the *nahual* IS the man. The smile takes over the face and swarms across reality itself, like the Cheshire Cat in *Alice in Wonderland*. ("I've often see a cat without a grin," thought Alice; "but a grin without a cat!"[52])

"The '*Sup* Marcos' is ready to take off his mask," states the Masked Man.

"But is Mexican society ready to take off its mask?"

"Don't forget to tune in to the next exciting episode of this story of masks and faces, this story that affirms and denies itself in the telling (if the warplanes, helicopters, and green and olive masks allow)."[53] A grin without cat, that's for sure.

At times, death and ghosts take the place of laughter. But the tantalizing presence generated by facelessness remains. *Los sin rostro*, the faceless ones. They diffuse through the communiqués, infinite in number, like Canetti's invisible crowd of the dead. They crowd the texts, crowding truth, crowding secrecy, into a corner. *Los sin rostro.* . . . A contagion of defacement more magical than any *nahual* = being hidden, enveloped, disguised, veiled, cloaked, hiding "in snow and sunlight on white walls and clouds and rocks," moving "down windy streets with blown newspapers and shreds of music and silver paper in the wind." Thus Margaras. The cat. This is *mana*, "mobile and fluid, without having to stir itself . . . spread throughout the tangible world where it is both heterogeneous and ever immanent."[54] The masquerade. Secrecy is the obsession. Truth is the obsession. How to speak it, even more than what it is. Witness the subcomandante's delight with the language, "mobile and fluid, without having to stir itself." Language as *mana*. Postscripts as *mana*.

This is a political movement that has transformed the notion of the political. It garners energy from masquerade, no less than did Montaigne adrift in a world of flux and deception in which nothing is what it appears to be; Montaigne meditating on physiognomy and the propriety of quoting and hence using, if not abusing, the authority of the ancients—such as Socrates, the beauty of his soul, the wretchedness of his face—not to mention admirable lessons to be learned from the way the French peasant faces death; Montaigne resigned to the impossibility of verbal defense in this culture of innuendo and mimetological malevolence. *And who has not faced it?* Here the plea for physiognomy strikes home.

For there is no ground on which evidence can rest secure.

Except the face—the evidence that makes evidence possible, says Levinas.

For there are propitious physiognomies.

Or, better still (as Montaigne's stories also instruct), become faceless and with that become animal, become multiple, *los sin rostro*, those who are the mountains, luminous in the dead body of the sleeper that is the nation-state that is the public secret that is *México tapado*. And not only Mexico. It is the mad dream of a revolutionary *nahual*—and so far it's done pretty good.

Erased from the Zapatista communiqués is all the bitterness and malignant sorcery of Indian and colonist communities turning with fear against the witch within. Erased, too, is the slightest hint of the malignancy of envy as the driving force of sorcery and what *that* might imply for a theory of justice and revolution and what shape the good society should have. Nor is there any mention of violence and rivalry between indigenous communities. Of these things there is little mention. Instead, death in the communiqués is the death whose dangerous powers, in the hands of the ancestors and the elderly, curers and sorcerers, becomes more like the death-kitsch to be found in the protocols of remembrance of nation-states, or else it is the death of public health statistics of children dying from malnutrition due to racism and other forms of exploitation, understandable and preventable deaths far removed from the unseemly act of murder of a fellow villager accused of sorcery. Here Marcos seems unable to tackle head-on the contradictions and war of stereotypes that such an admission to the outside world would involve, an admission that

would open the floodgates to a complexity overwhelming most of his readers. This seems to be the secret which even the masked ones falter to trans-
mit on their web page. Yet might not its secretive presence empower their determination to transform these Indian notions of transformation, using the
transforming power of secrecy to manifest the sorcery and *nahualism* at work
in national and international politics at the end of the twentieth century?

For the undoubted lesson is that sorcery and the *nahual* offer us a refreshingly
different way of relating to death and to the magic of transformation in the
secrecy that is, as Canetti remorselessly emphasized, and we all know too
well, so defining a power in modern politics. We have to reach "back" to a
virtual "prehistory" of sorcery and human-animal doubles to make sense of
such power in our midst. For me, this is the meaning in the photograph I described above of the masked figures negotiating with the state in San Cristóbal, mediated by the bishop. And just as it was pointed out that "the state is
always masked," so let me add that the state has always appropriated the powers of the *nahual*, and sorcery, too, attempting therewith to control transformation (as Canetti warns), and appropriate becomings (as Deleuze and Guattari point out), "in order to break them, reduce them to relations of totemic
or symbolic correspondences."[55] Hence the move from a mimetic to a metaphoric reality, from the smiling man *is* the animal, to the poetic reality, man
is *like* the animal, and especially man *has* the animal. "The use of the verb 'to
have' applied to *nahuals* is wrong. The Pinola Indian very seldom will express
in that way. To him man IS bull, ram, or horse."[56] But the appropriation of
the *nahual* war machine by the state war machine is inevitable. Every *nahual*
knows that and lives in that tension; appropriation, succeeded by reappropri-
ation. As in the photograph of the masked rebels, who see themselves as faceless, and the faceless bureaucrat, whom the rebels see as masked. Just the
whites of the eyes like stars scattered as an arch over the representative of the
state, the most masked entity of all possible beings to have ever crossed the
threshold of the human imagination. Up there in San Cristóbal. Window to
the soul, or mask? Which is which? "Our dead," it says in the communiqué,
"who are also the faceless ones who are the mountains who walk through the
night, declare . . . "[57] Always, so it seems, we turn to the living image of defacement, facelessness as prelude necessary to speech, certainly its postscript.
The *sub* of the *subcomandante*.

> The talent for transformation which has given man so much power
> over all other creatures has as yet scarcely been considered or begun
> to be understood. Though everyone possesses it, uses it and takes it
> for granted, yet it is one of the great mysteries and few are aware that
> to it they owe what is best in themselves.
>
> C A N E T T I,   *Crowds and Power* [58]

Crucial to the backfiring of the state's attempt at unmasking, was the role played by *refacement* as the state attempted to exercise its prohibition on transformation and becomings. By "refacement" I mean to draw attention to a ghosted return as a recuperation of surface, an inspired labor of the negative that does not so much reinstall the status quo as perturb it, the refaced face thus being the face of transgression, a defaced face, we could say, site of sacrilege animating the thing-world.

In the case of the figurehead from the mountains of southern Mexico, "refacement" refers to the remasking of the visage previously unmasked by the state in its attempt to dispel the mystique of the mask. But what the state didn't figure, and perhaps what most of us were previously blind to, is how such mystique can be created by just such an attempt at erasure of mystery through unmasking. The slightest knowledge of rites of unmasking in so-called primitive societies, such as the Selk'nam or Yamana, however, would have been enough to raise doubts about this hubris of "enlightenment" and, what is more, about the older metaphors of biblical and Platonic "revelation" on which such enlightening depends.

Now the state, of course, uses refacement in order to unmask, as with the police use of the "identikit." Here is an example, the case of the notorious Unabomber, a splendid yet nevertheless thought-provoking example, you will surely agree, of the roller-coastering proliferation of excess, thanks to un-

masking as refacement, laboring the negativity of the public secret of the Arab terrorist loose in our midst.

But what I want to draw attention to is another (perhaps related) dimension of refacement as that which occurs in *the history of reading*.

At first the child is read to, then as it gets older come the picture books, the captions slowly extending over the page to become a pictureless book, until

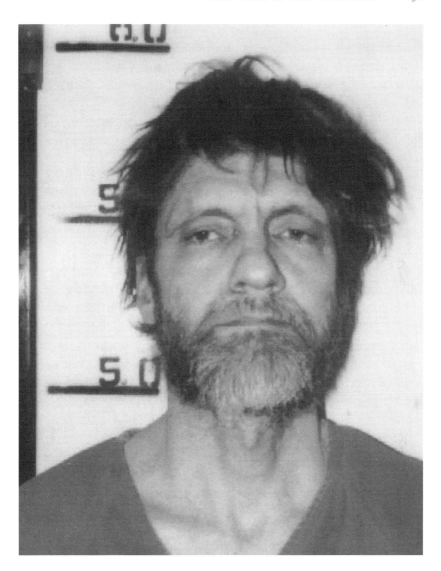

that day when the child, now pretty well ensconced in reading, suddenly con-
fronts a picture in the midst of the text, a depiction of the written. There is
often a shock and a special sadness at this moment, surely decisive to the history of the image and its relationship to the body and to bodily transformation, similar to seeing the movie after reading the book, and my assessment of
this moment, paradoxical as it may sound, is that it amounts to one of the first

and most profound indications of both prohibition of transformation *and* of possibilities for transformation, whereby the facelessness of the roving imagination is brought to stillness and shock by the graven image.

I wonder if we might generate insight into that omnivorous reader, Walter Benjamin, if we figure him, in our imagination, of course, as occupying precisely this history of this moment of refacement, where word and image come abruptly to rest, the shock propelling, the sadness restraining, such that masks and allegorical delights (as in his study of the Baroque *Trauerspiel*) could clinch, thereby, all the more securely with the profane illumination of the fetish of commodities he labored so long and well to craft? Be that as it may, refacement per unmasking would seem to have just this sort of potential given in the dialectic at a standstill for reconfiguring faciality as defacement.

For my understanding is that with refacement, as in my fictitious "history of reading," with this upsurge of the image in the midst of the text, most especially the image of the face, the smooth flow between word and referent is disjointed as the work of reading is reconfigured by what Benjamin called *allegory*, in which shock and sadness play a preeminent role. "Allegories become dated," he observed, "because it is part of their nature to shock. If the object becomes allegorical under the gaze of melancholy, if melancholy causes life to flow out of it and it remains behind dead, but eternally secure, then it is exposed to the allegorist, it is unconditionally in his power . . . a key to the realm of hidden knowledge."[59] It would be hard to imagine a face more dead from which life has been sucked than photo-ID state certifying portraits, in general, or the refacing photograph used to unmask the subcomandante, in particular. (We recall the distaste of Alma G.'s niece and the "milk toast" epithet, a white face of death, even a ghost?)

So, could the face, as both window and mask, ur-border and mother of all borders, be *allegory*, thus defined? Or at least this face, masked, then unmasked, and masked once again? And being masked once again—"yanking back the mask his pursuers had torn off"—*seems now strangely different to the first time around*, restless for a home, just about any home, it would seem, yet open to the winds of exposure and the mysteries of hidden innernesses. How we choose or are forced to cross and recross this border between the window to the soul that is also its mask will determine the intensity of its allegorical proclivities, the more so the more Baroque the political warfare. For an object that has become allegorical, advises Benjamin, is "incapable of emanating any meaning or significance of its own; such significance as it has, it acquires from the allegorist. He places it within it and stands behind it; not in a psychological but in an ontological sense . . . and it becomes for him a key to the realm of hidden knowledge."[60] This is what I assume to be the magical advantage of defacement handed to the subcomandante on a platter by the Mexican state. Welcome to your defacement and double welcome to your refaced face as the key in the hands of the allegorist.

Hence unmasking leads in my account to a certain refacement, but hardly the face we once knew. Something new has emerged. A mystery has been reinvigorated, not dissipated, and this new face has the properties of an allegorical emblem, complete with its recent history of death and shock, which gives it this strange property of "opening out."

Although Benjamin directs us to the caption of words the allegorist places below the image, whereas, for me, in my "history of reading," refacement is the placing of the image, notably the face, amidst the words that form the text, the outcome of these two procedures is the same. They converge when we consider that words come from the mouth (the *Trauerspiel* was, after all, *theater*), and it is a fact that speech in such plays has been compared to old paintings in which scrolls of writing emerge from the mouths of persons.[61] In that case the words come from the mouth; while in my "history of reading," the mouth and the face around it, emerge suddenly as pictorial illustration from the words.

In either case it would be an enormous error, as Benjamin counsels with regards to the scrolls, to see in these picturings a sudden freeze and cessation of movement. On the contrary, he detects not just movement in the static image with words pouring out the mouth, but an irregularity of movement that he calls an "irregular rhythm of the constant pause, the sudden change of direction, and consolidation into a new rigidity."[62] And it is precisely this irregularity which, in my opinion, characterizes refacement. The configuration of words to picture here has, Benjamin suggests, the same function as light has in a Baroque painting. "It is a flash of light in the entangling darkness of allegory."[63]

And here we cannot overlook the privileged function of *postscript* in the subcomandante's letters that emerge from his masked mouth as living but written speech to the people at large. For the postscript here is the same as the allegorical maxim or scroll. Moreover, there is something endearing, even magical, about the postscript. "In the letters I get from her," says Breton's

Nadja about her mother's letters, "what touches me most, what I'd give all the rest for, is the postscript." And of course Nadja was the serendipitous Event, a veritable postscript herself—"from which each of us is entitled to expect the revelation of one's life and meaning."[64]

"What I'd give all the rest for . . . " As if the corpus of the text could be traded in for its postscript in a continuous process of deferral. And at one point, in a further postscript from the mountains, the subcomandante suggests that a postscript is nothing more (and nothing less) than a letter in disguise—a masked letter, we might say.[65] It is clear, too, that the flamboyant use of the postscript indicates not so much "second thoughts" as continuous reconstruction elegantly staged as staggered and permanent incompleteness, as if reality is most heartfeltly always lagging behind its representability, and truth must never tire of the disguises with which power renders representation, very much including the representation of *that*. (In the first usage of the postscript, in the letter of February 6, 1994, there are, for instance, seven postscripts, each one referring to postscripture.[66]) It is also worth noting that, to my knowledge, neither video nor audiotaping amount to anything more than a small fraction of the representation of either the subcomandante's or the Zapatistas' presence. What we who live outside of certain small areas in Chiapas have beamed at us are *written words*—and *photos, by the score, of masked persons.* Indeed there is a striking photogenicity here; the more masked the reality, the more striking the drama and even the beauty of the photography, as if the masked face, here at least, is divinely preordained for the camera.

The subcomandante's writing exerts the presence of spoken speech, but of necessity has to be written so as to maintain the secrecy of the location and movement of guerrilla fighters. Indeed the more written it is, the more it comes across as living speech, but fractured on account of radical opposition to the state (the great force, of course, behind the Baroque). Thus in these conditions the more written it is, the more it is like living speech conveying presence, notably the presence of the person hidden behind the words behind the mask. And although addressed to the people at large, indeed, to the world, it is an intimate voice, as so easily obtained in the latitudes of familiarity the letter form allows.

This way of thinking the masked face, accentuated by its being unmasked, then remasked, as happened with the Mexican state working over the masked image of what must stand as one of its most talented Baroque antagonists in many a year, brings to mind the fearsomely magical force Giles Deleuze and Felix Guattari with such aplomb claimed for *defacialization* as the fast track to transformation, becoming clandestine and imperceptible, through quite special spiritual "becomings-animal"—and as such takes us back to the magical animation achieved by the defacement of statues described at the beginning of this book, no less than into the curious world opened up by Sergei Eisenstein's political state of double-men with animal heads, and to Roger Caillois, where the latter draws attention to a form of delirium and mimetic excess in which the subject "is not similar to something, but just *similar*," inventing spaces of which she or he is "the convulsive possession."[67]

Of all such invented spaces, does not pride of place have to go to the human face? And is not this seduction by space painfully similar to what Benjamin emphasizes as a major trope in the Baroque, the spatialization of tragedy "in which the events of history shrivel up and become absorbed in the setting," such that "everything about history that, from the very beginning has been untimely, sorrowful, unsuccessful, is expressed in a face—or rather in a death's head."[68] For Mexico, certainly, and to some degree the entire New World, this *setting* into which history shrivels must be Chiapas itself, expressed in the convulsions of the face that is the subcomandante's mask and postscript.

# UNMASKING AND PROLIFERATION

Everyone, including the *Sup* tears off their ski masks and faces . . .

Alma Guillermoprieto has characterized the postscript as the subcomandante's contribution to epistolary art. "Now swaggering, now full of righteous fury, now impudent and hip, the Marcos of the postscripts is at all times both elusive and intimate, and this seductive knack has allowed him to become a faceless stand-in for all the oppressed."[69] What is so wonderful here is that being "faceless" in this way is not so much being without a face as it is a reorganization of faciality creating a new type of face, collective and mysterious, wherein body and face coalesce. This type of face reconfigures the masquerade of history that is the public secret—that which is known but cannot be stated, of the face as both mask and window to the soul—such that there is a type of "release" of the fetish powers of the face in a proliferation of fantasy and of identities, no less than of the very notion of identity itself, a discharge of the powers of representation.

"Now the afternoon has followed the last of the journalists," begins yet another of the subcomandante's postscripts, this one in a communiqué transmitted just *before* the drama of the Convención Nacional Democrática staged by the Zapatistas in August 1994 at what they call Aguascalientes in the forested heart of their territory in Chiapas.

It continues (the subcomandante being known as the *Sup*, for short):

When they are alone, the *Sup* makes a sign. . . . Everyone, including the *Sup* tears off their ski masks and their faces. A multitude of fierce-

looking sailors appears, the *Sup* has a patch on his right eye and begins to
limp ostentatiously on his wooden leg. . . . The awning [of the convention in the jungle] is in reality a sail, the benches oars, the hill the hull
of a mighty vessel, while the stage becomes the bridge. . . . "Aguascalientes" unveils itself—*se devela y se revela*—a pirate ship, solitary and
magnificent, it begins its voyage into the night until the day following,
skull and crossbones fluttering.

There has to be order on the deck. I order that the helmsman be
thrown to the sharks. No one listens to me. I cut the throat of the first
sailor I find handy. The ship is foundering. I take the helm [and] at last
the ship seems to straighten its course and return to the bay that my
hopelessness brought us out of this dawn. . . .

Now I am a pirate. A pirate is tenderness that explodes in fury, is
justice that has not yet been understood, is disconsolate love, is a sad
battle and shared solitude, is an eternal navigating toward no port, is
perennial torment, is a stolen kiss, is always unsatisfied possession, is
no rest.

And he signs the letter:

Pirate without bearings
professional of hope
transgressor of injustice
robber of sighs
owner of the night
lord of the Mountain
man without face and with no tomorrow[70]

While in the next communiqué, five days later, the author refers to Aguascalientes as, amongst other things, "Fitzcarraldo's boat of the forest, the delirium of Neo-Zapatism, the pirate vessel."[71]

Everything seems to hinge not on the mask but on unmasking. *Everyone,
including the* Sup *tears off their ski masks and their faces.* When the state did the
unmasking, the mask became even more of a mask. It spread through society,
it became collective ("We are all Marcos"), and the appearance of depth and
mystery it created became even deeper. But when the Zapatistas do it to
themselves, tearing off the mask becomes like defacing-sport, exercises in
metamorphosis and the generation of *mana.*

It is also a Nietzschean and surrealist defacement of Marxist tradition from
within. The promise of depth gives way to exuberant teasing of that promise

"that Nietzsche never stopped maintaining"—that depth is "an absolutely superficial secret." Foucault continues in the best *nahual* mode: "The eagle's taking flight, the ascent of the mountain, all the verticality so important to Zarathustra, is, in the strict sense, the reversal of depth, the discovery that depth was only a game, and a crease in the surface."[72]

Side by side with real guns and real privation, this real play in the communiqués from the southeast of Mexico seems first and foremost out to take the macho violence out of revolutionary metaphysics too. The romantic hyperbole achieves this no less than the terrible seriousness with which we are enjoined to be mad. Ever vigilant to the claims of common sense and its staple utilitarianism, the *Sup* warns against readings of Don Quixote, for instance, which see the noble knight as a lapsed fool, a man who learned the error of his silly ways and returned to the plow. "This is what we have to avoid," advises the masked one. "Instead we have to maintain our madness till the end. The windmills of Quijote were the helicopters of Godínez Bravo."[73]

Real surrealism, too, New York City and Porteño variety, alongside real guns. In swift response to the accusation that the Zapatistas are financed by foreign powers, the communiqué of July 10, 1994, reminds us (in its third postscript) that in his story "Elephants, Ants, and Revolutions" Julio Cortázar reminds us that Marcel Duchamp claimed that elephants are contagious, to which Cortázar added that revolutions are contagious too. To which the *Sup* appends his own thoughts regarding the patient labor of ants consuming his modest living quarters, hidden in revolutionary tension there in the forest. His medical advisers want to destroy them. They are unhygienic. Just as revolutions are for neoliberalism, notes the *Sup*, who against the advice of the experts, approves of the ants. Perhaps they remind him of the Zapatistas? In any event he thinks peaceful coexistence with ants is called for and he suspects there is a secret between ants and elephants, whose astonishing shape and size remind him how much nature imitates art—hardly the sentiments of a social scientist, let alone an attitude congenial to a Marxist determinism. He suspects that those large floppy ears provide good hiding places for ants under siege, just as the ants diligently dig huge subterranean galleries for elephants when they are in trouble, as when they break away from their pickets at the circus and ravage the sugar candy.

And in meditating upon the contagious nature of elephants, ants, and revolutions, the postscript points out that this fable of Cortázar's is a story for children masked as adults, no less than it is a story for adults masked as children (*un cuento para niños disfrazados de adultos y para adultos disfrazados de niños*).[74] Thus what is exposed and set to work here is that enchanting element which no power—whether of the state or of revolution—can do without, namely the adult's imagination of the child's or, as Cortázar puts it, "a story for children masked as adults, no less than a story for adults masked as children." It's as if their very masks indicate a secret pact between adult and child, a pact no less necessary for the story to function than the persons addressed by it. And if this elusive child-adult hybrid, reflecting the Other's reflection, lies within the magic of the state, its banality and vulgarity no less than its grandeur, such a hybrid is no less capable of appreciating the absurd when, as with the contagion of elephants and revolution, nature imitates art—the very formula of the mimetic faculty as the nature that culture uses to create second nature. If revolution necessitates awareness as to the artificial quality of culture—that culture is a social construction, as current cliché would have it—then this must also involve a creative confrontation with the public secret that reality is really made up, that social life poses as natural so we can "get along" with our everyday lives. Surely, if the *Sup*'s communiqués mean anything, it is this? So, as with elephants, so for social action and revolution too. We expect nothing less than subterranean ant galleries and hidden recesses behind those ears turning secrecy itself inside out in sweet paroxysms of acoustic hypertrophy.

The *Sup*'s appreciation of the adult's imagination of the child's imagination seems boundless. This was brought home with remarkable finesse in a scandal that broke on March 10, 1999, embarrassing the U.S. National Endowment for the Arts. The Endowment had given a modest grant of $15,000 to Cinco Puntos Press in El Paso, Texas, to publish what journalists called an eye-catching bilingual Spanish and English book for children called *The Story of Colors*. It turns out to have been written by none other than the Subcomandante, whose picture appears, masked as usual, inside the back flap.

Elephantine, too, are these massive postscripts in relation to the tiny antlike body of the letter that is the communiqué. Does this mean that here, too, the postscript form, as much as the revolution, provides evidence as to how nature imitates art? The communiqué, in which the rebels tear off their masks and therewith their faces, for example, consists merely of one short paragraph of four lines. But its pirate postscript is three pages long! The postscript has, as it were, boarded the vessel of the letter and made off with it.

As for the body or the vessel of the communiqué itself, these pathetic four lines, they are no less tender than the pirate exploding in fury, no less mocking of the form itself. For like all the others, this communiqué is a burlesque of the paperwork of officialdom. "Today there is no communiqué," it begins. "I am just writing so those who can't make it to the delirium of the Neo-Zapatista Convention won't feel sad and abandoned." So this communiqué that is not a communiqué plunges us into the mysteries of social forms of address and control as it wavers between the letter, as bureaucratic communication—"everything must be in writing!"—and the letter as heartfelt personal form expressing secrets and emotion between two people, a bond too precious for speech alone.

What's more, this communiqué that is not a communiqué is dispatched *before* the convention in the jungle has begun, but its postscript evokes the timeless time just *after* the convention has ended. The "postscript" is not merely elephantine sizewise in relation to the "script" it *follows*, but is *ahead* of it, timewise, suggesting that all script is prescribed by the rolling aftermath of its language.

"How can one tell what in reality is hidden by Aguascalientes?" begins the postscript written ahead of time for these stay-at-homes like most of us so we won't feel left out of being let in. So right from its start, we sense the event of Aguascalientes is a mask being caressed by its wearer, pulling it aside in order to replace and hence reface it. "Now," it continues, "the afternoon has followed the last of the journalists . . . " The hand of the writer who has to stay behind lies outstretched to this straggling column of other writers winding their way into the night back to the city, leaving the mud churned under the first faint star. This is the timeless time of defacement, an expanding space wherein everyone tears off their mask *and therewith their face.* How could it be otherwise? Midday. Moment of the shortest shadow.

So the *mask* has led us away from concealed depths to the open stage of *theater*, in this strange new brand of revolutionary warfare undreamed of by previous generations of armed-struggle strategists from Lenin to Mao, from Che to the ultimate disillusion some twenty years after his ignominious capture and assassination in 1967. *¡Venceremos! Patria o Muerte!* Could there be anything sillier, more absurd, more sad? Beyond parody?. *Power comes from the barrel of a gun* was the sentiment in those days, not *defacement*. Of course all this gun-stuff has its own brand of theater and guile too, not to mention the occasional laugh. Witness this bumper sticker provided by the NRA-friendly Ulster County Sportsman's Association for the car in front of me at the supermarket parking lot, upstate:

> Kids who hunt, trap, and fish
> do not mug little old ladies

Looking to more autochthonous peasant revolt than achieved by Che, we note that neither Emiliano Zapata, the namesake of the contemporary Zapatistas, nor his followers in the Mexican revolution of the second decade of this century, felt the need to wear the mask or indulge in such theater. That was, I guess, a less self-conscious epoch. It was left to the nostalgic sentiments of succeeding generations to theatricalize their image and suffer through the intense image-making realities of institutionalized revolutionary parties and politics for the remainder of the century.

Doubtless the mask was adopted by the contemporary Zapatistas in response to the growing awareness of this new theatrical need of postmodern politics—and not only because, as the subcomandante said, he and many of the other guerrilla fighters were so ugly. And nothing would more miss the point than the claim that the mask is a utilitarian device for thwarting police identification. That would be to miss the potential for reconfiguration of the face with the body and therewith the reconfiguration of reality with fantasy—most especially concerning transformation and the proliferation of identities, including the identity of the nation-state. "I would like to focus on what I find most revealing," writes the Mexican intellectual, Roger Bartra, "the question of how it was possible for a war that only lasted ten days to so radically change the political culture of Mexico."[75]

You could sense the disposition for theatricality in unmasking in the very design of the amphitheater, beginning with the grandeur of its absurdity. To Alma Guillermoprieto it was a wonder. The proscenium was large enough for a military parade with a makeshift podium the size of the one in the

Chamber of Deputies in Mexico City. Not only was there a parking lot, but there was also an area designated for assassination attempts. And the hill around the theater, she wrote, had the exact contours of a Mayan pyramid (of which there are striking examples close by in the Chiapas forests).[76] In the black-and-white photograph taken by Paula Haro from the stage area, looking out at the sea of empty chairs and benches contouring the hillside in their regular rows, there is a huge white cloth draped over the upper third of the amphitheater.[77] Hung from a high wire stretched from the hilltop, uppermost folds draped over the hill from which it emerges, it has the striking profile of a church steeple. Or is it a circus tent? Tiny dark figures hover underneath.

This, then, is the mighty "sail" that, as energizing element for the transformation to the pirate ship of fools, bears an excruciatingly close relation to the mask. For as the white cloth floating majestically overhead becomes the sail, the *vela*, so the amphitheater is then *unveiled—se devela, se revela*—as a pirate vessel. Unveiling has led to and is part of the process of transformation, just as revolution is always about such fundamental transformations. Veil and sail. Sailing and unveiling. Gliding over uncharted space, unmasking means transformation.

There is no agency. It just happens, as the reflexive form of the language shows. *Se devela, se revela.* It just happens, as if Being itself hiccuped. Yet this transformation must be the consequence of a tearing, a tearing of tegument, as when plainly it is said, *Everyone, including the* Sup *tears off their ski masks and their faces.* Now we are in a thicket of tearing wherein *unmasking and deface-ment merge.*

As the deserted amphitheater is transformed into a pirate vessel, the *Sup* himself passes out of existence. Now he is the "ex-*Sup*," disappeared along with the tearing off of his mask which is his face, this man with no face, as the postscripts never tire of telling us. By virtue of this ex-ness, the unmasked *Sup* now speaks to us in the first person. Or rather, he murmurs to himself and perhaps we too are listening to ourselves, lost in thought, caught up in what he calls the delirium. "Now it's coming, the sea from the night. Now comes the wind. Now the cycle of fate is complete and we recommence our journey." ("Prohibitions on transformation are a social and religious phenom-enon of the greatest importance, which have never been properly considered and certainly never understood," writes Canetti in *Crowds and Power*.)[78]

Anticipating the *reconfiguration* of the self with one's body-parts as pro-voked by masking followed by unmasking, this ex-*Sup* deliriously speculates how "Admirals all over the world have put a price [not on my head but] on my facelessness—my *estar sin rostro*, my facelessness of being." The head has been displaced as the prized object by its face, by image and visage, so to speak, and this face is further displaced by its facelessness and a fearful scram-ble for bodiedness as traces, at the very least, of the wholesomeness of body that once was and should be. "They want my noble hair," he goes on to say, "my one and only eye, the grimace I sport instead of lips, my severed head as an adornment for their sumptuous feasts. 'Grab it!' they scream hysterically."

To the ex-*Sup* writing his postscripts (looking out from within the mask, and within from without), this theater stage of revolt was a mobile thing moving through the jungle in excesses of *neozapatismo* where the opposed forces of *neoliberalismo* and *neomarxismo* converge in the fantastic figure of a pirate ship—and I am reminded of William Burroughs, who but thirteen years earlier in a similar ascension of childhood fantasy begins his *Cities of the Red Night*: "The liberal principles embodied in the French and American revolu-tions and later in the liberal revolutions of 1848 had already been codified and put into practice by pirate communes a hundred years earlier."[79]

"Imagine a number of such fortified positions all through South Amer-ica," he continued,

> offering refuge to fugitives from slavery and oppression: "Come to us and live under the Articles." . . . Imagine such a movement on a world-wide scale [in which] the land would belong to those who used it. No white-man boss, no Pukka Sahib, no Patrons, no colonists. . . . The chance was there. The chance was missed. It died in the eighteenth century with Captain Mission. Only a miracle or a disaster could restore it.[80]

What we are left with is the magic of the state.

To *the man without a face and no tomorrow* the act of looking in from outside and looking out from within amounts to gymnastic exercises in physiognomy as soul and face alternately foreground one another. However, as opposed to the goal of a physiognomy that would "fix" the soul through a reading of face, such exercises in radical physiognomics free the soul for other destinies in a

series of identity deaths and transformations, as captured in a brilliant figure
by Walter Benjamin with his suggestion that the authority of the storyteller
relies heavily on death because it is death that releases from the face of the dying a sequence of images—"unfolding views of himself under which he encountered himself without being aware of it."[81]

To unfold views of the self as one dies, views in which one has encountered
oneself without being aware of it—to crystallize this sequence of othernesses
in the self at the point of dissolution of one's being, this is surely the epitome
and essence of defacement through masking, and we note that being faceless
in this de-territorializing mode allows for other plays with identity as well.

A reporter asked if Marcos is gay.

> Marcos is gay in San Francisco, black in South Africa, an Asian in
> Europe, a Chicano in San Ysidro, an anarchist in Spain, a Palestinian
> in Israel, a Mayan Indian in the streets of San Cristóbal, a gang member
> in Neza, a rocker in the National University, a Jew in Germany, an
> Ombudsman in the Defense Ministry, a Communist in the post–Cold
> War era, an artist without gallery or portfolio, a pacifist in Bosnia, a
> housewife alone on a Saturday night in any neighbourhood in any city
> in Mexico, a reporter filing stories for the back pages, a single woman on
> the subway at 10 P.M., a peasant without land, an unemployed worker, a
> dissident amid free-market economics, a writer without books or readers,
> and, of course, a Zapatista in the mountains of southern Mexico.[82]

The Secret of the Gift

My nine-year-old daughter finds it impossible to keep a secret. I would like to think, at least sometimes, that she doesn't even care. But that can't be, because I know she loves secrets. Yet no sooner had she and I bought her brother a Christmas present in December 1994 in La Sonora Market in Mexico City, a tiny tin boat driven by candlepower, than she had to tell him what it was. Secrets are to her what the candle is to the boat, as it noisily and magically putt-putts its way jerkily around the bathtub. No sooner does she come in possession of a secret than she has to reveal it. She can neither possess it nor let it possess her. All that Simmel so wisely says about secrets magnifying reality seems irrelevant here. She cannot inhabit a secret as adults do (or at least as adults like to think they do), and by the same token she and her brother are ruthless in secretly searching for Christmas presents placed in hiding in the days and weeks before that great day. And here I think a certain adult quality does, on occasion, creep in, as both she and he do seem to exercise skill in keeping their searches for those particular secrets secret. But then, do I really know what's going on?

Perhaps we should distinguish here not only children from adults with respect to discretion, but also the secret within the gift? Christmas is, after all, a prime example of the public secret—what is generally known but cannot be stated—in that adults pretend that children are not pretending (to believe in Santa Claus, for instance). And here, written into the adult's imagination of the child's, would seem to lie, if not the lie, then at least the secret in the gift itself—as something both altruistic and indebting, spontaneous and calculated. This has more commonly been seen as a contradiction in the gift, not a secret, but it is precisely the role of secrecy, specifically public secrecy, to control and hence to harness the great powers of contradiction so that ideology can function. And what is especially interesting with Christmas is the invocation of the child as the recipient of the gift in a one-way exchange from adult to child without any obligation to pay back—other than (and here's the rub) by having the child pretend to believe in Santa Claus, for instance, this cheery fat spirit of expenditure for its own sake alone, giving for the sheer love of giving. Yes! There is such a thing as a free lunch!

Why, then, are children in such a hurry to contest the reality of the fat man? Why do they positively delight in the revelation of secrets in general? (Why do they so love presents?) And why is discretion with regard to secrets so widely regarded by adults as a sign of social, if not biological, maturity, like developing secondary sexual characteristics or acne?

Are these little people, then, ruthless realists bent on exposing the games of adults? I think not. First, because although it is true that they derive pleasure from teasing the public secret (remember the little boy in Hans Christian Andersen's "The Emperor's New Clothes"?), we also have to consider the complicating fact that there exists a well-known other side—that kids are also thought to form some sort of fabulous reservoir for the otherwise feeble imagination of adults. There is no getting around it: children exist to make a mockery of Enlightenment. On the one hand, they serve as the mark of the world's infantile prehistory, when myth and fairy tales ruled consciousness; on the other, they are notoriously awful for telling it like it is. No small feat.

Yet children are also greedy, or if not exactly greedy, animated with an undying love to consume, in the very positive sense, of course, of *spending*, as in Georges Bataille's *dépense*, meaning love of wasting, blowing off the surplus.[1] As against more restricted views of the undoubted importance of exchange in grounding social life, involving the obligation to receive and to give back, this emphasis on giving for the sake of giving, on giving as expenditure *regardless of return*, was Bataille's contribution to social theory and draws attention to the logical, no less than historical necessity of such giving for the very notion of the gift, and hence society, to be effective. Even an old toughie like Brecht succumbs, as in his 1950 poem "Giving": "What I possess I cannot treasure / Without a mind to pass it on."[2] While for Zarathustra, child of Zoroastrian fire, the sun surely gives without receiving. "Bless the cup that wants to overflow. . . . This cup wants to be empty again."[3]

And here I think lies the child's love of revelation, because this is precisely what revelation is—the spending of the secret, the emptying of the cup. Indeed the child's inability not to reveal seems to me an enticement for more presents in the form of more secrets, each one of which shall, in its turn, be deliciously spent as revelation. The principle of *dépense* or expenditure would thus apply first and foremost to the childish demand for more and more secrets as presents to be revealed, and the cheery fat man is thus one of the great signs whereby gift and secrecy allow the adult's imagination of the child's imagination to sustain the theater of the social world as exchange.

Moreover, this comes about because of a strategic undecidability as to the moral responsibility of the child, which is one, very concrete, way of stating that social life depends more on rules honored in the breach than in their observance. An impossible situation, logically. But there it is and there it remains, a decided victory for the labor of the negative, its delirious creativity, its ceaselessly dissimulating energy.

My point is this: that the notion of expenditure can only apply to the child and the spending of secrets *if* that child recognizes the rule against telling. This act then corresponds to "the negation of the negation," to deploy that divinely dreadful Hegelian phraseology that, otherwise stated, means transgressing the rule in full consciousness as to the existence of the rule. Otherwise, if done in ignorance of the rule, if the child in this sense lacks "moral maturity," then the child is not a Bataillian creature bent on *dépense*. He or she is simply a creature of what we dubiously refer to as "instinct."

My point is this: thus the child as a morally ambiguous entity, a mysterious entity who knows and yet might not "fully" know the rule, is forever destined to sway on either side of what we might here call the "*dépense* rule," swaying between raw instinct, on the one hand, and a sophisticated negation of the negation, on the other. Thus swaying, thus indeterminate, the child can be given the benefit of the doubt, viewed as a mere bundle of raw perceptual energy bound to crude instinct—and the Emperor strides on, regardless, after a wholesome shudder.

And as I write these lines I shudder at the memory of my own childhood experience of revelation. So monstrous it was I cannot believe it was me, and surely this trauma is one of the main forces behind this book. I was about nine years old and had been a patient at the Children's Hospital in Sydney, bound wholly to my bed for some months, under strict vigilance not to move or strain myself. Christmas came and a party was organized downstairs in the orthopedic ward, whose patients, on account of the pulleys and levers to which their broken bones were attached, could not be moved. It was a liberating moment, to have my bed, with its red-cross bedspread, wheeled into the elevator and taken downstairs in company with my many sick companions, similarly red-crossed. My bed-centered view of the changing world was like a Cubist view of reality, with oblique and horizontal slices of things jerking in front of me as my bed went this way and that—a perspective on reality made all the more wondrous at journey's end by the forest of medieval forms of ropes and pulleys and plaster casts, through which my jovial and loving companions, two beautiful women nurses from my ward, steered me on my throne.

Situated on the outer perimeter of beds, the nurses, much to my delight, sat on my bed to watch the entry of Santa. I thus felt privileged, partly because of the bird's-eye view our outermost position could be thought of as bestowing, despite strict instructions to keep my head on the pillow, and partly because, as I overheard the nurses' conversation, and joined in, I thought of myself as somehow between the kids and the world of the adults and authorities.

Then it all went wrong.

Making a grand entrance, in walked Santa, not as fat as I thought he should be, but certainly jovial. You could feel the joy and expectancy.

"Doesn't Doctor Jones [I forget his real name, and far be it for me to reveal it, anyway] look beaut as Santa!" exclaimed one of the nurses, quite loud enough for me to hear and—given my newfound position as their bedmate, if not confidant, could be thought of as addressed, if somewhat ambiguously, to me too.

Like pulling a rip cord, like a flash of lightning or whatever it takes to turn day into night, and in total disregard of my cardiac future, not to mention doctors' orders, I propped myself up on my thin elbows and bellowed for all to hear:

"Hey kids! It's not Santa Claus! It's Doctor Jones!"

Events after that remain confused in my memory. I do remember being shamed beyond words by the reaction of my nurses. The red cross on my bedspread positively blanched. It was like I disappeared at that moment. Maybe I was wheeled out right then, as my memory says I was. But I find it hard to believe that as actual fact. More likely, I was psychically or morally removed, my own self wishing it no less and probably a good deal more than everyone else in the ward. Looking back, I want to say that I was a victim of the public secret, specifically of the place the child occupies on the crossroads of Enlightenment as both fabulist and as the one who is supposed to tell it like it is. I want to question the need of my beautiful bedmates to let me "know" the public secret, but when all of this questioning and pondering has gone its course, I wonder if I will ever understand why—and this is what I remember most vividly—I was so hurt, not so much by their revelation as by the artless, calm, matter-of-factness of their so doing. And this, of course, is the ultimate treason. For if, even back then, I had come to realize along with Nietzsche how deeply truth is sunk in untruth, I insist like Benjamin that truth demands of the secret that it be artfully revealed, in a manner that does justice to it, keeping the world aquiver with the feints and gesturing of gay science and its nervously nervous system. Thus I bring my book to finish, in arch-defacing mode, allowing (my) art to take its revenge on reality through the medium of an autobiographical detail plundered from the adult's imagination of the child's—a sacrilege, no less, that does not expose the secret so much as do justice to it. I hope. Midday: moment of the shortest shadow.

Reference Matter

PROLOGUE

1. Nietzsche, *The Gay Science*, p. 181.
2. Burroughs, *The Western Lands*, pp. 56–57.
3. Hegel, *Phenomenology of Spirit*, trans. Miller, p. 10.
4. Benjamin, *Origin of German Tragic Drama*, p. 31.
5. Ibid.
6. Elsaesser, "Dada/Cinema?" p. 25.
7. Frazer, *The Golden Bough*, vol. 1, part 1, *The Magic Art and The Evolution of Kings*, pp. 52–214.
8. Freud, *The Origins of Psycho-Analysis*, pp. 229–35.
9. Horkheimer and Adorno. *Dialectic of Enlightenment*, pp. 184–85.
10. Bataille, "The Jesuve," p. 77.
11. Foucault, "A Preface to Transgression."
12. Burroughs, "Last Words," p. 37.
13. Nietzsche, *Twilight of the Idols*, pp. 50–51.
14. Canetti, *Crowds and Power*, p. 290.
15. Nietzsche, *The Gay Science*, p. 181.
16. Ibid., p. 182.
17. Nietzsche, *Twilight of the Idols*, p. 51.

I. SACRILEGE

Epigraph: Hegel, *Phenomenology of Spirit*, trans. Miller, p. 10.

1. Horkheimer and Adorno, *Dialectic of Enlightenment*, p. 184.
2. Freud, *Standard Edition*, vol. 1, 14 November 1897, p. 270.
3. Horkheimer and Adorno, *Dialectic of Enlightenment*, p. 180.

4. Kafka, *Diaries 1914–1923*, p. 23.

5. Lewis, "What Is to be Done?" p. 3.

6. Weschler, "Slight Modifications."

7. Frazer, *The Golden Bough*, vol. 1, pt. 1, p. 55.

8. Musil, "Monuments."

9. White, *History of Australian Bushranging*, pp. 351–52.

10. Jones, *Ned Kelly*, p. 259.     11. White, p. 352.

12. Jones, p. 259.     13. Ibid., p. 324.

14. Hegel, preface to *Phenomenology of Spirit*, in Bataille, "Hegel, Death, and Sacrifice," trans. Strauss, p. 14.

15. Derrida, "From Restricted to General Economy."

16. Benjamin, "The Image of Proust," p. 208. My thanks to Richard Kernaghan for pointing this out to me.

17. Arendt, introduction to Benjamin, 1969, p. 45.

18. Ibid., p. 49.

## II. SECRECY MAGNIFIES REALITY

1. Freud, "The Uncanny," *Standard Edition*, vol. 17, pp. 217–52.

2. Foucault, "A Preface to Transgression."

3. Foucault, *History of Sexuality*, p. 35.

4. Foucault, "A Preface to Transgression," p. 30.

5. Ibid., p. 35.

6. Musil, "Monuments," p. 61.

7. Warner, *Monuments and Maidens*.

8. Kahn, *John Heartfield*, pp. 133–34.

9. Nietzsche, "On Truth and Falsity in Their Ultramoral Sense."

10. Simmel, "The Secret and the Secret Society."

11. Nietzsche, "Attempt at a Self-Criticism," 1886 preface, *The Birth of Tragedy*, p. 23.

12. Nietzsche, preface to the 2d ed., *The Gay Science*, pp. 32–38. See also Kofman, "Baubo: Theological Perversion and Fetishism," and Carson, "The Gender of Sound."

13. Canetti, *Crowds and Power*, pp. 290–96; Foucault, *History of Sexuality*, p. 86.

14. Pitt-Rivers, *The People of the Sierra*, p. xvi.

15. Ibid.

16. Ibid., p. 207.

17. Ibid., p. 208.

18. Ibid.

19. Ibid., pp. 139–40.

20. Mauss, *The Gift*, p. 1.

21. Pitt-Rivers, *The People of the Sierra*, pp. 200–201.

22. Ibid., p. 201.

23. Ibid., p. 206.

24. Ibid., p. xiv.

25. Ibid., p. xiv. Yet the relation between religion and anarchism in Andalusia is subject to heated polemics. The notion that there was a symbiosis can be found in Juan Díaz del Moral, *Historia de las agitaciones campesinas andaluzas* (1929), and Eric Hobsbawm, *Primitive Rebels: Studies in Archaic Forms of Social Movements in the 19th and 20th Centuries*, p. 74. The latter, first published in 1959 as *Social Bandits and Primitive Rebels*, with the emphasis on a millenarial, utopic, vision, is hotly disputed by historians of anarchism in Andalusia, such as Jerome Mintz, in his *The Anarchists of Casas Viejas*, p. 5, who sees a long-standing tendency to overrate the religious basis of southern anarchism. A similar argument was advanced earlier by Temma Kaplan, in *Anarchists of Andalusia, 1868–1903*.

26. Pitt-Rivers, *The People of the Sierra*, p. xiv.

27. Hobsbawm, *Primitive Rebels*, p. 74.

28. Pitt-Rivers, *The People of the Sierra*, p. xvii.

29. Ibid., p. xvii, note 1.

30. Freud, "Fetishism," *Standard Edition*, vol. 21, pp. 152–57.

31. I take this estimate of mortality from Payne, *The Franco Regime*, pp. 218–19.

32. Ibid., p. 399.

33. Fraser, *In Hiding*, p. 18.

34. Ibid., pp. 220–21.

35. Payne, *The Franco Regime*, p. 399.

36. Carr, *Michael Bakunin*, p. 308.

37. Ibid., pp. 419, 428.

38. Kaplan, *Anarchists of Andalusia*, p. 72.

39. Pitt-Rivers, *The People of the Sierra*, p. xxii.

40. Ibid.

41. Ibid., p. xxiii.

42. Ibid.

43. Marx, "The So-Called Primitive Accumulation," in *Capital*, vol. 1, pp. 755–56.

44. Ruskin, *The Stones of Venice*, p. 236.

45. Mann, *Death in Venice*, in *"Death in Venice" and Other Stories by Thomas Mann*. All citations following are from the edition cited in the Bibliography.

46. Ibid., p. 252.

47. Ibid.

48. Ibid., pp. 252–53.

49. Bataille, *The Accursed Share*, vol. 1, p. 28.

50. Ibid., p. 21.

51. Mann, *Death in Venice*, p. 197.        52. Ibid., p. 254.

53. Ibid., p. 255.        54. Ibid., pp. 255–57.

55. Ibid., p. 243.        56. Ibid., pp. 244–45.

57. Ibid., p. 216.        58. Ibid., p. 237.

59. Ruskin, *The Stones of Venice*, p. 236.

60. Mann, *Death in Venice*, pp. 233–34.

61. Ibid., pp. 196–97.        62. Ibid., p. 196.

63. Ibid., pp. 212–13.        64. Ibid., p. 249.

65. Ibid., p. 208.        66. Ibid., p. 197.

67. Ibid., pp. 208–9.        68. Ibid., p. 209.

69. Ibid.        70. Ibid., p. 213.

71. Ibid., p. 252.        72. Ibid., pp. 258–59.

73. Ibid., p. 206.        74. Ibid., p. 201.

75. Ibid., p. 208.

76. Foucault, *History of Sexuality*, p. 35.

77. Pitt-Rivers, *The People of the Sierra*, p. xvii.

78. Schopenhauer, *The World as Will and Idea*, vol. 3, p. 86.

79. Ibid., p. 88.

80. Freud, "Fetishism," pp. 152–53.

III. IN THAT OTHER TIME: ISLA GRANDE

1. Gusinde, *Los indios de Tierra del Fuego*, vol. 1, *Los Selk'nam*, pp. 888–99. Martin Gusinde was born in Germany in 1886. He became a Catholic missionary-priest studying in Mödlingen, near Vienna, and there studied anthropology with Father Wilhelm Schmidt as well. He went to Chile as a schoolteacher in 1913 and became involved in ethnographic study in Tierra del Fuego, undertaking four trips from December 1918 to 1924. As regards Isla Grande, this was the island where both Lucas Bridges and Gusinde spent most of their time in Tierra del Fuego. The Bridges's ranch was located there, and the ethnographic reference of both authors is mostly this island, so I have taken advantage of that name, Isla Grande, for my chapter title. But Tierra del Fuego is an archipelago of islands, peninsulas, and straits, and native peoples lived on many of them, not just on Isla Grande.

2. Gusinde, ibid., pp. 800–801.

3. Gusinde, ibid., pp. 131–35. The 1886 figure of two thousand comes from

Lucas Bridges's father, Thomas Bridges. The Salesian mission also calculated two thousand in 1887.

4. Bridges, *Uttermost Part of the Earth*, pp. 424–25.

5. Gusinde, *The Yamana*, p. 1293. The Yamana are also known in the ethnographic literature as the Yahgan.

6. Ibid.

7. Ibid., pp. 1293–94.

8. Ibid., p. 1294.

9. Hegel, *Phenomenology of Spirit*, trans. Miller, pp. 1–45.

10. Ibid.

11. Nietzsche, 1886 preface, *Human, All Too Human*, pp. 4–5.

12. Freud, *Totem and Taboo, Standard Edition*, vol. 13, p. 142. For another fascinating twist on Freud's story and secrecy, this time from Calcutta, read Ashis Nandy, "The Savage Freud: The First Non-Western Psychoanalyst and the Politics of Secret Selves in Colonial India."

13. Wilbert, ed., "The Origin of the Women's Kloketen," p. 147.

14. Ibid., p. 152.

15. Ibid., pp. 152–53.

16. Ibid., p. 152.

17. Ibid., p. 157. Here it is made clear that the first generation of women after the massacre had no idea of the appropriation of the secret that their mothers had held previously. However, Lucas Bridges cites clear evidence to the contrary in *Uttermost Part of the Earth*, p. 428.

18. Ibid., p. 157, passim.

19. Ibid., p. 157.

20. Gusinde, *Selk'nam*, pp. 661–62.

21. Bridges, *Uttermost Part of the Earth*, p. 435.

22. Chapman, *Drama and Power in a Hunting Society*, p. 84.

23. Wilbert, "The Origin of the Women's Kloketen," p. 156.

24. Chapman, *Drama and Power in a Hunting Society*, pp. 72–74.

25. Gusinde, *Selk'nam*, pp. 661–64.

26. Wilbert, "The Origin of the Women's Kloketen," p. 163.

27. Bridges, *Uttermost Part of the Earth*, p. 444. For the sake of consistency I have taken the liberty of replacing the name *Ona* by its equivalent, *Selk'nam*, in this quotation.

28. Gusinde, *The Yamana*, p. 1317.

29. Ibid., pp. 1317–18.

30. Bridges, *Uttermost Part of the Earth*, p. 263.

31. Ibid. Also see Gusinde, *Selk'nam*, pp. 716–19; *The Yamana*, pp. 1297–1367.

32. See, for instance, Stephen Hugh-Jones on the notion of "he" among the Barasana in the Vaupes region of the northwest Amazon, in *The Palm and the Pleiades*. For a more "acculturated" form, in the Putumayo highlands among the Kamsá, see Michael Taussig, "History as Sorcery," chapter 23 in *Shamanism, Colonialism, and the Wild Man: A Study in Terror and Healing*, pp. 366–92. Stephen Rubinstein tells me, from his fieldwork among the Shuar on the eastern slopes of the Ecuadorian *montaña*, that this invocation of a prehistory is also important in their shamanism.

33. Gusinde, *Selk'nam*, p. 897.

34. Ibid., p. 899.

35. Ibid., p. 871.

36. Ibid., p. 876.

37. Ibid., p. 868.

38. Ibid., pp. 883–86.

39. Ibid., p. 881.

40. Ibid., p. 1056.

41. Ibid., pp. 880–81.

42. Bridges, *Uttermost Part of the Earth*, pp. 424–25.

43. Ibid.

44. Ibid., p. 419.

45. Chapman, *Drama and Power in a Hunting Society*, pp. 74–75. Chapman writes *Hain* where I write *Big Hut*.

46. Ibid., p. 75.

47. Ibid., p. 71; Gusinde, *Selk'nam*, p. 887.

48. Chapman, *Drama and Power in a Hunting Society*, pp. 80–86. Information largely from her own informants, Angela and Frederico.

49. Ibid., p. 86.

50. Ibid., p. 93.

51. Ibid., p. 98, and pp. 174–75, note 9.

52. For fuller discussion of the trick, see Taussig, "Viscerality, Faith, and Skepticism."

53. Gusinde, *Selk'nam*, pp. 829–33.

54. Chapman, *Drama and Power in a Hunting Society*, p. 105.

55. Ibid., pp. 104–7. For her sources see p. 175, note 14. Some parts of this unmasking description come from her ethnographic diary compiled between 1966 and 1976.

56. Bridges, *Uttermost Part of the Earth*, p. 421. Bridges spells this spirit *Short* but I have followed Gusinde's spelling of *Shoort* for consistency.

57. Gusinde, *Selk'nam*, pp. 1013–17.

58. Chapman, *Drama and Power in a Hunting Society*, pp. 147–48.

59. Gusinde, *Selk'nam*, pp. 1018–21.

60. Ibid., p. 882.

61. Bridges, *Uttermost Part of the Earth*, p. 424.

62. Beckett, *Proust*, pp. 55–56.

63. Proust, *Swann's Way*, pp. 48–49.

64. Beckett, *Proust*, p. 23. Benjamin, "Some Motifs in Baudelaire," pp. 145, 113: "if we designate as aura the associations which, at home in the *mémoire involontaire*, tend to cluster around the object of a perception."

65. Beckett, *Proust*, pp. 55–56.

66. Hegel, *Phenomenology of Spirit*, trans. Miller, p. 19.

67. Gusinde, *The Yamana*, pp. 698–99.

68. Ibid., p. 699.

69. Ibid., p. 700.

70. Ibid., p. 701.

71. Ibid., p. 729.

72. Ibid.

73. Ibid., pp. 728–30.

74. Ibid., pp. 784–85.

75. Ibid., p. 764.

76. Nietzsche, *The Birth of Tragedy*, p. 39.

77. Bataille, *Erotism: Death and Sensuality*, p. 36.

78. Hubert and Mauss, *Sacrifice: Its Nature and Function*, p. 69.

79. Ibid., p. 79.

80. Ibid., p. 12.

81. Evans-Pritchard, *Nuer Religion*, p. 276.

82. Ibid., p. 279.

83. Hubert and Mauss, *Sacrifice: Its Nature and Function*, p. 77.

84. Foucault, *History of Sexuality*, vol. 1.

85. Hubert and Mauss, *Sacrifice: Its Nature and Function*, p. 33.

86. Ibid., p. 69; Frazer, *The Golden Bough*, vol. 2, *Spirits of the Corn and of the Wild*, pp. 4–6.

87. Lévi-Strauss, *The Savage Mind*, pp. 223–28, 51.

88. Benjamin, *Origin of German Tragic Drama*, p. 31.

89. Benjamin, "The Storyteller," p. 91, and "Art in the Age of Mechanical Reproduction." See Taussig, *Mimesis and Alterity*, for an extended discussion of this controversial and important point. Also note Sigmund Freud's method requiring of the patient a state of "double consciousness" somewhere between daydreaming and intellection in the form of "free association," both fixed and unfixed.

90. Gusinde, *The Yamana*, p. 798.

91. Benjamin, "The Storyteller," p. 91.

92. Benjamin, "Art in the Age of Mechanical Reproduction," pp. 237–39.

93. Benjamin, "A Glimpse into the World of Children's Books," p. 435. Henri Bergson claims the same thing for perception in general, in *Matter and Memory*, p. 75.

94. Benjamin, "A Glimpse into the World of Children's Books," p. 435.

95. Gusinde, *The Yamana*, p. 791.

96. Ibid., p. 779.

97. Ibid., p. 781.

98. Ibid., p. 791.

99. Ibid., p. 793.

100. Ibid., p. 796.

101. Ibid.

102. Ibid., p. 790.

103. Ibid., pp. 790–91.

104. Ibid., pp. 799–800.

105. Ibid., pp. 801–2.

106. Ibid., pp. 803–4.

107. Ibid., pp. 797–98.

108. Ibid., p. 798.

109. Ibid. In her article, "The Great Ceremonies of the Selk'nam and the Yamana: A Comparative Analysis," p. 94, Anne Chapman states that the last *Ciexaus* was held "during the early years of 1930 [*sic*]" on the Chilean shore of Canal Beagle on Isla Navarino.

110. Derrida, *The Gift of Death*, p. 37.

111. Gusinde, *The Yamana*, p. 644.

112. Ibid., p. 649.

113. Ibid.

114. Hoffmann, prologue to Gusinde, *Selk'nam*, pp. xiv–xv.

115. Gusinde, *Selk'nam*, pp. 795–96.

116. Bridges, *Uttermost Part of the Earth*, p. 428.

117. Bolle, "Secrecy in Religion."

118. The words were sounds, *o* and *a* that Freud and his daughter, the little boy's mother, interpreted as *Fort* and *Da*. For Lacan this is both relevant and irrelevant, first, in that "gone" and "there" strengthens the analysis of "absent presence" at a somewhat literal level, second, in that what underlies this is the production of difference as with *o/a*, or as Anthony Wilden puts it (in *Speech and Language in Psychoanalysis*, p. 163), "the binary opposition of presence and absence in the child's world." Why have otherwise astute observers misread the child's action as one of throwing the reel out of the crib, not into its curtained interior; Jacqueline Rose in *Feminine Sexuality* and Catherine Clement in *Lives and Legends of Jacques Lacan*, for example?

119. Freud, *Beyond the Pleasure Principle*, Standard Edition, vol. 18, p. 15.

120. Lacan, *Speech and Language in Psychoanalysis*, p. 84.

121. Ibid., p. 39.

122. Benjamin, "Surrealism," p. 190.

123. Joyce, *Stephen Hero*, p. 211. Thanks to Kostas Gounis for bringing this to my attention.

124. Gusinde, *Selk'nam*, p. 1054.

125. Ibid., p. 1055. But Anne Chapman in her *Drama and Power in a Hunting Society* presents quite a different view of sexual inequality and conflict among the

Selk'nam, including severe physical abuse by men of women (pp. 44, 60). Lucas Bridges's book is one source for her view.

126. Tuzin, *The Cassowary's Revenge*, p. 64.

127. Gusinde, *Selk'nam*, p. 1056.

128. Gusinde, *The Yamana*, p. 1296.

129. Lowie, review of Gusinde's *Die Yamana*, p. 503.

130. Gusinde states that he has discovered among the Tehuelche "the remains of a secret ceremony for men" that carries the same name for initiates as that used by the Selk'nam across the straits—although no mention is made of such a ceremony in the relevant essays in *Handbook of South American Indians*, by John M. Cooper, "The Yahgan," and "The Ona," first published in 1944.

131. Gusinde, *Selk'nam*, p. 123.

132. Ibid., p. 1029.

133. Ibid., p. 1027.

134. Bridges, *Uttermost Part of the Earth*, pp. 290–91.

135. Nietzsche, cited in Kofman, *Nietzsche and Metaphor*, pp. 130–31.

136. Crocker, "Being and Essence."

137. Ibid., pp. 160, 157.

138. Ibid., p. 158.

139. Ibid., p. 159.

140. Ibid., p. 160.

141. Ibid., p. 170.

142. Ibid., p. 175.

143. Gregor, *Anxious Pleasures*, p. 92.

144. Ibid., p. 104.

145. Ibid., p. 103.

146. Ibid., p. 98.

147. Ibid., p. 107.

148. Hugh-Jones, *The Palm and the Pleiades*, p. 247.

149. Goldman, *The Cubeo*, pp. 193–94.

150. Bamberger, "The Myth of Matriarchy," p. 275.

151. Ibid., p. 276.

152. Ibid., pp. 279, 280.

153. Ibid., p. 280.

154. Spencer and Gillen, *The Native Tribes of Central Australia*, p. 128.

155. Hiatt, "Secret Pseudo-Procreation Rites," pp. 77–78.

156. Ibid., p. 88.

157. Ibid., p. 88, note 18.

158. Ibid., p. 84.

159. Spencer and Gillen, *The Native Tribes of Central Australia*, pp. 363–64.

160. Warner, *A Black Civilization*, p. 227.

161. Ibid., p. 226.

162. Mauss, *A General Theory of Magic*, p. 111.

163. Spencer and Gillen, *The Native Tribes of Central Australia*, p. 364.

164. Hiatt, "Secret Pseudo-Procreation Rites," p. 84.

165. Spencer and Gillen, *The Native Tribes of Central Australia*, p. 366.

166. Stanner, *On Australian Religion*, p. 5.

167. Ibid., p. 257.

168. Ibid., pp. 112–14.

169. Ibid., p. 117.

170. Codrington, *The Melanesians*, p. 69.

171. Ibid., p. 96.              172. Ibid., p. 76.

173. Ibid.                      174. Ibid., p. 80.

175. Ibid., p. 97.             176. Ibid., p. 99.

177. Mauss, *A General Theory of Magic*, p. 111.

178. Turnbull, *The Forest People*, p. 88.

179. Nietzsche, *Twilight of the Idols*, p. 84.

180. Little, "The Poro Society," pp. 1, 4.

181. Ibid., pp. 3–4.

182. Little, *The Mende of Sierra Leone*, p. 235.

183. Little, "The Poro Society," p. 3.

184. Welmers, "Secret Medicines," pp. 209, 229. (I persist in using the slightly different Mende names for these societies.)

185. Ibid., p. 230.

186. Murphy, "Secret Knowledge as Property and Power in Kpelle Society," pp. 194, 199–200. Murphy does not mention clitoridectomy.

187. Bellman, *The Language of Secrecy*, pp. 43, 19.

188. Welmers, "Secret Medicines," p. 231.

189. Ibid.                      190. Ibid., p. 232.

191. Ibid., pp. 233–34.         192. Ibid., p. 239.

193. Bellman, *The Language of Secrecy*, p. 53.

194. Meyer, "'The Beast Within.'"

195. Bellman, *The Language of Secrecy*, pp. 53–58.

196. Shaw, "Secret Societies."

197. Welmers, "Secret Medicines," p. 241.

198. Ibid.

199. Bellman, *The Language of Secrecy*, pp. 84, 142.

200. Ibid., p. 43.

201. Picton, "What's in a Mask?" p. 196.

202. Ibid., p. 192.

203. Ibid., p. 193.

204. Little, *The Mende of Sierra Leone*, p. 226.

205. Nunley, *Moving with the Face of the Devil*, p. 68.

206. Little, *The Mende of Sierra Leone*, p. 227.

207. Ibid.

208. Evans-Pritchard, *Witchcraft, Oracles, and Magic Among the Azande*, p. 465.

209. Ibid., p. 441.

210. Little, *The Mende of Sierra Leone*, p. 228.

211. Bellman, *The Language of Secrecy*, p. 89.

212. Geschiere, *The Modernity of Witchcraft*. See also Mbembe, "The Banality of Power."

213. Gillison, "Images of Nature in Gimi Thought," pp. 144, 154.

214. Ibid., p. 149.

215. Ibid., 156.

216. Nietzsche, *Beyond Good and Evil*, p. 99.

217. Gillison, "Images of Nature in Gimi Thought," p. 156.

218. Glick, "Foundations of a Primitive Medical System."

219. See Terence E. Hays where he cites ethnography of the Yagara and the Fore, in "'Myths of Matriarchy' and the Sacred Flute Complex of the Papua New Guinea Highlands." According to Gillison, it is furthermore said by Gimi men that the "decorative incisions around the flute's blowing hole—it's 'mouth'—are identical to the tattoos applied around the bride's mouth some weeks before marriage. The bride's tattoos give her the appearance of having a beard"—which "according to the flute myth is actually female pubic hair," and other symbolic equivalencies can be inferred: the blowhole is the vaginal orifice, the nonsecret flutes that the bride brings to her wedding "symbolically represent her own detached penis," and so forth. Gillison, "Images of Nature in Gimi Thought," pp. 156–57. See also Berndt, *Excess and Restraint*, p. 50.

220. Gillison, "Images of Nature in Gimi Thought," pp. 152–53.

221. Ibid., p. 153.

222. Ibid.

223. Ibid., pp. 150, 153–54.

224. Silverman, *The Acoustic Mirror*, p. 7.

225. Lacan, *Speech and Language in Psychoanalysis*, p. 84.

226. Gillison, "Images of Nature in Gimi Thought," p. 160.

227. Ibid., p. 165.

228. Ibid., p. 168.

229. Berndt, *Excess and Restraint*, p. 68.

230. Ibid.

231. Ibid., pp. 68–69.

232. Ibid., p. 70.

233. Tuzin, *The Voice of the Tambaran*. Tambaran is the Melanesian pidgin lan-

guage form of a spirit variously known as known as Nggwal, Holof, and Waf, in the Arapesh language of East Sepik Province.

234. Ibid., pp. 22–23.

235. Ibid., p. 57.

236. Ibid.

237. Tuzin, *The Cassowary's Revenge*, p. 159.

238. Ibid., p. 57.

239. Lattas, "Trickery and Sacrifice." Lattas, however, is at pains to avoid using the word "sacred" for what he calls "immanent," as opposed to transcendent, religions.

240. Nietzsche, *The Will to Power*, p. 452.

241. Tuzin, *The Voice of the Tambaran*, p. 55.

242. Ibid., p. 71.

243. Barth, *Ritual and Knowledge Among the Baktaman of New Guinea*, pp. 218–19.

244. Tuzin, *The Voice of the Tambaran*, pp. 129–30.

245. Tuzin, *The Cassowary's Revenge*, p. 161.

246. Tuzin, *The Voice of the Tambaran*, p. 216.

247. Read, *Return to the High Valley*, p. 115.

248. Read, *The High Valley*, p. 115. The reference to "elaborate deception" and "charade" comes from his earlier article "Nama Cult," pp. 7–8.

249. Read, "Nama Cult," p. 8.

250. Tuzin, *The Voice of the Tambaran*, p. 57.

251. This 1952 article has been categorized as "classic," by Terence Hays, in "'Myths of Matriarchy,'" p. 98.

252. Read, "Nama Cult," p. 8.

253. Ibid.

254. Ibid., p. 7. We found this particular anxiety earlier, as with Martin Gusinde, perplexed as to the incongruity of the secret of the Yamana of Tierra del Fuego, for he could find no function for it in regulating gender and hence went searching for an ice bridge across which History could flaunt the straits of time.

255. Read, *The High Valley*, p. 113.

256. Ibid.

257. Ibid., p. 118.

258. Ibid., pp. 126–27, 117.

259. Ibid., pp. 116–17. This same point is repeated in the later book, *Return to the High Valley*, p. 215: "I don't think they [the women] accepted at face value the men's explanations for the cries of the *nama* flutes. There were numerous oc-

casions when the instruments were paraded along exposed ridges, when the processions were surely visible [and the screens made by the men] were mostly ineffective. In their excited state, the men seemed to forget their purpose, inadvertently lowering the boughs and leaving the players fully displayed in silhouette against the sky."

260. Read, *The High Valley*, p. 117.

261. Derrida, *Of Grammatology*.

262. Derrida, "Structure, Sign, and Play"; Nietzsche, *The Birth of Tragedy*, p. 103.

263. Read, *The High Valley*, p. 126.

264. Ibid., pp. 126–27. And elsewhere he remarks that the "secret of the flutes is the most important revelation given to the boys [although] the boy is probably well aware of the nature of the secret long before it is explained to him." "Nama Cult," p. 13.

265. Read, *The High Valley*, pp. 128–31.

266. Ibid., pp. 133–34. In modern Western medical science there is at least one research effort and therapy based on the assumption that there is a connection between nasal mucosa and the genitals of both sexes, and this very much includes the connection between that mucosa and menstruation. I refer to Freud's close friend and muse at the beginnings of psychoanalysis, Wilhelm Fliess. See the introduction, by Ernst Kris, to Freud, *The Origins of Psycho-Analysis*.

267. Read, *Return to the High Valley*, p. 199.

268. Berndt, *Excess and Restraint*, p. 57.

269. Herdt, *Guardians of the Flutes*, pp. 223–24.

270. Berndt, *Excess and Restraint*, pp. 56–57.

271. Read, *The High Valley*, p. 133.

272. Nietzsche, *Twilight of the Idols*, p. 121.

273. Read, *The High Valley*, p. 96.

274. Read, *Return to the High Valley*, pp. 207–8.

275. Finch, "Structure and Function in Papua New Guinea Highland Mythology," p. 208.

276. Berndt, *Excess and Restraint*, p. 69.

277. Tuzin, *The Cassowary's Revenge*, p. 20.

278. Gillison, *Between Culture and Fantasy*, p. 5.

279. Bateson, *Naven*, p. 136.    280. Ibid., p. 136, note 1.

281. Ibid., pp. 137–38.    282. Ibid., p. 135.

283. Tuzin, *The Cassowary's Revenge*, p. 1.

284. Ibid., pp. 1–2.

285. Ibid., pp. 64, 65, 181.

IV. THE FACE IS THE EVIDENCE THAT MAKES
EVIDENCE POSSIBLE

The title comes from Emmanuel Levinas, *Totality and Infinity*.

1. Levinas, *Totality and Infinity*; also "Dialogue with Emmanuel Levinas."
2. Levinas, *Totality and Infinity*, p. 202.
3. Burroughs, *The Western Lands*, p. 57.
4. Levinas, *Totality and Infinity*, p. 202.
5. Mann, *Death in Venice*, p. 256.
6. Montaigne, "On Physiognomy," pp. 311–42.
7. Ibid., p. 339.            8. Ibid.
9. Ibid., p. 341.            10. Ibid., p. 342.
11. Ibid., p. 338.
12. Eisenstein, "Film Form: New Problems," p. 127.
13. Benjamin, "A Small History of Photography," p. 251.
14. I take the term "double-men" from Canetti's discussion of "the double figure of the totem," in his section on transformation in *Crowds and Power*, pp. 348–57.
15. Horkheimer and Adorno, *Dialectic of Enlightenment*, p. 180.
16. Durkheim, *The Division of Labor in Society*.
17. Horkheimer and Adorno, *Dialectic of Enlightenment*, p. 234.
18. Adorno, "The Idea of Natural History."
19. Nietzsche, *Twilight of the Idols*, pp. 84–85; Burroughs, *The Western Lands*.
20. Metz, *The Imaginary Signifier*, p. 73. I am indebted to Professor K. Calhoon, of the Department of German at the University of Oregon, Eugene, for bringing this to my attention.
21. Ibid., p. 73.
22. Canetti, *Crowds and Power*, p. 378.
23. Guillermoprieto, "The Unmasking," p. 44.
24. Ibid.
25. Preston, "Mexican Gunmen Slay 45 in Southern Indian Village."
26. Photograph by Pedro Valtierra, in Guillermoprieto, "The Shadow War," p. 40. Anne Lovell drew my attention to this article.
27. Hermitte, "Supernatural Power and Social Control"; Guiteras-Holmes, *Perils of the Soul*.
28. Hermitte, "Supernatural Power and Social Control," p. 122.
29. Pitt-Rivers, "Spiritual Power in Central America," pp. 183, 203. In an article published in 1947, Alfonso Villa Rojas thought that such homicide in the

village he studied in Chiapas was rare because of the terror it would create in the mind of the killer. It would be the worst possible crime, he said, because if the killer was discovered, he or his children would become deathly ill. Villa Rojas, "Kinship and Nagualism in a Tzeltal Community," p. 585.

30. See, for example, the curing role of the "holy tiger" in James Greenberg's informant's account in Oaxaca, *Santiago's Sword*, p. 95. On friendliness combined with caprice see Bunzel, *Chichicastenango*, pp. 275, 317.

31. Foster, "Nagualism in Mexico and Guatemala."

32. Canetti, *Crowds and Power*, p. 337. This book is as concerned with magical transformation between humans and animals, with secrecy, and with death, as it is with the crowd. But Canetti never got to publish the promised second volume he said would deal more fully with such transformation. See his radio interview with Adorno (listed in Bibliography under the latter's name).

33. Benjamin, "On the Mimetic Faculty," p. 333.

34. See Burroughs, *The Western Lands*, p. 113, for a delineation of the Magical Universe. For a direct connection with the *nahual* in Burroughs's writing and painting, see Sobieszek, *Ports of Entry*, pp. 122, 134.

35. Burroughs, *The Western Lands*, pp. 56–57.

36. Caillois, "Mimicry and Legendary Psychaesthenia."

37. Burroughs, *The Western Lands*, pp. 56–57.

38. Mauss, *A General Theory of Magic*, p. 108. Much has been written on *mana* and the term has occasioned heated discussion since it entered the vocabulary of anthropology when Codrington's book put the term into circulation in the late nineteenth century. Notable are the reinterpretaions offered by Firth (1940), Keesing (1984), and Lévi-Strauss (1987). However, in my opinion all such efforts founder in either their push toward an empirical solution—so that, in Firth and Keesing's cases, they are put into a losing encounter with the magic of magic— or, in Lévi-Strauss's case, with his notion of *mana* as "floating signifier," whereby one mysticism is hijacked by another so as to form the point external to the semiotic system that shall ensure that system's systematicity.

39. Mauss, *A General Theory of Magic*, pp. 111, 117.

40. Ibid., p. 115. Mauss spells *nahual* as *naual*, but I have taken the liberty of adhering to my spelling for consistency. Other authors write *nagual*. Mauss's source on the *nahual* derives from the Spanish and Nahuatl illustrated manuscripts in the famous sixteenth-century survey by Father Sahagún, as translated and commented upon by Eduard Seler, "Zauberei und Zauberer im Alten Mexico," cited in Ibid., p. 16, note 4.

41. Ibid., p. 115.

42. Foster, "Nagualism in Mexico and Guatemala," pp. 88–89. Like Mauss,

Foster also uses Seler's research, as well as Fray Alonso de Molina, *Vocabulario de la lengua Mexicana*, 1571, and Jacinto de la Serna, "Manual de Ministros de Indios para el conocimiento de sus idolatrías, y extirpación de ellas," written in 1656. Foster warns against generalizations with the word *nagualism*, which he sees as acquiring, in the hands of anthropologists, a fictitious nature, like the concept "totemism." He emphasizes that "as a trait or complex there is no such thing as nagualism."

43. Foster, "Nagualism in Mexico and Guatemala," p. 92. Greenberg, *Santiago's Sword*, pp. 91–92.

44. Foster, "Nagualism in Mexico and Guatemala," p. 94.

45. Hermitte, "Supernatural Power and Social Control," p. 123.

46. Collier and Quaratiello, *Basta! Land and the Zapatista Rebellion*, p. 47.

47. Ejército Zapatista, *EZLN: documentos y comunicados*, 8 August 1994, pp. 49–66.

48. Marx, Letter to Arnold Ruge, p. 32.

49. Benjamin, "N," p. 1. Susan Buck-Morss was the first, as far as I know, to indicate the relevance of this "waking" in Benjamin's later work. See her eighth chapter, "Dream World of Mass Culture," in *The Dialectics of Seeing*, pp. 253–86.

50. Beckett, *Proust*, pp. 55–56.

51. Benjamin, "N," p. 9. He writes: "Then the moment of waking would be identical with the 'moment of recognition,' in which things put on their true—surrealistic—face. Thus, in Proust, the importance of committing the whole of life to its ultimate dialectical breaking point—waking." Note also that the figure of defacement occurs in many places in Benjamin's essay on surrealism. For example, it is revolutionary action that will reveal the "true face" of the city (of Paris). And the famous last lines of that essay referring to what Benjamin hopefully sees as the Marxist revolutionary impulse amongst surrealists, who, "exchange, to a man, the play of human features for the face of an alarm clock that in each minute rings for sixty seconds."

52. Carroll, *Alice's Adventures in Wonderland*, p. 43.

53. Ejército Zapatista, *EZLN: documentos y comunicados*, 20 January 1994, pp. 98–99.

54. Quotations are from Burroughs, *The Western Lands*, p. 57, and Mauss, *A General Theory of Magic*, p. 111.

55. Deleuze and Guattari, *A Thousand Plateaus*, pp. 247–48.

56. Hermitte, "Supernatural Power and Social Control," p. 121.

57. Ejército Zapatista, *EZLN: documentos y comunicados*, 26 February 1995, pp. 175–76.

58. Canetti, *Crowds and Power*, p. 337.

59. Benjamin, *The Origin of German Tragic Drama*, p. 183.

60. Ibid., pp. 183–84.          61. Ibid., p. 197.

62. Ibid.                       63. Ibid.

64. Breton, *Nadja*, pp. 68, 60.

65. Ejército Zapatista, *EZLN: documentos y comunicados*, p. 130.

66. Ibid.

67. Deleuze and Guattari, *A Thousand Plateaus*; Caillois, "Mimicry and Legendary Psychaesthenia," pp. 17–32.

68. Benjamin, *The Origin of German Tragic Drama*, p. 166.

69. Guillermoprieto, "The Unmasking," p. 42.

70. Ejército Zapatista, *EZLN: documentos y comunicados*, pp. 301–4. I have used some of the translation provided by Alma Guillermoprieto in "The Shadow War."

71. Ejército Zapatista, *EZLN: documentos y comunicados*, 8 August 1994, p. 305.

72. Foucault, "Nietzsche, Freud, Marx," p. 62.

73. Duran de Huerta, *Yo, Marcos*, p. 22.

74. Ejército Zapatista, *EZLN: documentos y comunicados*, pp. 288–89.

75. Bartra, "Tropical Kitsch," pp. 89–90.

76. Guillermoprieto, "The Shadow War," p. 42.

77. Ejército Zapatista, *EZLN: documentos y comunicados*, p. 281.

78. Canetti, *Crowds and Power*, p. 379.

79. Burroughs, *Cities of the Red Night*, pp. xiii–xiv.

80. Ibid., pp. xiv–xv.

81. Benjamin, "The Storyteller," p. 94.

82. This was mailed to me at Sydney in April 1995 by my friend Kostas Gounis from New York City, who got it in his e-mail.

## V. THE SECRET OF THE GIFT

1. Bataille, "The Notion of Expenditure."

2. Brecht, *Collected Poems*, p. 419.

3. Nietzsche, *Thus Spake Zarathustra*, p. 39.

Adorno, Theodor. "A Portrait of Walter Benjamin." In *Prisms*, translated by Samuel Weber and Shierry Weber, pp. 227–42. Cambridge: MIT Press, 1981.

―――. "The Idea of Natural History" (1932). Translated by Robert Hullot-Kentor. *Telos* 60 (1984): 111–24.

―――. Interview by Elias Canetti. In *Thesis Eleven*, no. 45 (1996): 1–16.

Arendt, Hannah. Introduction to Walter Benjamin, *Illuminations*, edited by Hannah Arendt, translated by Harry Zohn, pp. 1–51. New York: Schocken, 1969.

Bamberger, Joan. "The Myth of Matriarchy: Why Men Rule in Primitive Society." In *Women, Culture, and Society*, edited by Michele Z. Rosaldo and Louise Lamphere, pp. 263–80. Stanford, Calif.: Stanford University Press, 1974.

Barth, Fredrik. *Ritual and Knowledge Among the Baktaman of New Guinea*. New Haven, Conn. / Oslo: Yale University Press / Universitetsforlaget, 1971.

Bartra, Roger. "Tropical Kitsch: Melancholy and War in Cybernetic Space." *Lusitania* 8 (1996): 89–90.

Bataille, Georges. *The Accursed Share: An Essay on General Economy*. 3 vols. Translated by Robert Hurley. New York: Zone, 1988.

―――. "The Big Toe," "The Jesuve," "The Pineal Eye," "The Notion of Expenditure." In *Visions of Excess: Selected Writings, 1927–1939*, translated by Betsy Wing, pp. 20–23, 73–78, 79–90, 116–29, respectively. Minneapolis: University of Minnesota Press, 1985.

―――. *Erotism: Death and Sensuality*. San Francisco: City Lights, 1986.

―――. "Hegel, Death, and Sacrifice." Translated by Jonathan Strauss. *Yale French Studies* 78 (1990): 9–28.

Bateson, Gregory. *Naven*. 2d ed. Stanford, Calif.: Stanford University Press, 1958.

Beckett, Samuel. *Proust*. New York: Grove, 1957.

Bellman, Beryl Larry. *The Language of Secrecy: Symbols and Metaphors in Poro Ritual*. New Brunswick, N.J.: Rutgers University Press, 1984.

Benjamin, Walter. "The Doctrine of the Similar." Translated by Knut Tarnowski. *New German Critique*, no. 17 (Spring 1979): 65–69.

———. "A Glimpse into the World of Children's Books." In Walter Benjamin, *Selected Writings*, vol. 1 (1913–26), edited by Marcus Bullock and Michael W. Jennings. Cambridge: Harvard University Press, 1996.

———. "N [Theoretics of Knowledge; Theory of Progress]." *The Philosophical Forum* 15, nos. 1–2 (Fall–Winter 1983–84): 1–40.

———. *The Origin of German Tragic Drama*. Translated by John Osborne. London: New Left Books, 1977.

———. "A Small History of Photography." In *One Way Street, and Other Writings*, translated by Edmund Jephcott and Kingsley Shorter, pp. 240–57. London: New Left Books, 1979.

———. "Some Motifs in Baudelaire." In *Charles Baudelaire: A Lyric Poet in the Era of High Capitalism*, translated by Harry Zohn. London: New Left Books, 1973.

———. "The Storyteller," "The Image of Proust," "Art in the Age of Mechanical Reproduction." In *Illuminations*, edited by Hannah Arendt, translated by Harry Zohn, pp. 83–110, 201–16, 217–52, respectively. New York: Schocken, 1968.

———. "Surrealism: Last Snapshot of the European Intelligentsia," "On the Mimetic Faculty." In *Reflections*, translated by Edmund Jephcott, pp. 177–92, 333–36, respectively. New York: Harcourt Brace Jovanovich, 1978.

Bergson, Henri. *Matter and Memory*. New York: Zone, 1981.

Berndt, R. M. *Excess and Restraint: Social Control Among a New Guinea Mountain People*. Chicago: University of Chicago Press, 1962.

Bolle, Kees W. "Secrecy in Religion." In *Secrecy in Religions*, edited by Kees W. Bolle. New York: E. J. Brill, 1987.

Brecht, Bertolt. *Collected Poems: 1913–1956*, translated by John Willet and Ralph Mannheim. London: Methuen, 1979.

Breton, André. *Nadja*. New York: Grove, 1960.

Bridges, E. Lucas. *Uttermost Part of the Earth*. London: Hodder and Stoughton, 1951.

Brown, Norman O. "Dionysus in 1990." In *Apocalypse and/or Metamorphosis*, pp. 179–200. Berkeley: University of California Press, 1990.

Buck-Morss, Susan. *The Dialectics of Seeing: Walter Benjamin and the Arcades Project*. Cambridge: MIT Press, 1989.

Bunzel, Ruth. *Chichicastenango: A Guatemalan Village*. Locust Valley, N.Y.: J. J. Augustin, 1952.

Burroughs, William S. *Cities of the Red Night*. New York: Henry Holt, 1981.

———. "Last Words." *New Yorker*, August 18, 1997.

———. *The Western Lands*. New York: Viking, 1987.

Caillois, Roger. "Mimicry and Legendary Psychaesthenia." Translated by John Shepley. *October* 31 (Winter 1984): 17–32.

Canetti, Elias. *Crowds and Power*. Translated by Carol Stewart. New York: Farrar, Straus and Giroux, 1984. First published in German in 1960.

———. "Elias Canetti: Discussion with Theodor W. Adorno." *Thesis Eleven*, no. 45 (1996): 1–16.

Carr, E. H. *Michael Bakunin*. New York: Farrar, Strauss and Giroux, 1975.

Carroll, Lewis. *Alice's Adventures in Wonderland*. New York: Dover, 1993.

Carson, Anne. "The Gender of Sound: Description, Definition, and Mistrust of the Female Voice in Western Culture." In *Glass, Irony, and God*. New York: New Directions, 1995.

Chapman, Anne. *Drama and Power in a Hunting Society: The Selk'nam of Tierra del Fuego*. Cambridge: Cambridge University Press, 1982.

———. "The Great Ceremonies of the Selk'nam and the Yamana: A Comparative Analysis." In *Patagonia: Natural History, Prehistory, and Ethnography at the Uttermost End of the Earth*, edited by Colin McEwan, Luis A. Borrero, and Alfredo Prieto, pp. 82–109. London: Trustees of The British Museum, 1997.

Codrington, R. H. *The Melanesians: Studies in Their Anthropology and Folk-Lore*. 1891. Reprint, New York: Dover, 1972.

Collier, George. "The New Politics of Exclusion: Antecedents to the Rebellion in Mexico." *Dialectical Anthropology* 19, no. 1 (Spring 1994): 1–44.

Collier, George A., and Elizabeth Lowery Quaratiello. *Basta! Land and the Zapatista Rebellion in Chiapas*. Oakland: Institute for Food and Development Policy, 1994.

Cooper, John M. "The Yahgan," "The Ona." In *Handbook of South American Indians*. Vol. 1, *The Marginal Tribes*. New York: Cooper Square, 1963.

Crocker, Jon Christopher. "Being and Essence: Totemic Representation Among the Eastern Bororo." In *The Power of Symbols: Masks and Masquerade in the Americas*, edited by N. Ross Crumrine and Marjorie Halpin, pp. 154–73. Vancouver: University of British Columbia Press, 1983.

Deleuze, Gilles, and Félix Guattari. *A Thousand Plateaus: Capitalism and Schizophrenia*. Translated and with a foreword by Brian Massumi. Minneapolis: University of Minnesota Press, 1987.

Derrida, Jacques. *Dissemination*. Translated by Barbara Johnson. Chicago: University of Chicago Press, 1981.

———. *The Gift of Death*. Translated by David Wills. Chicago: University of Chicago Press, 1995.

―――. *Of Grammatology*. Translated by Gayatri Chakravorty Spivak. Baltimore: Johns Hopkins University Press, 1974.

―――. "From Restricted to General Economy: A Hegelianism Without Reserve," "Structure, Sign, and Play in the Discourse of the Human Sciences." In *Writing and Difference*, translated by Alan Bass, pp. 251–77, 278–94, respectively. Chicago: University of Chicago Press, 1978.

―――. *Specters of Marx*. New York: Routledge, 1994.

Díaz del Moral, Juan. *Historia de las agitaciones campesinas andaluzas*. 1929. Reprint, Madrid: Alianza Editorial, 1967.

Duran de Huerta, Marta, comp. *Yo, Marcos*. Mexico: Ediciones del Milenio, 1994.

Durkheim, Emile. *The Division of Labor in Society*. Translated by George Simpson. New York: Macmillan, 1933.

Eisenstein, Sergei. "Film Form: New Problems." In *Film Form: Essays in Film Theory*, edited and translated by Jay Leyda. New York: Harcourt, Brace, 1949.

Ejército Zapatista de Liberación Nacional. *EZLN: documentos y comunicados. Lo de enero-8 de agosto de 1994*. Prologue by Antonio García de León, commentary by Elena Poniatowska and Carlos Moinsiváis. Mexico: Ediciones Era, 1994.

Elsaesser, Thomas. "Dada/Cinema?" In *Dada and Surrealist Film*, edited by Rudolf Kuenzli, pp. 13–27. New York: Willis, Locker, and Owens, 1987.

Evans-Pritchard, E. E. *Witchcraft, Oracles, and Magic Among the Azande*. Oxford: Clarendon, 1937.

―――. *Nuer Religion*. Oxford: Oxford University Press, 1956.

Finch, John. "Structure and Function in Papua New Guinea Highland Mythology." *Oceania* 55, no. 3 (March 1985): 197–213.

Firth, Raymond. "The Analysis of Mana: An Empirical Approach." *Journal of the Polynesian Society* 49 (1940): 483–510.

Foster, George. "Nagualism in Mexico and Guatemala." *Acta Americana* 2 (1944): 85–103.

Foucault, Michel. *The History of Sexuality*. Vol. 1, *An Introduction*. Translated by Robert Hurley. New York: Vintage, 1980.

―――. "Nietzsche, Freud, Marx." In *Transforming the Hermeneutic Context*, edited by G. L. Ormiston and A. D. Schrift. Albany: State University of New York Press, 1990.

―――. "A Preface to Transgression." In *Language, Counter-Memory, Practice*, edited by Donald F. Bouchard, pp. 29–52. Ithaca, N.Y.: Cornell University Press, 1977.

Fraser, Ronald. *In Hiding: The Ordeal of Manuel Cortes*. New York: Pantheon, 1972.

Frazer, James George. *The Golden Bough: A Study in Magic and Religion*. 12 vols. 3d ed. London: Macmillan, 1912.

Freud, Sigmund. *Beyond the Pleasure Principle. SE*, vol. 18.

————. "Fetishism." In *SE*, vol. 21, pp. 152–57.

————. *The Origins of Psycho-Analysis: Letters to Wilhelm Fliess*. Edited by Marie Bonaparte et al. New York: Basic, 1977.

————. *Standard Edition of the Complete Psychological Works of Sigmund Freud*. 24 vols. Edited by James Strachey. London: The Hogarth Press and the Institute of Psycho-Analysis, 1960–74.

————. *Totem and Taboo. SE*, vol. 13.

————. "The Uncanny." In *SE*, vol. 17, pp. 217–52.

Geschiere, Peter. *The Modernity of Witchcraft*. Translated by Janet Roitman. Charlottesville: University of Virginia Press, 1977.

Gillison, Gillian. *Between Culture and Fantasy: A New Guinea Highlands Mythology*. Chicago: University of Chicago Press, 1993.

————. "Images of Nature in Gimi Thought." In *Nature, Culture, and Gender*, edited by Carolyn P. MacCormack and Marilyn Strathern, pp. 143–73. Cambridge: Cambridge University Press, 1980.

Glick, Leonard. "Foundations of a Primitive Medical System: the Gimi of the New Guinea Highlands." Ph.D. diss., University of Pennsylvania, 1963.

Goffman, Erving, "On Face-Work: An Analysis of Ritual Elements in Social Interaction." In *Interaction Ritual*, pp. 5–45. London: Penguin, 1972.

Goldman, Irving. *The Cubeo*. Urbana: University of Illinois Press, 1972.

Greenberg, James. *Santiago's Sword: Chatino Peasant Religion and Economics*. Berkeley: University of California Press, 1981.

Gregor, Thomas. *Anxious Pleasures: The Sexual Lives of an Amazonian People*. Chicago: University of Chicago Press, 1985.

Guillermoprieto, Alma. "The Shadow War." *New York Review of Books*, 2 March 1995, pp. 34–43.

————. "The Unmasking." *New Yorker*, 13 March 1995, pp. 40–47.

Guiteras-Holmes, Calixta. *Perils of the Soul: The World View of a Tzotzil Indian*. New York: Free Press, 1961.

Gusinde, Martin. *Los indios de Tierra del Fuego*. Vol. 1, *Los Selk'nam*. Translated by Werner Hoffmann. Buenos Aires: Centro Argentino de Etnología Américana, 1982.

————. *The Yamana: The Life and Thought of the Water Nomads of Cape Horn*. 3 vols. Translated by Frieda Schutze. New Haven, Conn.: Human Relations Area Files, 1961.

Gwertz, Deborah, editor. *Myths of Matriarchy Reconsidered*. Oceania Monographs 33 (1988).

Hays, Terence. "'Myths of Matriarchy' and the Sacred Flute Complex of the Papua New Guinea Highlands." *Oceania Monographs* 33 (1988): 98–120.

Hegel, G. W. F. *Phenomenology of Spirit.* Translated by A. V. Miller. Oxford: Oxford University Press, 1972.

Herdt, Gilbert H. *Guardians of the Flutes: Idioms of Masculinity.* New York: McGraw-Hill, 1981.

Hermitte, Esther M. "Supernatural Power and Social Control in a Modern Mayan Village." Ph.D. diss., Department of Anthropology, University of Chicago, 1964.

Hiatt, L. R. "Secret Pseudo-Procreation Rites Among the Australian Aborigines." In *Anthropology in Oceania: Essays Presented to Ian Hogbin*, edited by L. R. Hiatt and Chandra Jayawardena, pp. 77–86. Sydney: Angus and Robertson, 1971.

Hobsbawm, Eric J. *Primitive Rebels: Studies in Archaic Forms of Social Movement in the 19th and 20th Centuries* (originally published in 1959 under the title *Social Bandits and Primitive Rebels*). New York: Norton, 1965.

Hoffmann, Werner. Prologue to Martin Gusinde, *Los Selk'nam*, vol. 1 of *Los indios de Tierra del Fuego*. Buenos Aires: Centro Argentino de Etnología Américana, 1982.

Horkheimer, Max, and Theodor W. Adorno. *Dialectic of Enlightenment.* Translated by John Cumming. New York: Continuum, 1987.

Hubert, Henri, and Marcel Mauss. *Sacrifice: Its Nature and Function.* Translated by W. D. Halls. 1898. Reprint, Chicago: University of Chicago Press, 1964.

Hugh-Jones, Stephen. *The Palm and the Pleiades: Initiation and Cosmology in Northwest Amazonia.* Cambridge: Cambridge University Press, 1979.

Jones, Ian. *Ned Kelly: A Short Life.* Melbourne: Lothian, 1995.

Joyce, James. *Stephen Hero.* New York: New Direction, 1959.

Junod, Henri. *The Life of a South African Tribe.* 2 vols. Hyde Park, N.Y.: University Books, 1962.

Kafka, Franz. *Diaries 1914–1923.* Edited by Max Brod. Translated by Martin Greenberg. New York: Schocken, 1965.

Kahn, Douglas. *John Heartfield: Art and Mass Media.* New York: Tanam, 1985.

Kaplan, Temma. *Anarchists of Andalusia, 1868–1903.* Princeton, N.J.: Princeton University Press, 1977.

Keesing, Roger. "Rethinking *Mana.*" *Journal of Anthropological Research* 40 (1984): 137–56.

Kofman, Sarah, *Nietzsche and Metaphor.* Translated by Duncan Large. Stanford, Calif.: Stanford University Press, 1993.

———. "Baubo: Theological Perversion and Fetishism." In *Feminist Interpretations of Friedrich Nietzsche*, edited by Kelly Oliver and Marilyn Pearsall, translated by Tracy B. Strong, pp. 21–49. University Park: Pennsylvania State University Press, 1998.

Kris, Ernst. Introduction to Sigmund Freud, *The Origins of Psycho-Analysis: Letters to Wilhelm Fliess*, edited by Marie Bonaparte et al. New York: Basic, 1977.

Lacan, Jacques. *Speech and Language in Psychoanalysis: Jacques Lacan*. Translated with notes and commentary by Anthony Wilden. Baltimore: Johns Hopkins University Press, 1968.

Lattas, Andrew. "Trickery and Sacrifice: Tambarans and the Appropriation of Female Reproductive Powers in Male Initiation Ceremonies in West New Britain." *Man* 24 (1989): 451–69.

Levinas, Emmanuel. "Dialogue with Emmanuel Levinas." Interview by Richard Kearney. In *Face to Face with Levinas*, edited by Richard Cohen, pp. 13–34. Albany: State University of New York Press, 1986.

———. *Totality and Infinity: An Essay on Exteriority*. Translated by Alphonso Lingis. The Hague: Martinus Nijhoff, 1979.

Lévi-Strauss, Claude. *The Elementary Structures of Kinship*. Boston: Beacon, 1969.

———. *Introduction to the Work of Marcel Mauss*. Translated by Felicity Baker. London: Routledge and Kegan Paul, 1987.

———. *The Savage Mind*. Chicago: University of Chicago Press, 1966.

———. *Totemism*. Boston: Beacon, 1963.

Lewis, Mark. "What Is to be Done." In *Ideology and Power in the Age of Lenin in Ruins*, edited by Arthur Kroker and Marilouise Kroker, pp. 1–18. New York: St. Martin's, 1991.

Little, K. L. *The Mende of Sierra Leone*. London: Routledge and Kegan Paul, 1951.

———. "The Poro Society As An Arbiter of Culture (A Note on Cultural Inter-penetration)." *African Studies* 17 (March 1948): 1–15.

Lowie, Robert. Review of *Die Yamana*, vol. 2 of *Die Feuerland Indianer. American Anthropologist*, n.s., 40 (1938): 495–503.

Magee, Paul. "An Ethno-History of the White Colonial Subject Travelling Through Tierra del Fuego to a Time When the Sheep had Wings." Master's thesis, Department of History, University of Melbourne, 1997.

Mann, Thomas. *Death in Venice*. In *"Death in Venice" and Other Stories by Thomas Mann*, translated by David Luke. New York: Bantam, 1988.

Marx, Karl. Letter to Arnold Ruge, September 1843. In *The Letters of Karl Marx*, edited by Saul Padover. Englewood Cliffs, N.J.: Prentice-Hall, 1979.

———. *Capital*, vol. 1. New York: International, 1967.

Mauss, Marcel. *A General Theory of Magic*. Translated by Robert Brain. New York: Norton, 1972.

————. *The Gift: Forms and Function of Exchange in Archaic Societies*. Translated by Ian Cunnison. Norton: New York, 1967.

Mbembe, Achille. "The Banality of Power and the Aesthetics of Vulgarity in the Postcolony." *Public Culture* 4 (1992): 1–30.

Metz, Christian. *The Imaginary Signifier: Psychoanalysis and the Cinema*. Bloomington: Indiana University Press, 1985.

Meyer, Birgit. "'The Beast Within'": Juju and the Modern Family in Popular Ghanaian Video Movies." Paper presented at the conference "Magic and Modernity" at the Research Centre for Religion and Society, University of Amsterdam, 23–25 June 1997.

Michaels, Eric. "A Primer of Restrictions on Picture-Taking in Tribal Areas of Aboriginal Australia." *Visual Anthropology* 4, nos. 3–4 (1991): 259–75.

Mintz, Jerome. *The Anarchists of Casas Viejas*. Chicago: University of Chicago Press, 1982.

Montaigne, Michel de. "On Physiognomy." In *Essays*, translated by J. M. Cohen, pp. 311–42. London: Penguin, 1958.

Moore, Rachel. *Savage Theory*. Durham, N.C.: Duke University Press, 1999.

Murphy, William. "Secret Knowledge as Property and Power in Kpelle Society: Elders Versus Youth." *Africa* 50 (1980): 193–207.

Musil, Robert, "Monuments." In *Posthumous Papers of a Living Author*, pp. 61–64. Hygiene, Colo.: Eridanos, 1987.

Nandy, Ashis. "The Savage Freud: The First Non-Western Psychoanalyst and the Politics of Secret Selves in Colonial India." In *The Savage Freud and Other Essays on Possible and Retrievable Selves*, pp. 81–145. Oxford: Oxford University Press, 1995.

Nietzsche, Friedrich. *Beyond Good and Evil*. Translated by Walter Kaufmann. New York: Vintage, 1989.

————. *The Birth of Tragedy*. In *Basic Writings of Nietzsche*, translated and edited by Walter Kaufmann. New York: Modern Library, 1968.

————. *The Gay Science*. New York: Vintage, 1974.

————. *Human, All Too Human*. Translated by M. Faber with S. Lehmann. Lincoln: University of Nebraska Press, 1996.

————. *Thus Spake Zarathustra*. Translated by R. J. Hollingdale. London: Penguin, 1969.

————. "On Truth and Falsity in Their Ultramoral Sense." In *Early Greek Philosophy and Other Essays*, translated by M. A. Mugee, pp. 73–92. New York: Russell and Russell, 1964.

————. *Twilight of the Idols*. Translated by R. J. Hollingdale. London: Penguin, 1990.

————. *The Will to Power*. Translated by Walter Kaufmann and R. J. Hollingdale. New York: Vintage, 1968.

Nunley, John W. *Moving with the Face of the Devil: Art and Politics in Urban West Africa*. Urbana: University of Illinois Press, 1987.

Payne, Stanley G. *The Franco Regime, 1936–1975*. Madison: University of Wisconsin Press, 1987.

Perera, Victor, and Robert D. Bruce. *The Last Lords of Palenque: The Lacandon Mayas of the Mexican Rain Forest*. Berkeley: University of California Press, 1982.

Picton, John. "What's in a Mask?" *African Languages and Cultures* 3 (1992): 181–202.

Pietz, William. "The Problem of the Fetish, I." *Res* 9 (1985): 5–17.

Pitt-Rivers, Julian. *The People of the Sierra*. 2d ed. Chicago: University of Chicago Press, 1971.

————. "Spiritual Power in Central America: The Naguals of Chiapas." In *Witchcraft, Confessions, and Accusations*, edited by Mary Douglas, pp. 183–205. London: Tavistock, 1970.

Preston, Julia. "Mexican Gunmen Slay 45 in Southern Indian Village." *New York Times*, 24 December 1997, p. 1.

Proust, Marcel. *Remembrance of Things Past*. Vol. 1, *Swann's Way*. New York: Vintage, 1982.

Read, Kenneth. "Nama Cult of the Central Highlands of New Guinea." *Oceania* 23 (September 1952): 1–25.

————. *The High Valley*. New York: Scribner's, 1965.

————. *Return to the High Valley: Coming Full Circle*. Berkeley: University of California Press, 1986.

Remet, Anna E. "The Importance of Illustrations in Children's Books." Paper written for Columbia University undergraduate seminar, "Pirates, Boys, and Capitalism," 23 March 1998.

Roberts. Neil. *Media Dossier: "Down by the Lake with Phil and Liz."* Unpublished archive. Canberra National Sculpture Forum, c/o Galerie Constantinople, Queanbeyan, Australia, 1995.

Rubenstein, Steven. "Death in a Distant Place: The Politics of Shuar Shamanism." Ph.D. dissertation, Department of Anthropology, Columbia University, 1995.

Ruskin, John. *The Stones of Venice*. New York: Da Capo, 1960.

Schanoes, Veronica. "Personal Meditations on Illustrations and the Presentation of Books." Paper written for Columbia University undergraduate seminar, "Pirates, Boys, and Capitalism," 23 March 1998.

Schopenhauer, Arthur. *The World as Will and Idea*. 3 vols. Translated by R. B.

Haldane and J. Kemp. 1896 (London: Kegan Paul, Trench, and Trübner). Reprint, New York: AMS, 1977.

Shaw, Rosalind. "Secret Societies." In *The Encyclopedia of Africa South of the Sahara*, edited by John Middleton. New York: Scribner's, 1997.

Silverman, Kaja. *The Acoustic Mirror: The Female Voice in Psychoanalysis and Cinema*. Bloomington: Indiana University Press, 1988.

Simmel, Georg. "The Aesthetic Significance of the Face." In *Georg Simmel, 1885–1918*, edited by Kurt H. Wolff, pp. 276–78. Columbus: Ohio State University Press, 1959.

———. "The Secret and the Secret Society." In *The Sociology of Georg Simmel*. Edited and translated by Kurt H. Wolff, pp. 307–78. New York: Free Press, 1950.

Smith, Robertson W. "Sacrifice." In *Encyclopedia Britannica*, 9th ed., vol. 2. Edinburgh: Adams and Charles Black, 1886.

Sobieszek, Robert A. *Ports of Entry: William S. Burroughs and the Arts*. Los Angeles: Los Angeles County Museum of Art, 1966.

Spencer, Baldwin, and Frank J. Gillen. *The Native Tribes of Central Australia*. 1899. Reprint, New York: Dover, 1968.

Stanner, W. E. H. *On Aboriginal Religion*. Oceania Monograph, no. 11. Sydney: Australasian Medical Company Ltd., n.d. Reprints of articles that were published in *Oceania* from 1959 to 1963.

Taussig, Michael. *The Magic of the State*. New York: Routledge, 1997.

———. *Mimesis and Alterity*. New York: Routledge, 1993.

———. *Shamanism, Colonialism, and the Wild Man: A Study in Terror and Healing*. Chicago: University of Chicago Press, 1987.

———. "Transgression." In *Critical Terms for Religious Studies*, edited by Mark C. Taylor, pp. 349–64. Chicago: University of Chicago Press, 1998.

———. "Viscerality, Faith, and Skepticism: Another Theory of Magic." In *In Near Ruins: Cultural Theory at the End of the Century*, edited by Nicholas B. Dirks, pp. 257–94. Minneapolis: University of Minnesota Press, 1998.

Turnbull, Colin M. *The Forest People*. New York: Simon and Schuster, 1961.

Tuzin, Donald. *The Cassowary's Revenge: The Life and Death of Masculinity in A New Guinea Society*. Chicago: University of Chicago Press, 1997.

———. *The Voice of the Tambaran: Truth and Illusion in Ilahita Arapesh Religion*. Berkeley: University of California Press, 1980.

Villa Rojas, Alfonso. "Kinship and Nagualism in a Tzeltal Community, Southeastern Mexico." *American Anthropologist* 49 (October–December 1947): 578–87.

Warner, W. Lloyd. *A Black Civilization: A Social Study of an Australian Tribe*. New York: Harper and Row, 1937.

Warner, Marina. *Monuments and Maidens: The Allegory of the Female Form.* London: Weidenfeld and Nicolson, 1985.

Welmers, William E. "Secret Medicines, Magic, and Rites of the Kpelle Tribe in Liberia." *Southwestern Journal of Anthropology* 5 (1949): 208–43.

Weschler, Lawrence. "Slight Modifications." *New Yorker,* 12 July 1993, pp. 59–64.

White, Charles. *History of Australian Bushranging.* 2 vols. Hawthorn, Australia: Lloyd O'Neil, 1970.

Wilbert, Johannes, ed. "The Origin of the Women's Kloketen." In *Folk Literature of the Selknam Indians: Martin Gusinde's Collection of Selknam Narratives,* pp. 147–61. Los Angeles: UCLA Latin America Center Publications, 1975.

Wilden, Anthony. "Lacan and the Discourse of the Other." In *Speech and Language in Psychoanalysis,* by Jacques Lacan, pp. 159–311. Baltimore: Johns Hopkins University Press, 1968.

In this index an "f" after a number indicates a separate reference on the next page, and an "ff" indicates separate references on the next two pages. A continuous discussion over two or more pages is indicated by a span of page numbers, e.g., "57–59." *Passim* is used for a cluster of references in close but not consecutive sequence.

Library of Congress Cataloging-in-Publication Data

Taussig, Michael T.
  Defacement : public secrecy and the labor of the negative /
Michael Taussig.
      p.   cm.
  "The Raymond Fred West memorial lectures at Stanford University."
  Includes bibliographical references and index.
  ISBN 0-8047-3199-3 (alk paper). — ISBN 0-8047-3200-0 (pbk. :
alk. paper)
  1. Ethnology—Philosophy.   2. Secrecy—Cross-cultural studies.
I. Title.
GN345.T375   1999
305.8'001—dc21                                              99-27085

Original printing 1999

Last figure below indicates year of this printing:
08   07   06   05   04   03   02   01   00   99


Designed by Janet Wood
Typeset by James P. Brommer in 10.5/14 Bembo